"# The Free Society

JC
585
.P584
1996

THE FREE SOCIETY

Lansing Pollock

WestviewPress
A Division of HarperCollinsPublishers

All rights reserved. Printed in the United States of America. No part of this publication may be reproduced or transmitted in any form or by any means, electronic or mechanical, including photocopy, recording, or any information storage and retrieval system, without permission in writing from the publisher.

Copyright © 1996 by Westview Press, Inc., A Division of HarperCollins Publishers, Inc.

Published in 1996 in the United States of America by Westview Press, Inc., 5500 Central Avenue, Boulder, Colorado 80301-2877, and in the United Kingdom by Westview Press, 12 Hid's Copse Road, Cumnor Hill, Oxford OX2 9JJ

Library of Congress Cataloging-in-Publication Data
Pollock, Lansing.
The free society / Lansing Pollock.
  p. cm
Includes bibliographical references and index.
ISBN 0-8133-2719-9.—ISBN 0-8133-2720-2 (pbk.)
1. Liberty. 2. Representative government and representation.
3. Economic policy. 4. Libertarianism. I. Title.
JC585.P584 1996
320'.01'1—dc20   95-40706
                                                                                                         CIP

The paper used in this publication meets the requirements of the American National Standard for Permanence of Paper for Printed Library Materials Z39.48-1984.

10 9 8 7 6 5 4 3 2 1

Contents

Acknowledgments vii

Introduction 1

MORAL FOUNDATIONS

1. Moral Skepticism 6
2. The Freedom Principle 10
3. Evaluating Moral Theories 19
4. Liberalism 34
5. Why Be Moral? 45
6. Summary 52

LIBERTY AND GOVERNMENT

7. Legitimacy 58
8. Justice 62
9. The Constitution 73
10. Summary 83

LIBERTY AND ECONOMICS

11. General Observations 92
12. Poverty 103
13. The Taxpayer's Dilemma 110
14. Health Care 114
15. Education 123
16. Government Failure 129

LIBERTY AND REALITY

17. Optimisim and Pessimism   136
18. Strategies   142
19. Change   148

Notes   155
About the Book and Author   169
Index   171

Acknowledgments

I have tried to take the best in libertarian thought from all sources, classical to contemporary, and from different academic disciplines. As a result, my debts are enormous, too numerous to mention in the space normally allotted to acknowledgments. I recognize some of these debts in the text and the notes. Special mention should be made of some recent books that were crucial to my understanding of markets. They are *The Seven Fat Years* by Robert L. Bartley, *Forbidden Grounds* by Richard A. Epstein, *Recapturing the Spirit of Enterprise* by George Gilder, *Patient Power* by John C. Goodman and Gerald L. Musgrave, and *Politics, Markets, and America's Schools* by John E. Chubb and Terry M. Moe. *Knowledge and Decisions* by Thomas Sowell provided the general framework for understanding these works.

I thank John Carbonara, James Grunebaum, Diane Hess (my copy editor at Westview Press), George Hole, Jan Narveson, Robert Pollock, David Schmidtz, and Michael Stansbury for their comments, criticisms, and encouragement. My wife, Pam, and my daughter, Anne, deserve special thanks for trying to keep me in touch with reality.

I have borrowed liberally from Kant and Mill, the most fertile of the great moral philosophers. The book is dedicated to James Madison. If the United States has a reasonably free society 100 years from now, Madison will have proven to be one of the greatest benefactors of humankind.

Lansing Pollock

Introduction

Suppose we assume that morality requires respect for persons as free and equal beings.[1] What are the implications of this assumption? On a very general level, there is a surprising degree of agreement concerning what this requirement entails. For example, Kant, the preeminent rationalist, and Mill, the most sophisticated utilitarian, say very similar things:

> No one can compel me to be happy in accordance with his conception of the welfare of others, for each may seek happiness in whatever way he sees fit, so long as he does not infringe upon the freedom of others to pursue a similar end which can be reconciled with the freedom of everyone else within a workable general law—i.e., he must accord to others the same right as he enjoys himself.[2]
>
> The only freedom which deserves the name is that of pursuing our own good in our own way so long as we do not attempt to deprive others of theirs, or impede their efforts to obtain it.[3]

The values of freedom and moral equality can be combined in one fundamental right, the equal right to be free. If we borrow Mill's terminology, this right requires us to grant others the equal right to pursue their own good in their own way. I shall present a libertarian interpretation of this right. According to this interpretation, if we take the right seriously, much of the coercion by government that many take for granted is immoral.

In my defense of libertarianism, I shall contrast two approaches to moral thinking. According to the approach I call consequentialism, the primary concern of morality is to produce something or to bring something about. The theory that says we should produce the greatest balance of pleasure over pain (Bentham) and the theory that says we should bring about a just distribution of primary goods (Rawls) are examples of consequentialism. According to the approach I call Kantianism, the primary concern of morality is how persons should relate to each other.[4] There is of course much controversy concerning the correct interpretation of Kant's moral theory, but one thing at least is clear: Kant rejects consequentialism as I have defined it.[5] Consequentialism is rejected because it allows persons to be used as mere means to produce desired end-states (the greatest happiness, a just distribution of goods, etc.). Using persons as mere means is not permitted by Kantian theories.

Libertarianism, as I conceive it, is a Kantian theory. According to this conception, mutual consent is the ideal standard for judging relations between persons. When interactions are based on mutual consent, the equal right of each person to be self-directing is respected. When interactions result from coercion or decep-

1

tion, the relationships are inherently unequal. When someone gets me to go along with his scheme by deceiving me, I cannot consent to the interaction because I do not know to what I am agreeing. Coercion (in the broad sense) includes both the use of threats and the use of force. When a person responds to a threat (your money or your life), he is compelled to choose the lesser evil in a situation that has been structured unilaterally by the person issuing the threat. The successful application of (physical) force prevents a person from controlling his behavior and thus directly removes the possibility of consent. When deception or coercion are used, the agent treats his recipient as an object to be manipulated. In contrast, relationships based on mutual consent express the fundamental moral equality of persons.

To be governed is to be ruled by others. This raises the question of whether freedom and moral equality are compatible with having any government at all. A major theoretical problem for libertarians is to explain how a limited government can be funded without violating individual rights. This is one of the problems that Robert Nozick wrestled with in *Anarchy, State, and Utopia*. I shall propose a new solution to this problem, one that requires libertarians to abandon the orthodox view of how persons acquire rights to use natural resources.

Some libertarians will be satisfied with nothing less than anarchism. In my opinion, if libertarian rights entailed anarchism, this would be a fatal objection to libertarianism. My objections to anarchism are not new, and I see no need to dwell on them. However, for theoretical completeness, it is important to establish that government is necessary. I think that the most serious problems for anarchism have to do with the punishment of those who break the (natural) law. With no government to protect them, anarchists assume that individuals and businesses will hire private protective agencies. Suppose that I do not like my neighbor, and one of the things he does to annoy me is to play loud music. After many complaints and warnings, I ask my protective agency to arrest and imprison him for one year. Or suppose that a factory is dumping pollutants into Lake Ontario and environmentalists are so upset that they hire a protective agency to arrest the owners. What procedures will be used in determining guilt or innocence, and what punishments are appropriate for these "crimes"? In an anarchist society, how will children be protected from physical and sexual abuse by their parents? It is clearly no answer to say that they can hire an agency to protect them from their own parents. And what about unborn children? Suppose antiabortion activists try to prevent these "murders" by arresting doctors who perform abortions. What should be done with someone who clearly is a murderer? Who has the right to punish him? Will excusing conditions be recognized? Suppose that feminists and conservative Christians want protection from the moral decay caused by prostitution and pornography. Many more examples could be given, but the general point is that the risk that anarchism will lead to anarchy (in the pejorative sense of the term) is too great.

The opposite danger is that government will abuse its powers. The antidote, I shall argue, is to drastically reduce the size and scope of government. This was the answer that the Founding Fathers proposed by establishing a limited, constitutional government. With the failure of liberals to produce "the great society," it is time to take a fresh look at the wisdom of their answer. The main obstacle to this "fresh look" is ignorance of how free market economies work. Too many people believe that government regulation is beneficial not only to special interests but to the economy as a whole. I shall try to dispel some of these economic fallacies. I shall argue that when libertarian moral theory is combined with economic theory, a compelling conception of the good society emerges. A free society is both practical and inspiring.

The rejection of welfare rights is a defining characteristic of libertarian theories. This is a hard pill to swallow; I speak from experience, for I have wavered on this issue many times. I am now convinced, however, that the failure of government programs to reduce poverty means that a radically different approach is needed and that the libertarian solution is better than the alternatives. Many will want to reject these claims. If you are among them, I invite you to consider a different approach to this very difficult problem. The libertarian solution to poverty is discussed in "Liberty and Economics." The moral and political foundations for a libertarian society are examined in "Moral Foundations" and "Liberty and Government."

I have tried to write in a manner accessible to the general reader; however, non-philosophers may have difficulty with Sections 3 and 4 of "Moral Foundations." I urge these readers to persevere, with the understanding that subsequent sections are less difficult.

ONE

Moral Foundations

To suppose that any form of government will secure liberty or happiness without virtue in the people, is a chimerical idea. If there be sufficient virtue and intelligence in the community, it will be exercised in the selection of [virtuous and wise] men. So that we do not depend on their virtue, or put confidence in our rulers, but in the people who are to choose them.

James Madison, Speech to the Virginia Convention, 1788[1]

1. Moral Skepticism

In a healthy society, morality, like language, is a spontaneous order that develops without central control or direction.[2] It is a social practice that at its core has reasonably clear rules, but no person or group is responsible for establishing these rules. Instead, those of us who care about morality are involved in creating and reinforcing it. We do this by raising our children so that they will know the difference between right and wrong, and we do it by praising and criticizing the conduct of others. The moral skeptic intrudes on this comfortable scene by claiming that morality, even at its core, lacks a rational foundation.

Beliefs are rational when we have good reasons for accepting them.[3] Beliefs are irrational when we have good reasons for rejecting them. A belief is nonrational when reason gives us no guidance concerning whether to accept it or reject it. The moral skeptic claims that moral beliefs fit in the last category: Moral beliefs are nonrational. Are abortions immoral? According to the moral skeptic, reason cannot help us decide. Is this claim of moral skepticism true? It seems plausible when we think of very controversial issues like the morality of abortions. Still, there are moral beliefs that are widely accepted; for example, it is unjust to punish an innocent person, persons who break important promises are dishonest, no one should be held responsible for wrongdoing unless the person could have known that the action was wrong, attacking innocent people for amusement is immoral. Most of us, I assume, think that we have good reasons for accepting these beliefs. Are we mistaken about this, or is the moral skeptic mistaken?

When people argue about moral issues, they often think that they are giving good reasons for their views. Many of these arguments appeal to the rational canon of consistency. The opponent of abortion, for example, is accused of inconsistency if he supports capital punishment. If human life is sacred in one case (the fetus), why not in the other case? If the opponent of abortion believes that rational standards do not apply to moral beliefs, he should not be bothered by this charge. In fact, opponents of abortion usually feel the need to respond by claiming that there is a relevant difference between abortion and capital punishment: The fetus is an innocent life, whereas the convicted murderer is not innocent.

What underlies the appeal to consistency in moral arguments? For one thing, a moral judgment is more than a statement of personal preference. If I say that I like apple pie better than peach, I am stating a fact about me. When I say abortions are immoral, I am making a judgment about abortions. I could take the view that I don't care what others believe about abortion, but if I do care, to convince others that my view is correct, I have to do more than simply report my state of mind. I have to say what it is about abortions that makes them immoral—for example, human life is sacred. Once this move is made, opponents can ask whether my beliefs are consistent: Can I oppose abortion and support capital punishment?

Philosophers have noted that a singular judgment such as "It was wrong for Jones to steal my car" entails the generalization that it would be wrong for anyone to steal a car in similar circumstances.[4] The rational canon of consistency underlies this entailment; to be consistent, we must make the same judgments about relevantly similar cases. Let us call this the *generalization requirement*. This requirement provides the logical framework for Golden Rule arguments. We should obey the rules we think others should follow. Would the thief say it is wrong for someone to steal his property? If so, he should admit that it is wrong for him to steal. Of course the thief can claim that his case is special, but let us move to a deeper problem. Suppose that the moral skeptic concedes that the rational canon of consistency applies to moral judgments, but he points out that consistency provides no guarantee of truth. The thief can say that it is not wrong for him to steal, and it is not wrong for others to steal as well. At this point we might accuse the thief of insincerity: Does he really believe that he is not morally wronged when someone steals *his* property? Suppose the thief replies, "Yes, I really do believe that."[5]

When Golden Rule arguments do work, it is what I shall call the *reversibility requirement* that generates the moral conclusion.[6] The agent should be willing to be the recipient of his own rule of action. Can the thief honestly say this? If he says yes, where do we go from here? One possibility is to note the social role of moral rules. If stealing were *normal* behavior, economic cooperation could not take place and the thief might have nothing to steal. Suppose the thief grants this point, but he still sees no reason to change his opinion. Yes, he admits, life would be very difficult (if not impossible) for me if stealing were normal behavior; but fortunately it is not. Again, we can accuse the thief of insincerity; given this admission, surely he cannot believe that stealing is permissible. Suppose he replies that he does believe it—he just hopes that others continue to believe that stealing is wrong.

The rational canon of consistency is insufficient, by itself, to generate the conclusion we are looking for. Suppose we press on by saying that so far we have failed to fully appreciate the social nature of moral rules. We teach moral rules to our children so that they will know the difference between right and wrong, so that they won't grow up believing that stealing is permissible, which would, if acted upon, make social cooperation impossible. Moral rules are (inter alia) rules that we publicly advocate.[7] Let us call this the *publicity requirement*. The thief violates this requirement when he admits that he hopes that others will not share his belief about stealing. But this shows that his belief is not a moral belief; it is not the rule that should be taught to children. Let us call the rules that are necessary for social living the *basic moral rules*. Broadly interpreted, they include:

> It is usually wrong to lie.
> It is usually wrong to steal.
> It is usually wrong to attack others.

To see why these rules are necessary, ask yourself whether a social institution like a college could exist if violating these rules were normal behavior. I shall assume that your answer is no.

Our moral lives would be much simpler if moral rules did not have exceptions, but most of us do believe that lying, for example, is permissible in some cases. You may lie to a kidnapper if this will help you escape. The publicity requirement says that we must be willing to publicly advocate any exceptions to the basic moral rules. This requirement is stronger than the generalization requirement, but it also has its limitations. The president believes that he may lie when lying promotes national security. This belief is very vague. However, if the president tells us, with specificity, just when he thinks lying is justified, a lie will not be effective because no one will believe it. In addition, the skeptic can rejoin the argument by pointing out that people advocate moral views that others find abhorrent. Some people think that the economic inequalities in capitalist societies are terribly unjust; others strongly endorse the moral superiority of capitalism. Can these disagreements be settled in a rational way?

Suppose we say that moral rules should be acceptable to all rational persons. This is the move that supporters of contract theories make. Moral rules are the rules for behavior that all rational agents would agree to given a suitable analysis of rationality. What the contract theorist is seeking can be called hypothetical consent—the rules people would agree to *if* they were appropriately rational. John Rawls, for example, thinks that rational persons are strongly risk averse, and thus rational contractors will reject utilitarianism in favor of the principle that economic inequalities are justified only if they benefit the least-advantaged members of society.[8] Jan Narveson, in contrast, thinks that rational contractors will opt for laissez-faire capitalism.[9] T. M. Scanlon says that the correct moral rules are the ones that no one could reasonably reject: "An act is wrong if its performance under the circumstances would be disallowed by any system of rules for the regulation of behavior which no one could reasonably reject as a basis for informed, unforced general agreement."[10] Scanlon and Narveson agree that we do not need Rawls's "veil of ignorance" to make rational choices among various rules. However, they disagree about what rules would be chosen by rational contractors. Perhaps these disagreements show that the notion of a "contract" is misplaced.[11] The real work is being done by the analysis of rationality, and on this issue, very intelligent persons (Rawls, Narveson, and Scanlon) disagree. The moral skeptic is still smiling.

Suppose we jettison the idea of hypothetical consent in favor of actual consent. What could this mean? In the case of two persons, A and B, it means that they interact only when both give their consent. Otherwise, they leave each other alone. In other words, interactions are based on mutual consent. A asks B if B would like to play chess. If B says yes, they play. If she says no, that's the end of it. In more general terms, A and B respect the right of the other person to pursue her own good in her own way. When cooperation is mutually advantageous, according to their actual judgments, they cooperate. In addition, A may choose to help B (and vice versa) when B needs A's assistance. However, the refusal to cooperate (or to help) is simply the exercise of their fundamental right, the equal right to be free. The next section contains a general analysis of this right. I shall say more about moral skepticism in Section 3, where I argue that there are rational criteria for evaluating moral theories.

2. The Freedom Principle

In developing a moral point of view, a person must decide what position to accept regarding moral equality. In very general terms, there are two choices: an aristocratic view or an egalitarian view. An aristocratic view holds that some persons are morally superior. These persons are accorded greater rights or their interests are accorded greater weight (or both). An egalitarian view maintains that there is some fundamental sense in which all persons are moral equals. Egalitarian views differ depending on what their authors hold to be morally fundamental. The libertarian view that I am defending maintains that persons have one fundamental right, the equal right to be free. This libertarian view is incompatible with other egalitarian views that focus on different fundamental values.

I have proposed that our freedom should be limited by the equal right of others to be free. This constraint can be stated more formally by what I call the *freedom principle:* Each person ought to grant other persons an equal right to be free. The underlying idea is that interactions should (ideally) be based on mutual consent. When A and B agree to interact, the equal right of each person to be free is respected. In contrast, we usually violate the freedom principle when we cause others to behave involuntarily by coercing or deceiving them. Thus, as a general rule, this principle requires noninterference where interference is understood as causing another person to behave involuntarily. Let us call this requirement the *noninterference rule*. The noninterference rule has exceptions, which I shall examine shortly.

I have mentioned two ways in which we can cause others to behave involuntarily: coercion and deception. I am using the word 'coercion' in the broad sense, which includes both threats and the use of force. Much has been written about the difference between threats and offers. As with most concepts, there are clear cases, but there are also borderline cases where it is hard to say whether a threat or an offer has been made. In paradigm cases, the agent who issues a threat forces his recipient to choose between undesirable alternatives. The status quo (the way things were) is not an option, e.g., the gunman forces you to choose between handing over your money and risking injury or death. In paradigm cases of offers, the status quo is an option—you can refuse the offer and your life can continue as if no offer had been made. When the status quo is very bad, an offer can *seem* coercive in the sense that you "must" accept it. However, if a person accepts an offer in such circumstances, he does so because he believes that acceptance will improve his situation. This is not true of threats; the person who is threatened does not believe that choosing the lesser evil makes him better off than he was prior to receiving the threat. It is also worth noting that the person who issues the threat violates the freedom principle simply by making the threat. Suppose that you refuse to hand over your money to the gunman and he lets you walk away unharmed. He still forced you to accept the risk of harm, and in forcing you to make this choice, he has caused you to behave involuntarily. In contrast, acceptance of an offer can be completely voluntary. You are looking for a better job, and you respond to an ad in a local paper. The company offers you a better position, which you gladly accept. If this is a true description, there is no reason to think that the freedom principle has been violated.

There are borderline cases where it is difficult to say whether coercion has occurred. Suppose that A bothers B with requests for assistance. If B says "leave me alone," subsequent requests by A would be coercive. Forcing others to listen to you is coercive. This is obvious in the case of the Nazi who interrupts a Jewish religious service by shouting anti-Semitic slogans. In general, sounds can be coercive, including loud or obnoxious noises as well as words one doesn't want to hear. Whether an obnoxious noise is coercive often depends on how difficult it is to avoid it. Unpleasant sights can also be coercive. This is clear in the case of the exhibitionist who exposes himself to strangers, but in other cases, we may not be sure what to say. When we consider borderline cases, it is helpful to think of the libertarian ideal of mutual consent—when consent is lacking, the relationship is often coercive.

The basic moral rules (it is usually wrong to lie, it is usually wrong to steal, it is usually wrong to attack others) can be deduced from the freedom principle. When we manipulate another person by using physical force or deception, we do not respect the person's equal right to be free. Suppose that I hire someone to paint my porch, but after completion of the work I refuse to pay. Since the person would not have chosen to do the work had she known that I would break our agreement, I have caused her to behave involuntarily. Interactions should be based on mutual consent, but my victim did not agree to work without compensation. The prohibition of theft is more complicated because what counts as theft will depend on what rights persons have over things. I shall discuss this issue in Section 7, where I present a theory of property rights. For now, let us assume that persons do have rights over things and that the person who takes someone's property without the owner's consent violates the freedom principle.

Any moral theory worthy of consideration will entail the basic moral rules; the more difficult task is to explain the exceptions. When is lying, stealing, and attacking others permissible? Let us begin with a simple case: A threatens B with a gun and B (who has done nothing to provoke the threat) injures A while using physical force to take A's weapon. This act of self-defense does not violate the freedom principle. B does not assume that he has a superior right to be free; he defends his equal right to be free by ending an interaction to which he did not consent. Furthermore, B does not violate A's rights because A, according to the principle, has no right to threaten him. Since B has the right to defend himself, other persons would have the right to help B if that were necessary. A lie is also permissible when it is used for self-defense or the defense of others. If you lie to a kidnapper to help your spouse escape, you do not violate a right of the kidnapper because he has no right to hold your spouse captive.

Next let us consider the use of force and the threat of force in the apprehension and punishment of lawbreakers. If person A in our previous example is convicted of assault and subsequently punished, would this interference with his choices violate the freedom principle? The threat of punishment for assault does not violate a right of A because he has no right to threaten others. Furthermore, let us assume that the law prohibiting assault is well publicized so that A knows that he runs the risk of punishment when he breaks the law. In this case, A brings the punishment on himself by choosing to do what he had no right to do. To summarize, punishment is consistent with the freedom principle when two conditions are met: (1) the law prohibits acts that violate the freedom principle (which means the offender had no right to perform the act) and (2) the offender could have avoided the punishment by choosing not to break the law. Condition (2) entails the recognition of excusing conditions: When a lawbreaker has no real choice, he should not be held responsible. An example is a heart-attack victim who loses control of his automobile and kills a pedestrian. This rationale for excuses illustrates a difference between the freedom principle and the utility principle. We can agree with utilitarians that the primary purpose of the threat of punishment is to deter potential lawbreakers, and we can agree that the primary reason for actually inflicting punishment is to make the threat credible.[12] However, we should not pursue ends (such as deterrence) in ways that violate people's rights. In some circumstances the elimination of excusing conditions might increase deterrence, but according to the freedom principle, we have no right to punish persons who were not responsible for their illegal behavior. Rights set limits on the pursuit of ends.

I have noted that there are cases involving self-defense and punishment that are exceptions to the noninterference rule. These are not exceptions to the freedom principle; instead they are cases where interference does not violate the principle. Cases of paternalism constitute a third category of exceptions to the noninterference rule. Paternalism is interference with a person for what is seen to be that person's own good. When someone treats you paternalistically, he is assuming that you do not understand what your own good is or, if you do understand, you lack the self-control to behave appropriately. On the face of it, these assumptions seem inconsistent with the idea that persons should enjoy the *equal* right to be free. A paternalistic relationship is inherently unequal; the paternal agent assumes that he has a superior ability to determine what his recipient should do. From the libertarian point of view, there is at least a strong presumption that paternalism is impermissible. How might this presumption be rebutted?

To avoid confusion, let us begin with a case that some might think is an example of paternalism. Suppose you acknowledge that your doctor has superior knowledge of how to treat a disease. You accept her diagnosis and follow the treatment she recommends. This is not an example of paternalism because there is no interference, i.e., the doctor does not coerce or deceive you. To change the case, suppose that the doctor must lie to get you to follow her recommendations: She tells you that the disease could be fatal, knowing that this claim is false. This example fits our definition of paternalism. It also appears to be a clear violation of the freedom principle; genuine consent cannot be based on deception.

It is tempting to simply say that paternalism is unacceptable; however, a moment's reflection reveals that this approach is unrealistic. In some cases, persons are unable to make choices and thus cannot give consent. An unconscious accident victim is an example. In this case there is total (but not permanent) impairment of the ability to choose. Lesser impairments such as drunkenness must also be considered. You may prevent an inebriated friend from driving, for his own benefit as well as the safety of others. Furthermore, no one seriously disputes that young children may be treated paternalistically. The straightforward justification for this is to acknowledge the inequality between (normal) adults and young children. Children often lack the knowledge and self-control necessary for being self-directing agents. In *On Liberty*, Mill dealt with this problem by restricting the scope of his "liberty principle": ". . . this doctrine is meant to apply only to human beings in the maturity of their faculties. We are not speaking of children or of young persons below the age which the law may fix as that of manhood or womanhood. Those who are still in a state to require being taken care of by others must be protected against their own actions as well as against external injury."[13] If I wished to follow Mill on this issue, I would simply say that the freedom principle applies only to normal adults. However, I have claimed that the equal right to be free is the (only) fundamental moral right, and thus this approach would seem to entail that many human beings lack moral standing.

The freedom principle applies to persons. Who is included in this category? Let us begin with the most obvious candidates: normal adults. The normal adult has some (hard to define) minimum degree of knowledge and self-control. He understands what his important needs are and how these needs can be met in the society in which he happens to be living. He has the conceptual abilities necessary for formulating long-range plans, and he has the ability to control his behavior when he decides to pursue a goal. This last point is complicated because the failure to achieve a goal, such as stopping smoking, is not proof that the agent lacks self-control in the sense of lacking the capacity to control his behavior. Instead, he may simply lack the motivation necessary to achieve his goal. The smoker, for example, who really believes that his next cigarette would kill him could stop smoking—unless he is suicidal. Lacking this belief, he may not make the effort. The failure to make long-range plans is also not proof that the necessary capacities are missing. One may choose to live for today and not worry about tomorrow. Insofar as this approach to life is chosen, it is indicative of mental capacities that can recognize alternatives, including the possibility of long-range planning. To summarize, the normal adult has the capacities necessary for formulating and acting on different conceptions of how he should live his life. Let us say that persons who have these capacities are autonomous agents.

Should we say that persons simply are autonomous agents? Unfortunately (at least for those of us who prefer simple solutions) this proposal has serious problems. Do we want to say that someone who lacks the relevant capacities for a short period of time, say one hour, is not a person during this hour? This could mean that the unconscious accident victim has no moral standing. Assuming that this is not a conclusion we are willing to universalize, let us conclude that the temporarily comatose do have moral standing.[14] Suppose that we know that Jones will be comatose for exactly one year, and then he will regain his former capacities and thus become a self-directing agent. In this case, Jones is a person. This example suggests that the length of time it takes Jones to recover is not morally relevant. This idea can be applied to children as well. Children, like Jones, will acquire the capacities necessary for being autonomous agents. They differ from Jones because they do not yet have the capacities, but it is not clear why this difference should be morally relevant. Assuming that it is not, then children (at least normal ones) have moral standing. The upshot is that the word 'person', as it is used in the freedom principle, refers to actual and potential autonomous agents.

Some persons, young children for example, may be treated paternalistically. The young child has the equal right to be free, but it is not capable of exercising this right. Others therefore may take care of the child, including treating the child paternalistically until the child becomes an autonomous agent. When does this happen? I have no special insight into this very difficult question. Being overly protective can be a problem because children often learn by making mistakes. In contrast, many parents today are so unwilling to discipline their children that their parenting borders on legal neglect. There are no easy answers in this area.

What is the justification for interfering with otherwise normal adults who are temporarily impaired? Let us consider the case of the drunk who wants to drive home. We may of course wish to intervene to protect others, but for now I want to focus on the paternalistic reason for interfering. One rationale is that the drunk is childlike in his understanding of the situation and his lack of self-control. In addition, there is another possible justification—that the interference is consistent with the person's "real" values. This reason for interfering assumes that when the drunk sobers up (i.e., is in his right mind) he will appreciate the wisdom of the interference. I am sympathetic to this approach, but there is a clear danger that it will be overused.[15] It is easy to assume that a person's real values are the values that any reasonable person would have. This could lead some to conclude that a person with an unusually high tolerance for risky activity must not be in his right mind.

What landmarks does the libertarian view provide to guide us through this difficult area? Since the paternalistic relationship is inherently unequal, there is a strong presumption against the paternalistic treatment of adults. Interference is justified only when an adult is clearly incompetent, for example, persons who have suffered serious brain damage from an accident or stroke or persons in the later stages of Alzheimer's disease. Otherwise, adults must be allowed to pursue their own good in their own way. If this formula were followed, very few, if any, paternalistic laws aimed at adults would remain. Seat-belt laws, for example, interfere with normal adults, and thus they are clearly unacceptable. This example illustrates another difference between the freedom principle and the utility principle. There are good utilitarian reasons for requiring the use of seat belts: They save lives and reduce injuries. However, libertarians maintain that adults have the right to decide what risks they wish to take.

I shall conclude this section with an examination of Rawls's principle of equal liberty. Because of its apparent similarity to the freedom principle, it is important to establish that the two principles are very different. In *A Theory of Justice*, Rawls formulates the principle of equal liberty as follows: "Each person is to have an equal right to the most extensive total system of equal liberties compatible with a similar system of liberty for all."[16] The freedom principle applies to relations between individuals: Each person ought to grant other persons an equal right to be free. In contrast, Rawls's principles of justice regulate the basic structure of society. This makes his principle of equal liberty far more abstract than the freedom principle. The basic structure of society is determined by its major social institutions, which include "the political constitution and the principal economic and social arrangements" (7). The major social institutions are to be structured so that they provide the most extensive total system of equal liberties compatible with a similar system of liberty for all. What does this mean?

Rawls stipulates that an institution is "a public system of rules which defines offices and positions with their rights and duties, powers and immunities, and the like" (55). Rawls provides some examples to help us understand this very abstract definition. His examples include games and rituals, trials and parliaments, markets and systems of property, the monogamous family, and the legal protection of freedom of thought and liberty of conscience (7, 55). In addition to being able to identify particular institutions, the principle of equal liberty requires an assessment of the "total system" of institutions in terms of maximizing equal liberty.

> Now all the liberties of equal citizenship must be the same for each member of society. Nevertheless some of the equal liberties may be more extensive than others, assuming their extensions can be compared. More realistically, if it is supposed that at best each liberty can be measured on its own scale, then the various liberties can be broadened or narrowed according to how they affect one another. When lexical order holds, a basic liberty covered by the first principle can be limited only for the sake of liberty itself, that is, only to insure the same liberty or a different basic liberty is properly protected and to adjust the one system of basic liberties in the best way. The adjustment of the complete scheme of liberty depends solely upon the definition and extent of the particular liberties. Of course, this scheme is always to be assessed from the standpoint of the representative equal citizen. From the perspective of the constitutional convention or the legislative stage (as appropriate) we are to ask which system it would be rational for him to prefer. (204)

Is it realistic to think that normal moral agents can make these assessments?

The principle of equal liberty would be easier to understand and apply if its scope were limited. After giving his provisional formulation of the two principles of justice, Rawls proposes what appears to be a significant limitation on what the principle of equal liberty covers:

> ... these principles presuppose that the social structure can be divided into two more or less distinct parts, the first principle applying to the one, the second to the other. They distinguish between those aspects of the social system that define and secure the equal liberties of citizenship and those that specify and establish social and economic inequalities. The basic liberties of citizens are, roughly speaking, political liberty (the right to vote and to be eligible for public office) together with freedom of speech and assembly; liberty of conscience and freedom of thought; freedom of the person along with the right to hold (personal) property; and freedom from arbitrary arrest and seizure as defined by the concept of the rule of law. (61)

Are the freedom to choose one's occupation and the freedom to marry and raise children covered by the principle of equal liberty? In other words, are they included in the equal liberties of citizenship? Given the importance of these freedoms, it seems unlikely that the bargainers in the original position would allow them to be governed by Rawls's second principle of justice.[17] This would mean that any inequalities resulting from these choices would be allowed only if they benefit the least-advantaged members of society. Perhaps these freedoms are covered under the vague phrase "freedom of the person."

In *Political Liberalism*, Rawls reformulates the principle of equal liberty: "Each person has an equal right to a fully adequate scheme of equal liberties which is compatible with a similar scheme of liberties for all."[18] In this formulation, the words "a fully adequate scheme" replace the words "the most extensive total system." Rawls makes it clear that he has decided not to give a general interpretation of his first principle. Instead, the principle is a list of liberties.[19]

> A further preliminary matter is that the equal basic liberties in the first principle of justice are specified by a list as follows: freedom of thought and liberty of conscience; the political liberties and freedom of association, as well as the freedoms specified by the liberty and integrity of the person; and finally, the rights and liberties covered by the rule of law. No priority is assigned to liberty as such, as if the exercise of something called "liberty" has a preeminent value and is the main if not the sole end of political social justice.[20]

I assume that I am not alone in thinking that the rights on this list are extremely general and abstract.

In a public conception of justice, basic liberties cannot be basic simply because Rawls says they are. Thus, Rawls must do three things: (1) provide a general interpretation of each basic liberty (so that we can understand them), (2) explain why each liberty is on the list, and (3) explain why other liberties are not on the list (the problem of completeness). To me, these tasks seem more daunting than providing a general interpretation of the principle of equal liberty.

Why does Rawls want to avoid giving a general interpretation of his first principle? If Rawls gives a general interpretation of the principle, it would apply to economic freedoms that Rawls does not want to recognize.[21] Given the lexical priority of the first principle, if a general right to participate in capitalistic acts were recognized, Rawls's second principle of justice could become irrelevant. This may also explain why a Lockean conception of justice does not appear on the list of alternatives the representatives in the original position consider (124). This exclusion is not consistent with Rawls's stated methodology: "The source of the alternatives is the historical tradition of moral and political philosophy. We are to regard the original position and the characterization of the deliberations of the parties as a means of selecting principles of justice from the alternatives already presented."[22] In the American political tradition, Locke is more important than the utilitarians. Yet various versions of utilitarianism are on the list of alternatives, but Locke is not.

In addition, it can be misleading to present a general principle, such as the principle of equal liberty, and then not give a general interpretation of this principle. A less misleading presentation would simply say, Here are the basic liberties (given by a list). To summarize this list in the form of a general principle gives the impression that the list is deduced from the principle. However, this cannot be the case, since no general interpretation of the principle has been given. The principle is simply a name for the list. Historically, general moral principles have been used in the deduction of moral conclusions. Thus, it is easy to be misled and think that this is what Rawls is doing. This misunderstanding may lead one to think that Rawls has a more systematic (less ad hoc) justification of his basic liberties than he actually has.

Rawls's principle of equal liberty is abstract and vague, yet Rawls wants his principles of justice to serve as a *public* conception of justice (5). This requires that normal persons can understand them so that they can decide whether their society satisfies the principles. I do not understand the principle of equal liberty sufficiently to know what it requires.[23] Unless my capacity for understanding moral principles falls below that of normal moral agents, the principles cannot be the basis for a public conception of justice. I take up these issues again in Section 3, where I examine simplicity as one of the criteria for judging moral theories.

Unlike the principle of equal liberty, the freedom principle applies directly to real individuals and its requirements can be stated clearly and succinctly. As a general rule, it is wrong to cause other persons to behave involuntarily by coercing or deceiving them. This follows from the assumption that interactions should be based on mutual consent. Interference is defined as causing another person to behave involuntarily, and thus the freedom principle usually requires noninterference. Some cases of self-defense, punishment, and paternalism are exceptions to the noninterference rule. There will of course be hard cases—that is, situations where it is difficult to determine what the principle requires. For example, it is clear that young children may be treated paternalistically, but we may be uncertain what to say about a case involving a 12-year-old. The freedom principle does not provide a mechanical decision procedure for all cases. Some cases call for judgment, and getting it right depends on the wisdom of the judge. However, the basic ideas underlying the freedom principle are clear, and normal moral agents can understand why the hard cases are difficult.

3. Evaluating Moral Theories

Are there rational criteria for evaluating moral theories? Let us begin to answer this question by considering what a moral theory is. The moral theorist seeks to give a systematic account of moral thought and practice. This project assumes that morality has an underlying structure that the theorist wishes to reveal. This is done by showing that the seemingly disparate elements of morality can be accounted for by the theory's fundamental values. How does the moral theorist know whether he or she has successfully achieved this goal? I believe that there can be no final determination of truth in this area, but I also reject moral skepticism because there are rational standards for evaluating moral theories. These criteria allow us to make comparative judgments—that one moral theory is better than another. In this regard, moral theories are like scientific theories, and the standards used for choosing between rival scientific theories can also be used to evaluate moral theories. These standards include explanatory power, simplicity, coherence, and empirical content. An examination of each criterion follows. Along the way, I shall contrast the libertarian theory with utilitarianism and some other moral views.

Explanatory Power

Why are some acts wrong? I shall examine two approaches to this question: consequentialism and Kantianism.[24] Consequentialism maintains that acts are wrong when they have bad consequences. Kantianism holds that the primary concern of morality is how persons should relate to each other: It requires respect for persons as free and equal beings. According to the libertarian interpretation of this requirement, the ideal interaction is based on mutual consent, and thus it is usually wrong to coerce or deceive others. Let us consider a specific example in order to illustrate these very general remarks.

Why is cheating wrong? Suppose that Jack cheats on an exam that is not graded on a curve, and he gets a B when he would have gotten a C without cheating. Since the exam is not graded on a curve, Jack's grade does not affect the grades of the other students in the class. Given that Jack is happy to get the better grade and no students are harmed, what is wrong with this act of cheating? Presumably, consequentialists will look for bad consequences, which are not immediately obvious. Perhaps by cheating instead of studying Jack did not learn something that he will need to know later. This suggestion is very speculative, and as a consequentialist, Jack may wonder why he should choose an uncertain future benefit over a present benefit. Perhaps Jack will develop a bad character that will cause problems in the future. Again, this is speculation, and we can add further details to the case that cast doubt on it. Suppose that Jack studies very hard in the courses he considers important and only cheats in required courses where he sees no benefit in learning what is being taught.

So far we have assumed that the course is not graded on a curve. Let us change this assumption so we can identify a student who is harmed by Jack's cheating. When Jack gets a B instead of a C, the student who would have gotten the lowest B gets a C instead. It is now clear that the cheating produces a bad consequence, but all we can conclude so far is that Jack benefits and another student is harmed. Perhaps Jack needs the B more than the other student, and thus the cheating still produces, on balance, good consequences. Suppose that Jack gets a B when he would have gotten a D without cheating. Now two students are harmed: the one who would have received the lowest B and the one who would have received the lowest C. Since two students are harmed and only Jack benefits, can we now conclude that the cheating, under these assumptions, is wrong?

From a Kantian point of view, the consequential approach to cheating is wrongheaded from the beginning. What is wrong with cheating is the deception that is involved. Suppose the instructor would have flunked Jack had he known that Jack cheated, and thus successful cheating requires that Jack deceive the instructor. In the process, he uses the instructor as a mere means to his own end. The primary concern of morality is how persons should relate to each other, not how to produce the best consequences.

When dealing with complex issues it is usually helpful to begin with what we know best, which in the case at hand is the core of morality, the basic moral rules. Every moral system contains prohibitions against aggression, theft, and deception. However, when it comes to the exceptions to the basic moral rules, there is considerable variability in what different systems allow. Suppose that an act utilitarian, Jill, borrows money, promising to repay the loan on a specific date. When the time to pay up arrives, Jill decides that the money could be put to better use relieving starvation in Somalia, so she donates the money to CARE. Jill believes that this use of the money produces the best consequences, since the Somalis have greater needs than her creditor. According to the freedom principle, in contrast, Jill should repay the loan; otherwise she will cause her creditor to behave involuntarily, since he would not have loaned the money had he known that Jill would not repay.

In general, act utilitarians say that moral rules may be broken when doing so maximizes utility. Many critics have rejected this explanation on the ground (among others) that act utilitarianism could require violations of rights. Suppose that five lives could be saved if an innocent person is killed and his heart, liver, pancreas, and kidneys are used for organ transplants. In some circumstances this act could maximize utility, but most persons find it hard to believe that the act could be morally justified. A hardheaded utilitarian could claim that our beliefs, in this case and others like it, need revision. Those who are reluctant to change their views can look for an explanation of why the act is wrong; one possibility is rule utilitarianism.

John Harsanyi claims that one of the strengths of rule utilitarianism is its explanatory power: "One important virtue of rule utilitarian theory is its remarkable *explanatory power* as a theory of morality. I take it that the explanatory power of a philosophic or scientific theory is directly related to the number and complexity of the facts it can explain, and is inversely related to the number and complexity of the explanatory principles it needs to accomplish this task."[25] Harsanyi argues that rule utilitarianism has great explanatory power because it is able to explain the moral "facts" with one basic principle. A similar claim cannot be made on behalf of act utilitarianism, according to Harsanyi, because it oversimplifies and distorts the nature of morality. In particular he states that act utilitarianism is an unsatisfactory theory of morality because "it cannot avoid assigning absolute priority to social expediency over standards of justice, over individual rights, and over personal obligations."[26] Let us consider whether rule utilitarianism is vulnerable to a similar objection. Suppose that a society contains a racial minority whose members are enslaved. Could the rules that define this practice be justified on utilitarian grounds?[27] The answer would seem to depend on how many benefit from the practice of slavery in comparison to how many are harmed. It is perfectly consistent with the utilitarian outlook to sacrifice some persons in order to benefit others. When benefits outweigh the harms, a system of slavery would be required by rule utilitarianism so long as no other alternative had higher utility.

This ground, of course, has been covered before, and utilitarians have their responses. One response is to claim that in the real world, circumstances in which slavery maximizes utility would never arise. A critic might respond by asking whether a milder form of discrimination, one that lacked actual ownership, could be justified. But this line of inquiry shows that something is seriously amiss. As Bernard Williams insists, "How many racists are involved cannot begin to be an acceptable consideration on the question of whether racism is acceptable."[28] I take Williams's point to be that even if utilitarianism requires us to reject racism, it does so for the wrong reason. It does not provide a satisfactory explanation of why racism is wrong.

In an earlier article, Harsanyi maintains that antisocial preferences such as "sadism, envy, resentment, and malice" should be excluded from utilitarian calculations.[29] He claims that preferences based on hostile feelings conflict with the spirit of goodwill that forms the basis of the utilitarian outlook. This exclusion, however, does not remove the possibility of utilitarianism justifying a system of slavery; support for slavery could be based on a desire to benefit the majority rather than on ill will toward the minority. I think that Harsanyi goes astray in part because of his failure to recognize and deal with the problem of conflicting rules. A rule utilitarian theory would probably contain a number of rules that, when considered by themselves, would preclude slavery and other less objectionable forms of discrimination. These rules are likely to be negative in that they require us to refrain from harming or interfering with others. However, these rules could conflict with positive rules that require us to benefit others. When rules conflict, presumably the rule utilitarian would follow the rule that, given the circumstances, would maximize utility. Thus, rule utilitarianism is vulnerable to many of the same objections as act utilitarianism.

In the important book *Moral Realism and the Foundations of Ethics*, David O. Brink defends a utilitarian theory that he calls objective utilitarianism (OU).[30] Most of the book consists of a careful and sophisticated defense of moral realism; however, in the last chapter Brink outlines a version of utilitarianism that is not, he claims, vulnerable to the standard objections to utilitarianism. Brink believes that OU escapes the standard objections because (1) it employs an objective theory of value, in contrast to the usual subjective theories (hedonism and various desire-satisfaction theories), and (2) it treats the utility principle as a criterion of rightness and not a decision procedure. Let us begin our analysis of OU by considering Brink's theory of value.

Brink proposes a theory of human welfare that "counts reflective pursuit and realization of agents' reasonable projects and certain personal and social relationships as components of valuable lives" (231). The pursuit and realization of permissible projects and personal and social relationships that exhibit respect for persons have *intrinsic* value. The factors that enable us to realize these values, such as freedom, education, and the conditions of basic well-being, have *extrinsic* value. I find Brink's theory of value to be intuitively attractive; however, he admits that he has presented "a very rough account of the probable relations of the various goods involved" (230).

The utility principle, in Brink's moral theory, is a criterion of rightness: It is the standard for determining which acts are right. Acts are judged by the actual value realized, and thus Brink rejects rule utilitarianism, which can "justify actions that are not optimific" (237). The utility principle is not a decision procedure because persons will often produce the best consequences by following moral rules rather than applying the utility principle directly. Consider the case where Jill decides not to repay a loan and instead donates the money to famine relief. In regard to this kind of case, Brink says the following:

> ... the causal sequences initiated by keeping and violating promissory agreements are quite complex; our time, information, and cognitive abilities are limited; and our calculations are subject to various forms of bias and distortion. For these reasons, we are unable to discriminate reliably for cases in which the results of breaking our promises would be marginally better than keeping them. We are cognitively and motivationally such that by utilitarian reasoning we could violate a promise and so maximize welfare in one case, only by being such as to violate promises in cases where this fails to maximize welfare. Therefore, utilitarianism requires us to act from sturdy motives and direct appeal not to utilitarianism, but to rules of promise-keeping. (265–266)

I have two problems with this defense of OU. First, Brink has rejected rule utilitarianism: Sometimes we should apply the utility principle directly instead of following rules. How can we know this? Brink tells us that utilitarian reasoning is necessary when rules conflict (258), but how often does this occur? Consider the cheating example. Suppose that Jack's list of rules includes Do not cheat and Please your parents. He can please his parents by getting a better grade through cheating. Does his situation call for the direct application of utilitarian reasoning? An open-ended rule such as Help the needy will generate conflicts continually, for we could always do more to help the needy. Thus, if we choose to do anything else, such as go to a concert or read a book, our actions will conflict with this rule. Presumably, the rules about helping the needy will be more specific, but what exactly will they require of us? Without a list of rules, there seems to be no way of knowing how often rules will conflict. If rules often conflict, OU will usually require utilitarian reasoning.

Brink also tells us that we may break moral rules when it is clear that doing so will produce the best consequences (258). But given our liabilities as utilitarian reasoners (lack of information, bias, etc.), how can we be trusted to decide when direct application of the utility principle is called for? This raises the possibility that OU should be an esoteric morality known only to the utilitarian elite who can correctly decide when the utility principle should be used as a decision procedure. However, this "solution" cannot be implemented so long as conflicts between rules must be settled by utilitarian reasoning. And this leads back to the question, How often would conflicts occur? I shall say more about conflicts between rules in the section on coherence.

How would Brink deal with the case where welfare is maximized if an innocent person is killed and his organs used to save the lives of five persons? Since the details can make a difference, more needs to be said about the circumstances of this case. Suppose that a doctor is treating six patients. Five of them need organ transplants and the sixth patient, Joe, is in a temporary coma due to a motorcycle accident. Joe is unmarried, has fathered no children, and no one has come to visit him. The doctor can kill Joe so that it will appear that he died of natural causes, and then he can "legally" use Joe's organs to save the lives of his other patients. If the doctor accepts OU, should he kill Joe and save the others? One thing at least is clear: If killing Joe and saving the others maximizes welfare, it is the right thing to do according to OU. In fact, since OU is the criterion of rightness, it would be wrong not to kill Joe and save the others. No shifting back and forth from the criterion of rightness to the correct decision procedure should obscure this fact. If you believe that it is wrong to kill Joe even when it maximizes welfare, you are not a utilitarian.

Another standard objection to utilitarianism is that its requirements are excessively burdensome because it would often require the sacrifice of our personal projects and relationships in order to promote the welfare of others. This conclusion seems to flow directly from the utilitarian conception of moral equality: The welfare of each person counts equally (234, 284). Brink admits that this objection has some force against classical utilitarianism, but he thinks that OU is not similarly vulnerable. OU has an objective theory of value that counts pursuit of personal projects as a primary component of valuable lives. Also, OU is not a decision procedure, and it is difficult to know how to help strangers. We usually do better at promoting the general welfare if we help those we know best, such as friends and family members. Finally, Brink claims that our obligations to promote the welfare of strangers "can be carried out in predictable and minimally intrusive ways" (275). What Brink has in mind is contributing our fair share to welfare programs and charities.

This last point may be true if one focuses only on the society one happens to be living in. For example, in a wealthy country such as the United States, contributions to welfare programs and charities may meet our obligations to members of *this society*. However, equal concern for the welfare of *all* persons (not just Americans) would require radical changes in our lifestyles. Consider, for example, the suffering in the former Soviet Union caused by enormous environmental problems and the lack of modern medical care. Similar observations could be made about many countries in Africa and some countries in Asia and South America. If the welfare of these people counts equally with our own, how can we continue to spend money on luxuries like sports, entertainment, and philosophy courses? On a smaller scale, suppose that a stranger suffering from kidney disease will die unless she receives a kidney transplant. You have two healthy kidneys. Is it your *duty* to donate one of them? If you are required to count the welfare of others as equal to your own, the answer seems to be yes.

Bernard Williams presses a somewhat different objection: The demands of utilitarianism are unreasonable because they require us to push aside the personal projects and commitments that make our lives worth living.

> The point is that he [an agent] is identified with his actions as flowing from his projects and attitudes which in some cases he takes seriously at the deepest level, as what his life is about. ... It is absurd to demand of such a man, when the sums come in from the utility network which the projects of others have in part determined, that he should just step aside from his own project and decision and acknowledge the decision which utilitarian calculation requires. It is to alienate him in a real sense from his action and the source of his action in his own convictions. It is to make him into a channel between the input of everyone's projects, including his own, and an output of optimific decision; but this is to neglect the extent to which *his* actions and *his* decisions have to be seen as the actions and decisions which flow from the projects and attitudes with which he is most closely identified. It is thus, in the most literal sense, an attack on his integrity.[31]

Brink believes that OU is not vulnerable to Williams's objection because his theory of value directly assigns importance to personal projects and relationships. However, since OU maintains that the welfare of all persons is equally valuable, it entails that the permissible projects of others are just as valuable as your own. Thus, the person who accepts OU has a deep personal commitment to her own projects (since they provide the meaning and significance for her life) while at the same time holding that it would be wrong to give preference to her own projects. At best, this is a difficult balancing act; at worst, it could engender paralyzing confusion.

The freedom principle has its own interpretation of moral equality: It requires us to grant others the *equal* right to be free. This requirement, however, can usually be met by leaving others alone. Furthermore, since there are no unchosen duties to help others, we can control our positive obligations by limiting the commitments we make. Thus, the libertarian account of moral equality permits a deep commitment to personal projects and relationships.

Let us conclude this section by reviewing what the freedom principle requires in some of the cases we have considered. In the case where Jack cheats on the exam, he violates the principle by deceiving the instructor. When Jill chooses not to repay her loan, she causes her creditor to behave involuntarily, since he would not have loaned her the money had he known she would default. In the doctor case, the temporarily comatose Joe is a potential autonomous agent, and thus he is a person. As such, he is covered by the freedom principle. Since there is no reason to believe that he would consent to being used for spare parts, killing Joe is impermissible. The application of the freedom principle in each of these cases is straightforward: The victim does not consent to being used by the agent and none of the exceptions to the noninterference rule (self-defense, punishment, and paternalism) apply. One of the advantages of the freedom principle is its simplicity.

Simplicity

The idea of simplicity, as it applies to moral theories, is complex. This can be seen in the example of act utilitarianism. On the surface it appears to be a very simple theory, for it purports to reduce the complexity of our moral lives to a single injunction: Maximize utility. However, the calculations necessary to determine which acts would actually maximize utility can be exceedingly complex. Act utilitarians usually bypass this difficulty by dealing with hypothetical cases where the relevant facts are stipulated. This prompts Alan Donagan to comment, "What ought to astonish readers of their work is neither the complexity nor the difficulty of their calculations, but their absence."[32] For our present purposes, the lesson to be learned is that the simplicity of moral theories can be judged on at least two levels: simplicity of structure and simplicity of application.

Why should we prefer that a moral theory have a simple structure? This question can be answered by considering the goal of the moral theorist, which is to demonstrate that valid moral claims form a rationally understandable system. As Harsanyi notes, the alternative would seem to be that our moral beliefs consist of "a long list of logically independent and irreducible moral 'facts,' each of them directly given to our moral intuition without any real possibility of a deeper rational explanation."[33] The theorist wants to uncover connections between the seemingly disparate elements of morality, connections that reveal that morality has an underlying structure. This structure is revealed by reducing morality to its fundamental values and showing that specific claims are deducible from (or at least implied by) these general values. There is no reason to accept three fundamental moral values if two will do the job. The ideal would be the reduction of morality to one general principle. The obvious danger in the pursuit of this ideal is oversimplification; it is likely that morality is too complex to be explainable by a single principle. The need for simplicity of application, however, may push us in the direction of oversimplification. We want, I assume, a moral theory that can be understood and used by normal moral agents.

This point is stressed by Gert:

> [A moral system] must not only be simple enough that it is understood and can be applied by moral agents, there is a sense in which it must be known by all moral agents. A moral system that is significantly novel, or that can be understood or applied only by philosophers, is obviously inadequate. A moral theory may be somewhat more complex, but if it provides essential support for the moral system, it must also be understandable by and acceptable to all those who are subject to moral judgments. Otherwise, one would make moral judgments of people using a moral system which one could not defend or justify to them.[34]

The need for a simple theory follows from the normative ideal of moral equality: We do not want a theory that only the moral "experts" can understand. I think that Gewirth's moral theory, for example, violates this requirement. His theory is based on the Principle of Generic Consistency (PGC): Act in accord with the generic rights of your recipients as well as of yourself. The theory contains rights to freedom and well-being. The right to well-being includes rights to basic goods, nonsubtractive goods, and additive goods. The goods that are the objects of the right to well-being must be given generic-dispositional interpretations. Gewirth's theory provides three criteria for resolving conflicts between rights: prevention of the violation of rights, degrees of necessity of action, and indirect applications of the PGC based on the rules of justified institutions. It contains two kinds of justification for institutions, procedural and instrumental. In addition, specific institutional activities must promote the ultimate moral end, equality of generic rights. How would this theory be taught to children, or to adults who have not had many years of philosophical training? In response to a somewhat different problem, Gewirth stresses "the universality of the PGC as a principle addressed to and capable of being understood by all rational agents. . . ."[35] I think that this assumption is true only under a very elitist assumption of who counts as a rational agent. Unless we are willing to accept an esoteric morality, a satisfactory moral theory must be simpler than Gewirth's.[36]

I have said that the freedom principle is the fundamental moral principle. Can a single principle do justice to the complexity of morality? The freedom principle covers one area of morality, moral requirements. Different values are needed for understanding morally good acts that are beyond the call of duty. In addition, libertarian theory needs a principle of justice governing severity of punishment. I discuss these matters in Sections 5 and 8, where I conclude that a moral theory with one fundamental moral principle can recognize additional moral values and that these values can help us choose between alternatives that do not violate the fundamental principle.

Coherence

A moral theory that entails the prescriptions "Do X" and "Do not do X" will obviously fail as an action guide, at least in the relevant circumstances. Such a theory is incoherent in that it yields contradictory prescriptions. This type of incoherence should not be a problem for moral theories with one fundamental value, but a problem of practical incoherence could arise if the value is used to justify moral rules. One rule may tell us to do X and another to do Y, but a person may find herself in circumstances where she cannot do both. At this point, one can return to the fundamental value to resolve the conflict. As I have noted, this would seem to be the natural strategy for a rule utilitarian to employ, but it is a strategy that rule utilitarians should be wary of, for it may collapse the distinction between act and rule utilitarianism.

To see the problem, let us construct a simple rule utilitarian theory. In addition to the basic moral rules (Do not lie, Do not steal, and Do not attack others), let us add three more: Keep your promises, Take care of your children, and Help the needy. I have left out the "usually" qualification, but let us assume that a rule may be justifiably broken when the rule conflicts with another rule and it is determined that utility would be maximized (in the particular circumstances) by following the other rule. Which rules are likely to conflict? Since we can always leave others alone, the basic moral rules will not conflict with each other. The additional rules, in contrast, are positive in that they require us to do things for other persons. They can conflict with each other and they can conflict with the basic moral rules. For example, in order to keep your promise to repay a loan, you may have to steal some money. Which rule should you follow and which one should you break? According to our theory, you should follow the rule that, given your circumstances, would maximize utility. In this case, there seems to be little difference between our rule utilitarian theory and act utilitarianism.[37] As noted when I examined Brink's moral theory, whether this is typical will depend on how often moral rules conflict. The rule requiring us to help the needy presents an obvious problem. Given the amount of suffering in the world, more could always be done for the needy. So unless we see a dramatic reduction in poverty, disease, natural disasters, mental illness, war, and so on, this rule will conflict with whatever else we choose to do. Thus, our rule utilitarian theory collapses into act utilitarianism, for we would appeal invariably to the utility principle to determine what to do.

To preserve the theory, we must replace the "needy" rule with rules that are less open-ended. A wishy-washy rule such as "Provide some help to the needy" is too vague to be useful as an action guide. More promising is the rule that makes the duty to help categorically binding in emergency situations where the agent is the only one in a position to help. A moment's reflection, however, reveals that even this rule is unacceptable, for it may be the case that providing aid is risky. Hence, an attempt to help may be counterproductive, resulting, say, in the deaths of two persons rather than one. An act utilitarian will point out that what is needed is a calculation concerning whether the risk is worth the gamble. Furthermore, he can claim that an agent cannot determine whether she is in an emergency situation without doing what looks suspiciously like a utilitarian calculation. So what is the difference between act and rule utilitarianism?

Problems in formulating rules about helping others make the libertarian view seem more attractive. According to the freedom principle, we have no unchosen duties to aid other persons. Helping the needy is good, but unless the agent and recipient have a special relationship, it is beyond the call of duty. Libertarians do recognize positive duties, but only when they are voluntarily assumed. If you promise to help someone, you have a duty to help. If you choose to have a child, then you have a duty to take care of it. Such positive duties can conflict with the basic moral rules (and with each other), but the likelihood of conflicts is greatly reduced. Furthermore, one can control how likely they are by limiting one's commitments.

Let us next consider a rights-based moral theory called dualism. In addition to positing the fundamental right of libertarianism, the equal right to be free, dualism adds a second fundamental right, the equal right to basic goods. The idea of basic goods is more complex than one may initially think, but let us ignore these problems and assume that it includes the basic necessities of life such as food, shelter, clothing, and in some cases medical care. How does dualism differ from libertarianism? A case from Peter Singer can get us started: "The path from the library at my university to the Humanities lecture theater passes a shallow ornamental pond. Suppose that on my way to give a lecture, I notice that a small child has fallen in and is in danger of drowning. Would anyone deny that I ought to wade in and pull the child out?"[38] According to libertarianism, saving the child is a good thing to do, but it is not a moral requirement. Since there are no unchosen duties to help others, a Good Samaritan law requiring a passerby to help would violate libertarian rights. The dualist maintains that the child has the equal right to basic goods (in this case oxygen), and the duty to save the child would fall on whoever is in a position to help. What would a dualist say about a Good Samaritan law that requires passersby to help? To answer this question, the dualist needs a rule (or rules) for handling conflicts between the fundamental rights. A dualist can support Good Samaritan laws only if the equal right to basic goods takes precedence over the equal right to be free. There is an obvious reason for thinking that basic goods are primary: One has to be alive to make choices, and thus freedom has value only for persons who have access to basic goods.

Dualism has different practical implications than libertarianism only in cases where the equal right to basic goods takes precedence over the equal right to be free. Dualism is a much simpler theory if, in cases of conflict, the equal right to basic goods always overrides the equal right to be free. Is this a plausible view? Suppose that persons with kidney disease are dying because not enough kidneys are being donated for transplants. Do those of us with two healthy kidneys have a *duty* to become donors? I have found few people who think that morality requires this sacrifice. How does this case differ from saving the life of the child? An obvious reply is donating a kidney involves a much bigger sacrifice than saving the child. When is a sacrifice too much to demand? Gewirth's moral theory, which is based on rights to freedom and well-being, recognizes a positive duty to help others achieve well-being when they are unable to do so through their own efforts. This duty holds when assistance can be given at no comparable cost to oneself. In the context of discussing the duty to contribute to welfare programs, Gewirth states: "The PGC (Principle of Generic Consistency) by itself provides sufficient ground for the conclusion that positive beneficence of the differential-distributive kind is a strict duty of those who are most fortunate. For their being the most fortunate entails that they can engage in such action at no comparable cost to themselves."[39] This statement suggests that the phrase "no comparable cost" can be interpreted to mean, If your beneficiary gains more than you give up, you ought to help. In the kidney example, this would mean that those of us with two healthy kidneys have the duty to become donors. It is hard to see how a more moderate interpretation of the duty to help could be consistent with the dualist's assumption of moral equality, namely, that persons have the equal right to basic goods.

Dualism recognizes positive duties that libertarianism rejects. What are the practical implications of this difference? Let me begin to answer this question by stipulating that a moral theory is logically incoherent when it yields prescriptions that would be incompatible in any possible world. A theory that entails the prescriptions "Do X" and "Do not do X" is logically incoherent. A theory is contingently incoherent when, given the way the world is, its prescriptions are incompatible. Dualism, for example, is contingently incoherent when the equal right to basic goods requires a society to have a welfare system but the taxes necessary to fund the system violate the equal right of persons to be free. Contingent incoherence holds only in cases where both rights cannot be satisfied. The ideal solution to the problem of poverty, according to dualism, would be voluntary programs to help the indigent. In this case, no one's rights would be violated. Thus, it is possible to be a theoretical dualist and a libertarian in practice. All that is needed is the empirical belief that voluntary efforts to help the needy would be as effective as tax-funded programs, and therefore each person's right to basic goods would, as nearly as possible, be satisfied. I take up these matters again in Section 8.

Logical incoherence and contingent incoherence are negative criteria in the sense that they disqualify, or tend to disqualify, moral theories. Under a broad interpretation, coherence is a positive criterion in the sense that a coherent theory is more likely to be true. This point is stressed by Brink:

> Coherentism makes justification a matter of relations among beliefs: other things being equal, the more interconnections and mutual support among beliefs, the better justified those beliefs are. Coherentism places a premium on systematic explanation. Coherentism, therefore, favors unified moral theories over nonunified or fragmented theories. Indeed, coherentism not only favors unified moral theories but also unification between moral theories and our nonmoral beliefs. Insofar as a moral theory explains the connections among moral considerations and arranges them in a systematic fashion, as unified theories do, it makes our beliefs more coherent and better justified.[40]

Coherentism requires that our beliefs, both moral and nonmoral, be mutually supporting. A comprehensive conception of the good society includes moral, social, political, legal, and economic views. The coherence of the conception is enhanced when these views are mutually supportive. For example, the plausibility of libertarian moral theory is enhanced by its compatibility with economic theory, and the plausibility of free market economics is enhanced by a moral theory that supports the justice of free market outcomes. The plausibility of libertarian moral theory is enhanced by showing that it promotes important human values such as health and happiness (well-being). An analysis of the idea of happiness reveals the importance of freedom in the achievement of worthy lives. Such explanatory interconnections yield a web-of-belief where moral and nonmoral beliefs are mutually supportive.[41] Is libertarian moral theory more coherent than Brink's version of utilitarianism? There is no mechanical procedure for answering this question. We have to compare the theories and make a judgment as to which one is more consistent with what we know about morality, human nature, and society.

Empirical Content

Every moral theory makes assumptions about human nature and society. These assumptions should be compatible with what is known about human beings and their social relations. The failure to pass this test can provide rational grounds for rejecting moral theories. Consider a moral theory where the theorist accepts a hedonistic theory of value, and this assumption is based on the "fact" that human beings seek pleasure and shun pain.[42] Do human beings shun pain? An objective observer, one whose vision was not clouded by a desire for a reductionist theory of motivation, would not reach this conclusion. Even if we limit our observations to physical pain, we must acknowledge that persons often engage in activities that are known to be painful. What motivates boxers and football players? Perhaps they are seeking fame and glory, but clearly the avoidance of pain is not high on their list of values. As for emotional pain, some persons aspire to the achievement of difficult goals, and in doing so they leave themselves open to the pain of rejection and failure. Moreover, the struggle to achieve goals such as wealth and power is often painful. We can add further complexity to the motivational picture by noting that persons can be motivated by love and benevolence. These concerns have little to do with seeking pleasure and avoiding pain.

Bentham's version of utilitarianism is unacceptable because his hedonistic theory of value is false.[43] Specific utilitarian recommendations can also be refuted by showing that the proposals are counterproductive. An example is the minimum-wage law designed to help the poor, which in fact makes things worse for the people it is supposed to help. As we shall see, many liberal policies fail this test: They harm the people who need assistance.

On a larger scale, visions of the good society can fail because they make unrealistic or implausible assumptions about the perfectibility of human beings. Socialist Michael Harrington provides an interesting example. His utopian vision includes the abolition of money and the abolition of compulsory work.

> It is the idea of an utterly new society in which some of the fundamental limitations of human existence have been transcended. Its most basic premise is that man's battle with nature has been completely won and there is therefore more than enough of material goods for everyone. As a result of this unprecedented change in the environment, a psychic mutation takes place: invidious competition is no longer programmed into life by the necessity of a struggle for scarce resources; cooperation, fraternity and equality become natural. In such a world man's social productivity will reach such heights that compulsory work will no longer be necessary. And as more and more things are provided free, money, that universal equivalent by means of which things are rationed, will disappear.
>
> That, in very brief outline, is what socialism ultimately is. It will never come to pass in its ideal form, yet it is important to detail the dream in order to better design each approximation to it.[44]

To progress toward this vision of the good society, the government should provide "more and more goods and services free: medicine, housing, transportation, a healthy diet, etc."[45] These "free" goods and services would be paid for, at least initially, by a steeply progressive income tax and an effective inheritance tax.[46]

> The standard response of many economists to such a proposition is that cliché of Economics 1: there is nothing that is really free. All commodities cost something to produce, and if the individual does not pay for them directly, someone does indirectly. But this is to miss the enormous social gain that would occur if society were to decide to pay for all the collective fundamentals of life. The change in moral atmosphere such a new mode of distribution would portend would be profound.[47]

The plausibility of Harrington's dream depends on the "psychic mutation." He tells us that persons living in capitalist societies are competitive and acquisitive. But this egoism, according to Harrington, is not a fixed part of human nature: Change the society in the proper ways and "cooperation, fraternity and equality become natural." Is there any empirical evidence that supports this claim? More specifically, can Harrington point to a socialist society where the psychic mutation has taken place? The obvious answer is no.

Harrington is asking us to take a huge gamble. His policy proposals require a tremendous concentration of economic power in the hands of government officials. If these officials use this power to their own advantage, as they did in the former Soviet Union, the result will be totalitarian socialism, not the democratic socialism Harrington favors. There is ample empirical evidence that persons tend to be corrupted by power; there is no empirical evidence that Harrington's psychic mutation will occur, at least on a wide enough scale. Harrington's gamble is not reasonable.

Is the libertarian view of human nature too optimistic? A common criticism is that a libertarian society allows too much freedom, i.e., government would not provide enough direction and control. What must the libertarian assume about human nature to answer this charge? For a libertarian society to work well, most persons (but not all persons) must be self-reliant and compassionate. Is this too optimistic? When I say that most persons must be self-reliant, I do not mean that they are able to live on their own without the benefits of social cooperation. Instead, I mean that they are able to take care of their own basic needs through voluntary agreements (e.g., by working) so that they do not need assistance from government or charities. For various reasons, some persons will not be able to meet their own basic needs. The libertarian assumes that most people are compassionate, to a degree, and that they will voluntarily help those who need assistance. At the very least, these assumptions are not wildly optimistic. Furthermore, rejection of these assumptions poses a serious problem for the normative ideal of moral equality. The pessimistic view says that normal persons cannot be trusted to take care of themselves and the less fortunate members of society by voluntary means. Unless they receive more direction and control from government than they would get in a libertarian society, too many will make the wrong choices about whether to help others or how to take care of themselves. If some persons should be followers (because they cannot be trusted to make the right decisions), then others must be leaders. Some persons, presumably the best and the brightest, should be rulers, and the rest should be ruled. On the conflict between paternal government and moral equality, Kant wrote:

> A government might be established on the principle of benevolence towards the people, like that of a father towards his children. Under such a paternal government (imperium paternale), the subjects, as immature children who cannot distinguish what is truly useful or harmful to themselves, would be obliged to behave purely passively and to rely on the judgment of the head of state as to how they ought to be happy, and upon his kindness in willing their happiness at all. Such a government is the greatest conceivable despotism, i.e., a constitution which suspends the entire freedom of its subjects, who thenceforth have no rights whatsoever.[48]

In noting the conflict between paternal government and moral equality, I am doing more than making an empirical observation. However, empirical assumptions about human nature are relevant to assessing the elitist criticism that the libertarian view of human beings is too optimistic. This is another example where moral and nonmoral views are mutually supportive.

4. Liberalism

Contemporary liberals such as Rawls, Scanlon, and Nagel focus on the worst-off members of society. For example, Rawls's "difference principle" entails that inequalities that do not benefit the least-advantaged members are unjust. These theorists use contract arguments to explain and defend their views. What is sought is the hypothetical consent of rational contractors. Contract arguments vary according to (inter alia) the author's analysis of rationality, the information the contractors have, and what they are deciding. In Rawls's famous version, the rational contractors are self-interested persons who do not know what talents and abilities they have, nor do they know their actual place in society. They are deciding on the fundamental principles of justice that will govern the basic structure of society.

Rawls imagines his rational contractors behind a veil of ignorance. What do they know and what information do they lack? As a test of the meaning of the difference principle, let us suppose that the contractors' list of alternative conceptions of justice includes the difference principle (inequalities must benefit the least-advantaged members of society) and a version of dualism called Friedmanism. The Friedman scheme includes a "negative income tax" where persons with incomes below a certain threshold are given a subsidy from the government.[49] This subsidy is tied into a flat-rate income-tax system. Say that personal exemptions are worth $5,000. A family of four with a $20,000 income pays no income tax. Income above $20,000 is taxed at a 20 percent rate. If the family's income falls below $20,000, the family receives 50 cents in subsidy for each dollar below the threshold. If its earned income is $12,000, for example, the family receives a subsidy of $4,000, so its net income is $16,000. Unlike our present welfare system, the poor are always better off (financially) if they earn money. To summarize, under the Friedman system (1) the poor are guaranteed a minimum income, (2) the working poor get a subsidy, and (3) the rest of the economy is organized according to free market capitalism. Free market capitalism is discussed in "Liberty and Economics"; for now I shall assume that we know, at least roughly, what it is.

To simplify matters I shall focus on the primary good of income. There is a clear difference between the Friedman system and the difference principle: Under Friedmanism the poor are guaranteed a minimum income; under the difference principle the income of the worst-off should be as high as possible (incomes will be equal unless inequalities increase the incomes of the poorest members of society). Which scheme would Rawls's rational contractors choose? The answer depends in part on what information they have. Let us consider how Friedmanism and the difference principle would work over time. If the Friedman system were started in 1990, say, the income floor for a family of four would have been $10,000; under the difference principle the same family receives $20,000. In Rawls's society, no family has an income above $200,000; in Friedman's society some persons have incomes as high as $100 million. Let us assume that large-scale income redistribution is a disincentive to production. In this case, the Friedman economy would grow at a faster rate than the Rawlsian. The Friedman economy grows, on average, say, at 3 percent per year, and real incomes double in 23 years. The much more highly regulated Rawlsian economy grows at 1 percent per year, and real incomes double in 70 years. On these assumptions, after 23 years the guaranteed income for a family of four in Friedman's society would rise to $20,000. The same family in Rawls's society would have a $24,930 income. After 46 years, the guaranteed income in Friedman's society would be $40,000, and under the difference principle, $31,420.

Would Rawls's rational contractors choose the difference principle over free market capitalism with a guaranteed income? One thing the veil of ignorance excludes is knowledge of which generation the contractors belong to. They do not know, for example, whether they will be living in the eighteenth, nineteenth, twentieth, or twenty-first centuries. How can they make rational choices without this information? Rawls assumes that his contractors are very risk averse: They will choose the highest minimum (the maximin strategy). In our example, they reject Friedmanism and choose the highest minimum ($20,000). In my opinion, this choice is not rational. Since the guaranteed income under Friedmanism exceeds the lowest income in Rawls's society in about 31 years, I would choose Friedmanism. Apparently, I am not as risk averse as Rawls's rational contractors.

What knowledge of economics do Rawls's contractors have? Do they know, for example, how inefficient central planning is? In *Theory*, Rawls says that his principles of justice do not require socialism but do not preclude it either (271–274). Perhaps we can grant that in 1971, when Rawls wrote *Theory*, the problems of socialism were not "general knowledge" that we would expect the contractors to have. This assumption seems much less plausible today. Many left-wing economists now concede that Mises and Hayek were right: Socialist planners cannot get the information they need to make good economic decisions. In commenting on the economic problems of the former Soviet Union, Robert Heilbroner states that "the system deteriorated to a point far beyond the worst economic crisis ever experienced by capitalism, and that the villain in this deterioration was the central planning system itself. The conclusion one inevitably comes to is that to whatever extent socialism depends on such a system it will not work. . . . It turns out, of course, that Mises was right. The Soviet system has long been dogged by a method of pricing that produced grotesque misallocations of effort."[50] Since the failure of central planning is general knowledge, there is no rationale within Rawls's system for keeping this information from his "rational" contractors (158). Likewise, they should know that societies with highly taxed and regulated economies have lower economic growth than societies with free market capitalism. But perhaps this knowledge would be irrelevant because their extreme risk aversion forces them to take a short-range point of view. This is reflected in their choice of the difference principle. My general point is this: If we assume that economic systems produce rising living standards (at varying rates), the first generation is the least-advantaged group (in comparison to other generations). Furthermore, the beginning distribution within a generation establishes who belongs to the worst-off group within that generation, and Rawls maintains that we should "not say that the hardships of the poor are justified by the greater welfare of later generations" (299). I do not think that this extreme short-range point of view is rational.

What is the moral motivation behind Rawls's acceptance of the difference principle? His two principles of justice are a special case of a more general conception of justice. "All social values—liberty and opportunity, income and wealth, and the bases of self-respect—are to be distributed equally unless an unequal distribution of any, or all, of these values is to everyone's advantage" (62). This general conception is motivated by a desire for a theory of justice "that nullifies the accidents of natural endowment and the contingencies of social circumstance as counters in the quest for political and economic advantage. . . . They express the result of leaving aside those aspects of the social world that seem arbitrary from a moral point of view" (15). Natural and social circumstances, like one's talents and abilities or one's place in society, are morally arbitrary. No one deserves a greater share of primary goods because of special talents or family connections. Since these advantages are undeserved, they do not justify unequal shares.

As Nozick points out, Rawls's concern over not deserving our natural talents and abilities is puzzling because he explicitly rejects distribution according to moral desert (310), and his difference principle does allow larger shares because of differences that are arbitrary from a moral point of view.[51] Presumably it is the more talented members of society who are given special incentives to be productive. What is also puzzling is that Rawls's remedies are so indirect and halfhearted. Jack is blind, and Jill has two good eyes. Giving Jack more money will not "nullify" this accident of natural endowment. If eyeball transplants were possible, giving Jack one of Jill's eyes would rectify the problem. Jill, after all, does not deserve to have two good eyes. Nozick notes that such counterexamples seem "slightly hysterical," but there is a serious point here: Rawls owes us an explanation as to why more aggressive remedies are not called for.[52]

For example, why not attack these morally arbitrary differences in natural talents and abilities at their source? Suppose that the worst-off group in the United States is composed of persons who lack the capacities necessary for being productive workers. This group includes persons who are mentally retarded and persons with serious physical handicaps. The main reason for their status as least-advantaged is the problem of reduced self-respect caused by their dependence on others. This makes the problem difficult to solve, since it cannot be dealt with simply by transferring more resources to these people. There is, however, another way to deal with it. We could reduce the size of this group by instituting licensing requirements for the right to bear children. Teenagers and women over 40 are more likely to produce offspring with mental and physical handicaps. Licenses could be limited to healthy women between the ages of 20 and 40. In addition, licenses could be denied to women who are carriers of recessive genes that could be passed on to disadvantaged offspring. Similar rules would of course apply to men where appropriate. Suppose a wife is licensed but her husband isn't. This problem could be dealt with by using artificial insemination with government-approved sperm.

Another possibility would be to prohibit procreation by sexual intercourse altogether. Eggs could be fertilized artificially, and the eggs and sperm could be carefully screened to reduce the chances that children will be born with mental and physical handicaps. In the future, there is the possibility of cloning, which would permit us to avoid moral arbitrariness by ensuring that everyone has the same natural talents and abilities. To avoid confusion, I should stress that I am not at this point examining Rawls's principles of justice, at least not directly. My concern is with an underlying assumption, that differences in natural talents and abilities are undeserved. It may be that the principle of equal liberty rules out eugenics programs such as limiting childbearing to women who are licensed.[53] I cannot comment on this because I do not understand the principle of equal liberty. I do not know what its scope is (what it covers), nor do I know how to apply it.

So far we have not looked carefully at the meaning of 'undeserved.' Let us begin the analysis by considering Rawls's companion phrase, 'arbitrary from a moral point of view.' This phrase is ambiguous. It could mean (1) there is no moral reason for X to be the way it is, or (2) there is a moral problem with the way X is. A similar ambiguity infects the word 'undeserved.' To say that a benefit is undeserved often carries the connotation that someone has done something wrong. The good grade is undeserved because the student cheated. The word 'undeserved' could also mean not deserved in the sense that there is no moral reason for one person to get the benefit rather than another person. When the word is used in this sense, it does not imply that anyone has done anything wrong. To avoid confusion, let us use the word 'nondeserved' in cases where the notion of desert does not apply, and let us reserve the word 'undeserved' for cases where there is wrongdoing.

Rawls's principle of redress states that "undeserved inequalities call for redress; and since inequalities of birth and natural endowment are undeserved, these inequalities are to be somehow compensated for" (100). The initial plausibility of this principle is diminished when we substitute the word 'nondeserved' for 'undeserved.' If inequalities are the result of wrongdoing, it seems natural to suppose that compensation is called for. If the inequalities are nondeserved, so that the notion of desert does not apply, why should there be compensation? Should the lucky lottery winner compensate those who bought losing tickets? Rawls admits that the inequalities he is concerned with are nondeserved:

> It seems to be one of the fixed points of our considered judgments that no one deserves his place in the distribution of native endowments, any more than one de-

serves one's initial starting place in society. The assertion that a man deserves the superior character that enables him to make the effort to cultivate his abilities is equally problematic; for his character depends in large part upon fortunate family and social circumstances for which he can claim no credit. The notion of desert seems not to apply to these cases. (104)

Putting so much of what individuals are and what they do into the nondeserved category is dangerous. Nozick notes that this creates a problem within Rawls's theory:

> This line of argument can succeed in blocking the introduction of a person's autonomous choices and actions (and their results) only by attributing *everything* noteworthy about the person completely to certain sorts of "external" factors. So denigrating a person's autonomy and prime responsibility for his actions is a risky line to take for a theory that otherwise wishes to buttress the dignity and self-respect of autonomous beings; especially for a theory that founds so much (including a theory of the good) upon persons' choices. One doubts that the unexalted picture of human beings Rawls' theory presupposes and rests upon can be made to fit together with the view of human dignity it is designed to lead to and embody.[54]

Like so many contemporary liberals, Rawls has stood classical liberalism on its head. Classical liberals like John Locke, Adam Smith, and Frederic Bastiat emphasized the importance of individual freedom and personal responsibility. In place of individual freedom, Rawls's principle of equal liberty applies to "representative persons" in social institutions, and in place of personal responsibility, these social institutions determine one's place in society. This radical change in outlook has had profound effects on American society, to which I shall return shortly.

When I read *Theory* initially I was surprised by Rawls's neglect of punishment. In a book over 500 pages long, punishment is mentioned three times. It no longer surprises me that Rawls ignored this topic. He rejects utilitarianism, but it is not clear that he has another basis for justifying punishment. If the diligent and hardworking cannot claim responsibility for their success, then it is hard to maintain that lawbreakers can be held responsible for what they do. From a Rawlsian point of view, what could justify punishment? More specifically, how can Rawls justify punishment in a way that does not use lawbreakers as mere means to an end (the end being the suppression of crime)?

I think that there is a fundamental problem underlying the difficulties we have found in Rawls's conception of justice. Christine Korsgaard has found the problem, although surprisingly, she claims that Rawls avoids it: "To later generations, much of moral philosophy of the twentieth century will look like a struggle to *escape* from utilitarianism. We seem to succeed in disproving one utilitarian doctrine, only to find ourselves caught in the grip of another. I believe that this is because a basic feature of the consequentialist outlook still pervades and distorts our thinking: the view that the business of morality is to *bring something about*."[55] As an alternative, Korsgaard suggests, "The subject matter of morality is not what we should bring about, but how we should relate to one another."[56] She goes on to state that Rawls understands this point: "If only Rawls has succeeded in escaping utilitarianism, it is because only Rawls has fully grasped this point. His primal scene, the original position, is one in which a group of people make a decision together. Their task is to find reasons they can share."[57]

Contrary to Korsgaard, I claim that Rawls's thinking is still distorted by his consequentialist outlook: For Rawls the primary concern of morality is to bring something about, namely a just distribution of primary goods. What else can explain the failure to see that treating the distribution of the natural abilities of individuals as "a collective asset" is to use persons as mere means? Rawls states that his principles of justice "are equivalent to an undertaking to regard the distribution of natural abilities as a collective asset so that the more fortunate are to benefit only in ways that help those who have lost out" (179). Yet he assures us that his principles "rule out even the tendency to regard men as means to one another's welfare" (183). If natural talents and abilities are a kind of communal property, what rights do members of the community have over these assets? In his analysis of the concept of property, James O. Grunebaum notes that ownership rights can include (and usually do include) the right to manage and the right to income. If members of the community (collectively) have management rights over natural abilities, the community could dictate the schools a person attends, what occupation the person trains for, whether the person can smoke, eat fatty foods, and so on. Grunebaum assumes that this interpretation would violate the principle of equal liberty. He concludes that the most plausible interpretation of Rawls's view is that members of the community have a right to the income from the employment of natural talents and abilities.[58] Thus, persons can keep the income they earn only if this benefits the least-advantaged members of society. Perhaps Rawls's abstract person does not complain of being used as mere means. Once everything that is "morally arbitrary" is stripped away—all attachments to particular persons and all preferences for one morally permissible activity over another—the abstract person has few grounds for complaining about anything.[59] It is this stripped-down person, cleansed of the morally arbitrary, who agrees to treating his natural talents and abilities as a common asset. But real people who must pay the taxes to fund the redistributive programs Rawls favors may see themselves as being used as means to another's welfare.

Earlier we noted that contract arguments vary according to the author's analysis of rationality, the information the contractors have, and what they are deciding. Suppose we take seriously Korsgaard's suggestion that the primary concern of morality is how persons should relate to one another, not what outcome we should produce. Consider how different a contract argument would look under this assumption. Unlike Rawls, we would not be seeking agreement on how to divvy up the good things in life. Instead we would be considering, for example, if anyone ever has the right to coerce another person, and if so, under what circumstances. We would quickly conclude that slavery is unacceptable because rational contractors could not agree to it. Other inherently unequal relationships would also be rejected for the same reason. We would be left with the idea that interactions (ideally) should be based on mutual consent. This is the only conclusion consistent with the assumption of moral equality.

Korsgaard writes that consequentialism conceives of ethics as "the most sublime form of technical engineering, the one that tells us how to bring about The Good."[60] It has been my contention that this description applies to Rawls. It applies as well to other liberal thinkers such as T. M. Scanlon and Thomas Nagel. Scanlon recommends the following interpretation of the difference principle: "First maximize the income, wealth, etc. of the worst-off representative person, then seek to minimize the number of people in his position (by moving them upwards); then proceed to do the same for the next worst-off social position, then the next and so on, finally seeking to maximize the benefits of those in the best-off position (as long as this does not affect others)."[61]

Scanlon is assuming that social engineers have sufficient understanding of complex markets and sufficient knowledge of human psychology to move persons from one social class to another. It is doubtful that anyone has the knowledge to accomplish this task. The wide dispersal of information in market economies is one problem. Another problem is that it is very difficult to help the poor without encouraging the behavior that produces poverty. I discuss these problems in "Liberty and Economics." A third problem is the rejection of personal responsibility implicit in Scanlon's proposal. If the poor are not as well off as they could possibly be, the society is unjust. Thus, if the lives of the poor could be improved, they are victims of unjust social conditions. Improvement depends on manipulation of the social institutions that determine their fate. When the poor accept this view, they no longer believe that they can improve their lives through their own efforts. This mind-set can be a cause of poverty. It can also be a cause of crime. If the poor are victims of an unjust society, then crime can be rationalized as a rebellion against unjust social conditions. Inequalities of wealth and income are justified (according to Scanlon and Rawls) only if they "pay their way," i.e., if the least-advantaged are better off because of the inequalities. However, since no one has sufficient information to determine this, poverty can always provide a handy rationalization for crime. The poor can claim that they could be better off under different social arrangements, and no one can refute this claim. Furthermore, since those who are well off do not deserve their comfortable lifestyles, it is all right for those who are least advantaged to take the "undeserved" possessions of the better off. Insofar as the difference principle provides a rationalization for crime, Rawls's principles of justice will not promote the stable political union he seeks.

Nagel accepts Scanlon's criterion of nonrejectability: "… I have adopted the central feature of Scanlon's account of contractualism—the idea that the right principles to govern a practice are those which no one could reasonably reject, given the aim of finding principles which could be the basis of general agreement among persons similarly motivated."[62] Like Rawls, Nagel argues that preference should be given to the worst off.[63] Nagel's methodology requires him to show that it is unreasonable to reject this view. A clear implication of his view is that a society with institutions that work well for 90 percent of the population is unjust if the 10 percent who are not well off (comparatively) could be better off under a different social arrangement. Nagel writes:

> ... the acceptance of a serious egalitarian ideal would have to appeal to a notion of negative responsibility, on the part of the society, for failing to arrange things differently in ways that it could. If it is possible for people to be economically rewarded more equally under another arrangement, then maintenance of a system which allows rewards to be proportional to productivity would have to be regarded as a social choice to permit rewards to depend substantially on differences in natural talent, education, and background. Noninterference requires justification as much as interference does: Every arrangement has to be justified by comparison with every other real possibility. ...[64]

Suppose that a market economy rewards people for being responsible and hardworking employees. Under this system, 90 percent are better off than they would be under a system with greater government involvement in the economy (e.g., higher taxes and more regulations). If government programs could improve the lives of the remaining 10 percent, Nagel must hold that this society is unjust. After studying Nagel's arguments, I still think that it is reasonable to prefer the society where 90 percent are better off to the society where 10 percent would be better off.

Also at issue is the question of which policies are most likely to reduce poverty. A good antipoverty program should encourage persons to change behaviors that produce poverty. An important ingredient would be to teach children that they have the freedom to live valuable lives, that they are personally responsible for the choices they make, that the value of their lives should be judged by the strength of their character, and that strength of character is exhibited in the virtues of self-discipline, courage, perseverance, and moral goodness. This approach does *not* tell children that the failure to live a good life is excusable because they are victims of an unjust society. Some persons start life with mental, physical, and material handicaps. However, since the value of one's life is measured (in large part) by the strength of one's character, such handicaps should be seen as challenges, not as excuses.

One reason for telling children that strength of character is what really matters is that if persons adopt this view, poverty is more likely to decline. How can a libertarian defend this practice using a consequential (utilitarian) argument? The libertarian can appeal to other values when choosing between alternatives that do not violate the freedom principle. Teaching children about the importance of personal responsibility and strength of character does not violate the freedom principle. In addition, to teach children in the United States that they are victims of an unjust society would violate the freedom principle because it is false.

By accepting Scanlon's criterion of nonrejectability, Nagel also accepts unanimity as the ideal standard of legitimacy. Political arrangements are legitimate to the extent that all reasonable persons should support them and accept their results. Nagel seeks unanimity "among persons in many respects as they are, provided they [are] also reasonable and committed within reason to modifying their claims, requirements, and motives in a direction which makes a common framework of justification possible."[65] A political system is illegitimate when some persons can reasonably claim that their interests have not been adequately accommodated.

> The idea is that behind the coercion that has an unavoidable role in any political system there should be independent reasons for everyone to cooperate voluntarily in the maintenance of such a system and to respect its results. Coercion is not the basis of a legitimate political system, but merely one feature that plays an instrumental role, however essential, in its operation and the maintenance of its stability—a feature that is warranted only in virtue of the legitimacy of the system which contains it.[66]

Nagel notes a similarity between the criterion of nonrejectability and Kant's categorical imperative. A moral rule that no one can reasonably reject is a rule that everyone can will as a universal law insofar as they are rational agents. Kant's second formulation of the categorical imperative can also be interpreted along the same lines: "On one reading of this principle, it implies that if you force someone to serve an end that he cannot be given adequate reason to share, you are treating him as a mere means—even if the end is his own good, as you see it but he doesn't. In view of the coercive character of the state, the requirement becomes a condition of political legitimacy."[67] To his credit, Nagel recognizes a presumption against coercion, that coercion requires justification. The question then is, What can Nagel say to persons who study his arguments and still disagree with his liberal outlook? More specifically, what can he say to those of us who do not share his belief in the great importance of economic equality?

Moral equality is very important, but Nagel has, in my opinion, focused on the wrong value—economic equality. I think that his materialistic outlook is fundamentally misguided; there are more important things in life than how much money a person has. A thought experiment borrowed (with some changes) from Charles Murray illustrates this point.[68] Imagine that you must pick the family your child will be raised in. You have two choices. The first option is a wealthy childless couple who will provide all the advantages money can buy: private schools, music lessons, summer camps, and so on. The husband and wife are primarily concerned with their own careers, and they will spend little time with your child. If the second option is chosen, your child will be raised in a family of modest means: The husband's income covers little more than the basic necessities of life. The wife has chosen to stay home to raise their two (natural) children, and she (and her husband) will provide love and emotional support missing in the first family. Surely it is not unreasonable to prefer the second option.

Rawls, Scanlon, and Nagel give the worst off a veto over economic policies. The worst-off veto illustrates how multiply ambiguous the idea of moral equality is. It (the worst-off veto) assumes that equal concern for the welfare of each person leads to the conclusion that each person's share of material things should be equal unless the worst off would get a larger share if the division were unequal. As I have noted, this view has the implication that social arrangements that work well for 90 percent of the population are unjust if the remaining 10 percent could be better off under different arrangements. Suppose that the 90 percent complain that the worst-off veto does not treat them equally—they think that giving 10 percent of the population the right to determine economic policies is a strange interpretation of moral equality. If everyone's welfare counts equally, then why should 10 percent of the population have the ultimate say in economic policy? Nagel's methodology requires him to show that it is unreasonable to reject the worst-off veto. I doubt that he can meet this burden of proof.

What can Nagel say to persons like me who do not want to be included in his egalitarian programs? One thing he cannot say is "You go your way and I'll go mine." Nagel must include me in his plans because he must tax me to pay for the redistributive programs he favors. Nagel might reply that my situation in a liberal society is analogous to what his would be in a libertarian society. Just as I do not want to live in a liberal society, Nagel does not want to live in a libertarian society. This disagreement must be settled by the political process, namely by voting. This reply, however, ignores an important disanalogy in our situations. The libertarian *can* say to Nagel, "You go your way and I'll go mine." No one will prevent Nagel from helping the poor in a libertarian society. He can join with others who agree with him, and they can establish whatever programs they favor. The libertarian society restricts Nagel's freedom to help the poor only by preventing him from coercing others. Only coercive programs are prohibited; voluntary programs are not.

The Amish are an embarrassment to liberals for a number of reasons. For one thing, they often reject (when they can) many of the government "benefits" such as public schools and Social Security that liberals want them to have. More important, they are an example of what like-minded persons can do voluntarily to establish communities where coercive government programs are not needed. As Nozick points out, one of the great advantages of a libertarian society is the "experiments in living" that it allows.[69] Those who want to live in socialist communities where the distribution of goods is based on need can do so. Those who favor industrial democracy where workers control their factories can join with others who prefer these arrangements. There can be networks of communities, each one with a large degree of autonomy, that also belong to and participate in larger organizations. The possibilities are limited only by the imagination and the willingness of individuals to participate. Given human diversity, there is no reason to think that there is one community or even a small number of communities that are best for everyone.

I shall conclude this section with some general observations about contract arguments. Historically, contract arguments have been used to justify the authority of the state. Using the device of hypothetical consent, contract theorists have argued that political authority is legitimate because rational persons would agree that they have good reasons for accepting it. Contemporary contract arguments often take the legitimacy of political authority for granted, and they seek to justify a specific political agenda.[70] Contemporary versions differ according to the author's analysis of rationality, what information the hypothetical contractors possess, and what the contractors are deciding. Depending on how these variables are fleshed out, there are contract arguments for (inter alia) materialistic egalitarianism, various versions of utilitarianism, and libertarianism.[71] I think that it is unlikely that a methodology that can produce such diverse results will lead to a convergence on one moral and social system.

5. Why Be Moral?

The person who asks "Why be moral?" may be seeking clarification concerning the content of morality. For example, a person may see no point in following a moral rule until she understands why the rule is important in promoting human interests. In this case, the questioner will know what to do once she understands the reasons for thinking that an act is right or wrong. Conversely, the questioner could be asking for a motive for being moral: She knows what morality requires and how acting morally promotes human interests (in general), but she wonders why *she* should act morally. To answer the motivational interpretation of the question, we need to connect morality to something the person cares about. I shall seek an answer by exploring the connection between morality and happiness.

It is commonly assumed that acting morally can conflict with the pursuit of one's interests. When a person pursues her own interests, what is she pursuing? One interpretation, which I call the value-neutral analysis, connects self-interest with the satisfaction of the agent's desires. This view takes an agent's desires as a given and assumes that it is in her interest to satisfy them. Pursuit of self-interest in this sense can be difficult. An agent will need to recognize when her desires conflict, and she may need considerable self-control in order to forgo immediate gratification. She will also require the necessary information for knowing what she must do to satisfy her desires. Thus, this analysis of self-interest allows us to criticize other agents. For example, we might criticize a friend for lacking the self-control to defer gratification with the result that she satisfies a less important desire at the expense of a more important one. We could also criticize an agent for adopting ineffective means to her chosen end. However, whereas an agent is not immune from criticism on this conception of self-interest, she is the final judge of what she desires, and of the relative importance of her different desires.

The second conception of self-interest, which I call the normative analysis, is based on the assumption that it is in one's interest to live a good life. Furthermore, a person can desire things that are not good, and thus it would not be in the person's interest to satisfy these desires. According to this interpretation, it is not obvious that acting morally and acting according to one's self-interest conflict. Suppose that I am the owner of a small business and I receive a duplicate payment from one of my customers. Should I keep the money or return it? A person in this situation might worry about losing a customer if the customer discovers the duplicate payment and the money has not been returned. But suppose that I decide to return the money because (I believe) it is the moral thing to do. Furthermore, I do not see this situation as one in which morality and self-interest conflict; instead, I believe that it is in my interest to be a good person, and thus it is in my interest to act morally.

The normative analysis of self-interest assumes that it is in one's interest to live a good life. Can we give some content to this very general (and very vague) assumption? Let us begin by examining a desire that, if not universal, comes close to being so, namely the desire for happiness. If you want to be happy, what should you do? One response is "seek happiness." Why is this response so unenlightening? Happiness is not a feeling like physical pleasure, that can be sought directly. When you are happy, you are more satisfied than dissatisfied with the way your life is going. This feeling of satisfaction is secured through the pursuit and achievement of other values. In order to be happy, you must care about other things besides happiness. Suppose Jill believes that three values are of primary importance in her life: loving relationships with members of her family, success in her career, and participation in enjoyable activities. If we ask Jill whether she is happy and she takes our question seriously, she will base her answer on how she is doing in terms of realizing her important values.

If we want to convince Jill that she should add moral goodness to her list of values, how would we proceed? We could start by pointing out that it is important to Jill that *others* act morally. It is important first off because social cooperation would be impossible if the prohibitions against aggression, theft, and deception were commonly ignored. On a more personal level, it is important to Jill that she and the persons she cares about not be victims of immoral behavior. Since the same reasoning applies to each of us, we have a reason for endorsing morality as a general practice.

Can one endorse morality, which at a minimum means endorsing prohibitions against aggression, theft, and deception, while at the same time exempting oneself from these requirements? This question is ambiguous, for it could be referring to what a person can do or to what a person can believe. It is the latter interpretation that interests me at this point. Can I, for example, believe that others should refrain from stealing while also believing that this requirement does not apply to me? If I could believe that there is something special about me, so that I am relevantly different from other persons, then I could believe this. However, I am not relevantly different. All persons are social beings, and our survival as well as the good things in life depend on social cooperation. In this regard, I must recognize that everyone, including me, is in the same boat.

My argument assumes that it is a fact of human psychology that belief is not voluntary, at least not with regard to this issue. In other words, persons cannot choose to believe that they are special in a way that exempts them from the moral requirements that apply to other persons.[72] Thus, the belief that there is a good answer to the question "Why should we be moral?" leads to the belief that there is a good answer to the question "Why should I be moral?" Persons should be moral, and this judgment applies to each of us. Let us now consider how this conclusion connects up with happiness.

I have defined happiness as feeling satisfied with one's life. Since few persons, if any, are completely satisfied with their lives, let us say that the happy person is more satisfied than dissatisfied. Happiness comes in degrees: The more satisfied (and less dissatisfied) you are, the happier you are. Happiness is sought indirectly through the pursuit and realization of other values. Should we say that these other values have instrumental value, that they are valuable only as a means to securing happiness? This would be a mistake for the following reason. If Jill, for example, did not care about being successful, achieving success in her career would not give her satisfaction. As noted before, we must care about other things in order to be happy.

I have argued that one of the things we should care about is morality: We have good reasons for believing that it is important for persons to act morally. When this conclusion is combined with the normative interpretation of self-interest, we can conclude that it is in one's interest to be a morally good person. It is in one's interest to live a good life, and acting morally is good. The (internal) penalty for acting immorally is a loss of self-respect. To feel satisfied with your life, you need to believe that you are a good person. But this is hard to do if you act contrary to your own moral beliefs.

The conclusion we have reached is that acting morally is an important component of living a good life. What has not been shown is that moral values are always overriding. To prove this one would have to show that moral values are always more important than other values. Gauguin has been used as an example to illustrate how hard it is to prove that moral values are always more important than other values. Let us assume that Gauguin acted immorally when he left his wife and children. In addition, suppose that Gauguin would not have created great works of art had he remained in Paris with his family. What scale of values allows us to determine that moral values are more important than aesthetic values in Gauguin's case?

The Gauguin example involves a momentous choice between keeping his marriage vows and developing his artistic talent. Value conflicts are usually more mundane. I take a small towel from a motel to clean bugs from my windshield. I regret taking the towel, but the increased safety and the enjoyment of looking through a clean windshield seem more important. I fail to keep an appointment to meet a student because a friend asks me to go fishing and I know that he won't go by himself. What is more important—friendship or keeping my word? We should note that in both of these examples it would have been better to avoid the conflict: I can carry paper towels in my car and fishing trips can be planned in advance.

One of the keys to finding a reasonable answer to the "Why be moral?" question is to give up the vain hope of proving that moral values are always overriding. There are, after all, other important values such as love, friendship, and artistic excellence. We can often arrange our affairs so that our values do not conflict, but we are not sufficiently prescient to anticipate every circumstance in which acting morally will be incompatible with the realization of other values. When important values conflict, there is no objective decision procedure we can call upon to determine what to do.

I have assumed that normal persons want to be happy, that is, to feel satisfied with their lives. To be happy, we must be able to think of ourselves as being good persons, and this will usually mean that we must act morally. This answer to the motivational interpretation of the "Why be moral?" question depends, as it must, on the facts of human psychology. The facts are that we want to be happy and that belief (in the relevant sense) is not voluntary. The latter point assumes that normal persons can understand the reasons for endorsing morality as a social practice, and they cannot believe that they (as individuals) are exempt from the moral demands that apply to others. Thus, to the degree that persons act contrary to their moral beliefs, they will be less able to think of themselves as being good persons. This provides us with a strong, but not necessarily overriding, reason for acting morally.

The theory known as psychological egoism appears to challenge commonsense morality. Most of us think that morality requires concern for the rights and interests of *other* persons. But according to the psychological egoist, each person is only concerned with his or her own interests. Whether psychological egoism really is a problem for morality depends on how we interpret the idea of self-interest. According to the normative interpretation, it is in one's interest to live a good life. According to this interpretation, Mother Teresa is an egoist because she is trying to live a good life. However, if Mother Teresa is an egoist, then psychological egoism is not a threat to morality. This of course trivializes psychological egoism, but that is the point. Surely, it is not in one's interest to live a bad life, and this shows that we cannot talk about self-interest without considering what is involved in living a good life.

So far I have focused on moral requirements. In doing so, I have neglected an important part of morality—morally good acts that are beyond the call of duty. I shall call these acts beneficent. Beneficence includes charitable acts and acts of kindness. From the libertarian point of view, the category of beneficent acts is quite large because libertarians recognize duties to help others only when special relationships exist between agents and recipients. These special relationships are created by voluntary choices such as making a promise or choosing to have a child. What motive do we have for performing beneficent acts? For example, why should we practice the virtue of being charitable? We have the same motive as we have for doing our duty, namely, we want to be good persons. Beneficent acts are good, and it is in one's interest to live a good life.

We have noted that a libertarian society would not have a tax-funded welfare system because such coercive programs violate the freedom principle. The libertarian takes the optimistic view that enough people will recognize that helping the needy is good and they will act accordingly, so that voluntary assistance will be adequate. This libertarian view has been challenged by Nagel:

> Most people are not generous when asked to give voluntarily, and it is unreasonable to ask that they should be. Admittedly there are cases in which a person should do

something although it would not be right to force him to do it. But here I believe that the reverse is true. Sometimes it is proper to force people to do something even though it is not true that they should do it without being forced. It is acceptable to compel people to contribute to the support of the indigent by automatic taxation, but unreasonable to insist that in the absence of such a system they ought to contribute voluntarily. The latter is an excessively demanding moral position because it requires voluntary decisions that are quite difficult to make. Most people will tolerate a universal system of compulsory taxation without feeling entitled to complain, whereas they would feel justified in refusing an appeal that they contribute the same amount voluntarily. This is partly due to lack of assurance that others would do likewise and fear of relative disadvantage; but it is also a sensible rejection of excessive demands on the will, which can be more irksome than automatic demands on the purse.[73]

Nagel's comments raise a number of important issues, but for now I will focus on one, that being charitable places "excessive demands on the will." The moral excellence of being charitable is not achieved by the government taking part of your income and giving it to the poor. Instead, the charitable person incorporates helping the needy into his personal projects. This requires giving some thought to which charities actually help the needy—as opposed to encouraging behavior that produces poverty. Nagel sees this as an "irksome" demand; he doesn't want to be bothered. Nagel raises that free-rider "problem"—that the charitable person is at a relative disadvantage in comparison to the selfish person. This is a problem only if being charitable is a burden, and thus it is upsetting when others do not share the load. For the charitable person, however, helping the needy is not an unwelcome burden; it is part of living a good life, of being a good person. If others fail to achieve moral excellence, it is their loss.

Douglas Den Uyl makes a helpful distinction between "supply-sided" and "demand-sided" accounts of the morality of helping others. Demand-sided accounts focus on the recipient who needs help, and supply-sided accounts focus on the agent who provides assistance. "In a significant sense, classical virtue ethics is inherently supply-sided, since it places the bulk of its attention on the agent's own character, defines moral goodness in terms of the agent's nature, and expects that goodness to be the direct product of the agent's own actions. Moreover, the 'beneficiary' of the conduct is the agent himself."[74] Modern theories that stress welfare rights are demand-sided: They focus on what agents owe recipients. If you help a person because he has a right to your assistance, you are only doing what morality requires. Such views leave little room for the virtue of charity.

Nagel is concerned that the demands of what he calls the impersonal point of view will overwhelm our legitimate interest in personal projects and relationships. "The impersonal standpoint in each of us produces ... a powerful demand for universal impartiality and equality, while the personal standpoint gives rise to individualistic motives and requirements which present obstacles to the pursuit and realization of such ideals."[75] Let us say that a moral theory is strongly impartial when it requires us to give equal consideration to the interests of others. Moral theories that are strongly impartial devalue both charity and friendship. Preference for friends over nonfriends is at the core of what friendship is: We treat our friends differently than we do strangers.[76] For example, we help a friend even though there are strangers who are more needy. We go to dinner with a friend instead of donating the money to famine relief. In Nagel's ideal world, the demands of the impersonal standpoint would be handled by political institutions requiring, for example, that we contribute our fair share to welfare programs. Having done our part as citizens and taxpayers, we can then have special relationships with friends and family members. In the real world, this "solution" works only if you ignore the suffering of persons outside the society you happen to live in. If the interests of *all* persons count equally, there is no political solution to Nagel's problem: The demands of the impersonal standpoint overwhelm our interest in personal relationships.

From the libertarian point of view, we are not required to save the world, and thus you do not neglect a duty if you buy a ticket to a hockey game instead of donating the money to famine relief. The libertarian view does have its own interpretation of impartiality: We should grant others an *equal* right to be free. This fundamental right generates negative rights, such as freedom of religion, that are held by all persons. However, general rights for the libertarian are always negative—they can be satisfied by noninterference. One of the strengths of the libertarian view is that it does not devalue commitments to personal projects and relationships.

David Schmidtz distinguishes "concern" from "respect": "Insofar as one's other-regard takes the form of caring about other people's welfare, one exhibits *concern*. Insofar as one's other-regard takes the form of adherence to constraints on what one may do to others, one exhibits *respect*. As I see it, we manifest concern for people when we care about how life is treating them (so to speak), whereas we manifest respect for people when we care about how *we* are treating them, and constrain ourselves accordingly."[77] Schmidtz thinks that morality requires us to respect everyone, but he doubts "very much that morality requires us to care about everyone."[78] If morality did require universal caring, I do not think that we could give a reasonable answer to the "Why be moral?" question. If we were required to count the welfare of *everyone* equally and act accordingly, we could not give preference to friends and family members. Peter Singer endorses equal concern for everyone's welfare, and he recognizes how radical this view is. In a world where millions live in absolute poverty, where their lives are shortened for lack of food and medical care, this view would require us to give to others until we reach the level of marginal utility, that is, to give until by giving more we would reduce ourselves to absolute poverty.[79] For the libertarian, such sacrifice for others is beyond the call of duty.

I shall conclude this section with some remarks about happiness and the moral excellence of charity. Most of us would welcome assistance if we were in desperate need of food, shelter, or medical care. Thus, it is easy to understand why charitable acts are thought to be good. However, there is a downside to charity from the recipient's point of view; namely, it is not good to be dependent on others. It is a sobering thought that any of us could become permanently dependent. You or I, for example, could suffer brain damage caused by a stroke or an accident. Such cases are tragic, and permanent dependency should be avoided where possible. It is far better to be the person who gives assistance than the one who needs help. Mere survival is not satisfying. We want to be happy—to feel satisfied with our lives. We can help others survive, but we cannot make them happy. Genuine happiness can be achieved only by persons who take responsibility for living good lives.

6. Summary

I have proposed that persons have one fundamental right—the equal right to be free. In most cases, interactions should be based on mutual consent, and thus it is usually wrong to coerce or deceive others. I have stipulated that an agent interferes with another person when the agent causes his recipient to behave involuntarily. An agent can cause his recipient to behave involuntarily by using force, a threat, or deception. The basic right entails the noninterference rule—it is usually wrong to cause others to behave involuntarily. There are cases involving self-defense (and the defense of others), punishment, and paternalism that are exceptions to the noninterference rule. These exceptions were discussed in Section 3, and more cases will be considered in subsequent sections.

A moral theory with one fundamental right can recognize other values. The additional values can be used to choose between alternatives that do not violate the fundamental right. In these cases, consequential values can play an important role in determining what to do. For example, the reason for exercising the right to punish is to reduce crime. Concern for consequences also enters into my account of morality at a deeper level. I have said that the primary concern of morality is how persons should relate to each other, not what ends to produce. This claim is about what morality is concerned with. To ask why we should be concerned about morality is to raise a different issue. The need for social cooperation is the ultimate reason for being concerned about morality. In other words, it is the reason for adopting the moral point of view. It is from within the moral point of view that we see that the primary concern of morality is how persons should relate to each other. My reason for adopting the moral point of view is consequential, but it is definitely not utilitarian: Avoiding disaster is very different from maximizing the good.

The need for social cooperation is the bedrock of morality, and in this regard, morality has a teleological ground. Deontological considerations come into play when we try to understand the content of morality. It was my intuitions concerning moral equality that first led me to libertarianism. I could not accept the elitist view that some persons have the right to rule while others should docilely accept their inferior position. I resented being treated paternalistically. This resentment came easily, for it is not flattering to be the recipient of paternalistic treatment. The paternal agent is assuming that (1) the recipient doesn't know what his own good is, or (2) if he does know, he lacks the self-control to behave appropriately. I could not concede that others should have the right to determine what I should do for my own good. And I could not believe that I should determine what is good for other autonomous agents. These beliefs provided the deontological basis for the libertarian view that morality requires respect for persons as autonomous agents.

A deontological view, no matter how intuitively attractive, is incomplete: Consequences matter, and a moral view that would have disastrous consequences is unacceptable. So I asked the obvious question: What must we assume about human beings in order for a libertarian society to function well? I concluded that most persons (but not all) must be self-reliant and compassionate. Self-reliance, in this context, does not mean living on one's own without the benefits of social cooperation. Instead, I am making the more modest assumption that most persons are capable of taking care of their basic needs through voluntary means such as working. In addition, most persons are compassionate, and they will voluntarily help those who need assistance. In subsequent chapters, I shall argue that the libertarian view of human nature is realistic. In addition, I shall argue that the libertarian society is better than its competitors in promoting health and happiness (i.e., human well-being).

Earlier I used the metaphor "the web-of-belief." Coherence is one of the criteria for judging moral theories, and coherentism requires that our beliefs, both moral and nonmoral, be mutually supporting. We seek explanatory interconnections between moral theory, political theory, economic theory, and social theory. This is the task of the remaining chapters. The more considerations that support a moral view, the better.

Before I move on, some criticisms and objections should be considered. Some readers may object to my failure to provide an analysis of the concept of freedom. I do not believe that there is a neutral analysis of this concept. In other words, I do not think that there is an analysis that all moral and political thinkers should accept regardless of their substantive views.[80] My use of the word 'freedom' is both contextual and normative. Its meaning emerges in the explanation of the freedom principle. This meaning should be accepted or rejected based on the normative implications of its use within the theory. On the general issue of whether the analysis of concepts can yield substantive results, I agree with Rawls: "A theory of justice is subject to the same rules or method as other theories. Definitions and analyses of meaning do not have a special place: definition is but one device used in setting up the general structure of theory. Once the whole framework is worked out, definitions have no distinct status and stand or fall with the theory itself."[81]

On a related issue, I should say something about my use of the word 'autonomy.' As I use the term, it refers to certain capacities that normal adults have and many children have to lesser degrees. An autonomous agent has the capacities necessary for formulating and acting on different conceptions of how one should live one's life. This use of the term is descriptive: An autonomous agent has (in fact) certain capacities. In contrast, the phrase 'respect for autonomy' is normative: It refers to the treatment of others, namely respecting their equal right to be self-directing.

In his monumental work *The Methods of Ethics*, Henry Sidgwick presents some criticisms of the kind of view that I am defending: "All natural Rights, on this view, may be summed up in the Right to Freedom; so that the complete and universal establishment for the Right would be the complete realization of Justice—

the Equality at which Justice is thought to aim being interpreted as Equality of Freedom."[82] Sidgwick points out that there is a problem in determining the extension of "Equality of Freedom":

> In the first place, it seems obviously needful to limit the extent of its application. For it involves the negative principle that no one should be coerced for his own good alone: but no one would gravely argue that this ought to be applied to the case of children, or of idiots, or insane persons. But if so, can we know *a priori* that it ought to be applied to all sane adults? Since the above-mentioned exceptions are commonly justified on the ground that children, etc., will manifestly be better off if they are forced to do and abstain as others think best for them; and it is, at least, not intuitively certain that the same argument does not apply to the majority of mankind in the present state of their intellectual progress.[83]

In reply to Sidgwick, I should note that paternalism is a difficult topic for all moral theories, and thus we would have a reason for rejecting the libertarian view only if another theory provides better solutions. Sidgwick questions whether all "sane adults" should enjoy the equal right to be free. My position is that normal adults should not be treated paternalistically, but I have admitted that application of this rule can require difficult judgment calls. For example, how inebriated must the drunk be before we may take the keys to his car? No plausible moral theory that I am aware of provides an easy answer to this type of question. The quotation from Sidgwick entertains the possibility that the "majority of mankind" lacks the intellectual abilities for being self-directing. There is much more at stake here than a factual question: Moral equality is at issue. Does Sidgwick think that there is a class of superior persons, philosopher kings perhaps, who have the right to rule over the rest of us?

Sidgwick wonders whether the idea of freedom applies only to physical constraint, in which case equality of freedom would not rule out many annoying actions: "But, again, the term Freedom is ambiguous. If we interpret it strictly, as meaning Freedom of Action alone, the principle seems to allow any amount of mutual annoyance except constraint. But obviously no one would be satisfied with such Freedom as this."[84] My view is that interactions should be (ideally) based on mutual consent. This rules out annoying acts like forcing others to listen to you or forcing them to see things they do not want to see. Again, there are difficult judgment calls in this area, but this is true for every theory.

Sidgwick's third criticism seems to assume that the theory he is criticizing calls for maximizing freedom:

> Thirdly, in order to render a social construction possible on this basis, we must assume that the right to Freedom includes the right to limit one's freedom by contract; and that such contracts, if they are really voluntary and not obtained by fraud or force, and if they do not violate the freedom of others, are to be enforced by legal penalties. But I cannot see that enforcement of Contracts is strictly included in the notion of realizing

Freedom; for a man seems to be most completely free when no one of his volitions is allowed to have any effect in causing the external coercion of any other.[85]

My theory does not call for maximizing anything, including freedom. Again, the primary concern of morality is how persons should relate to each other. More specifically, it is usually wrong to cause others to behave involuntarily. If you contract with someone (e.g., hire a person to perform some service), you will usually violate the freedom principle if you do not keep your agreement. For example, you will cause the person to behave involuntarily if you do not pay for the service rendered.

Sidgwick concludes his criticisms by questioning whether the proponents of equal freedom have developed a coherent and plausible theory of property rights. On this issue, I agree with Sidgwick: The libertarian view needs a new theory of property rights. I discuss these matters in the next section.

TWO

Liberty and Government

The legislative powers vested in Congress are specified and enumerated in the eighth section of the first article of the Constitution, and it does not appear that the power proposed to be exercised is among the enumerated powers ...

James Madison, Veto Message to Congress, 1817[1]

7. Legitimacy

For rights-based moral theories, the primary concern of government must be protection of the rights of individuals. We seek a government that is strong enough to protect rights but that does not violate rights. This constitutional problem has a theoretical component and a practical component: We need assurance that it is theoretically possible to have a government that protects rights without violating rights; the practical problem is to identify the political institutions that are most likely to produce this result. Given human fallibility, there can be no guarantee that a government will never violate anyone's rights, but we should be able to devise political institutions that do not violate rights systematically, that is, moral lapses should be exceptions and not the rule.

We begin with the funding problem. According to many libertarians, taxes are theft on a large scale. If taxes violate property rights, how can government services be funded? One answer is user fees. For example, I receive water and sewer services from the city of Buffalo. In return for these services, I pay a quarterly fee. If I chose not to pay for the services rendered, the city would stop the delivery of water to my home, and I would have to find alternative means of meeting this need.[2] Thus, I can choose not to have the service and thereby avoid paying the fee.

User fees are appropriate for private goods, that is, when the beneficiary of the service can be identified and the benefit withheld from the person who prefers not to pay. This leaves us with the problem of public goods. A public good is a benefit that cannot be given to some individuals and withheld from others. National defense is the clearest example. In the 1980s the nuclear weapons of the Soviet Union were the primary military threat to the United States. The threat of nuclear retaliation was the primary defense against this threat. All citizens were protected, taxpayers and nonpayers alike. The preservation of order through law enforcement is another public good. Since we are social beings, everyone benefits from maintenance of the order that is necessary for social living. Even the thief benefits on the assumption that there must be some minimum level of protection of property rights for economic activity to take place. Law enforcement and the provision of national defense are generally recognized as essential functions of governments. How can these activities be funded without violating rights?

We can expand that idea of user fees to include the leasing of natural resources. Suppose the government leases rights to drill for oil on public lands. Businesses that wish to acquire these rights submit bids, and leases are awarded to the highest bidders. Since no one is required to bid, the subsequent payments are voluntary; lessees are willing to pay for the benefit. We can push this one step further by holding that all persons who have exclusive rights to use natural resources should pay for these rights. Homeowners, for example, should pay for the right to use land. As a practical matter, leasing this land may be both disruptive and cumbersome. A reasonable alternative would be a resource tax based on the market value of the land. In other words, the tax should be equal to what the land would lease for—if it were leased. Similar procedures could apply to other users of land such as businesses, private clubs, and churches. Rights to use natural resources are not just moral rights; they are legal rights protected by the military and police power of government. Persons who enjoy this protection can pay for it by paying for the exclusive rights to use natural resources. One result is that resource taxes are analogous to user fees: The taxpayer is paying for a benefit, the protected right to use a resource. If she refuses to pay, she forfeits the benefit, namely the exclusive right to use the resource. Thus, revenue raised by leasing natural resources and from resource taxes can be used to fund national defense and law enforcement.

How much revenue would be raised in the United States by leasing natural resources and from resource taxes? I have seen one estimate: David Friedman estimates that the value of natural resources is (roughly) 5 percent of national income.[3] I think that this estimate is conservative because it is based on the rental value of land and "minerals." There are many other valuable resources, for example, the airwaves (for broadcasting) could be leased, air routes (for travel) could be leased to airlines, air pollution could be controlled by charging for this use of the air, timber-cutting rights could be leased, the harvesting of fish could be controlled by selling fishing rights, and grazing rights could be leased. Assuming that the Friedman estimate is somewhat low, at present about $300 billion could be raised by resource taxes and the leasing of natural resources.[4]

In the United States, the mechanisms for collecting property taxes are already in place at the local level. A resource tax would differ from property taxes because property taxes are usually based on the assessed value of the land and any improvements to the land such as buildings. A resource tax, in contrast, would simply be based on the market value of the land. Thus a vacant lot would be taxed at the same rate as a comparable piece of property with a house on it. A resource tax has the advantage of not penalizing owners for improving their property. It would also encourage the efficient use of land by making it difficult for speculators to withhold land from the market in the hope that its price will rise in the future. I discuss additional economic advantages of resource taxes in Section 13.

The federal system in the United States makes the collection of revenue complicated, but not excessively so. I assume that most revenue would be collected at the local level through resource taxes on the rental value of land. This is convenient because law enforcement is primarily a local matter. A certain percentage of this revenue could be sent to the state and federal governments to fund the enforcement of state and federal laws. An additional percentage could be sent to the federal government to help pay for national defense.

The leasing of natural resources and resource taxes can provide federal, state, and local governments with legitimate sources of revenue. Other taxes, such as the income tax and sales taxes, violate property rights.[5] This conclusion follows from the precept that persons have the right to own things that they produce from resources they have the right to use. In *Principles of Political Economy*, Mill provides a succinct summary of this view: "The institution of property, when limited to its essential elements, consists in the recognition, in each person, of a right to the exclusive disposal of what he or she have produced by their own exertions, or received either by gift or by fair agreement, without force or fraud, from those who produced it. The foundation of the whole is, the right of producers to what they themselves have produced."[6] To take what a person has produced without the person's consent is theft. It is a violation of the freedom principle because it causes the producer to behave involuntarily: When you take what others have produced, you force them to work for you. Ownership rights over what one has produced include rights of voluntary exchange. "The right of property includes, then, the freedom of acquiring by contract. The right of each to what he has produced, implies a right to what has been produced by others, if obtained by their consent; since the producers must either have given it from good will, or exchanged it for what they esteemed an equivalent, and to prevent them from doing so would be to infringe their right of property in the product of their own industry."[7] Mill goes on to note that the rationale for ownership rights over what one has produced does not extend to natural resources: "The essential principle of property being to assure to all persons what they have produced by their labour and accumulated by their abstinence, this principle cannot apply to what is not the produce of labour, the raw material of the earth."[8]

The theory of property rights that I am defending challenges the orthodox libertarian view. Most libertarians believe that natural resources should be privately owned, and thus all taxes, including a resource tax, are illegitimate. The fundamental problem for this view is to explain how persons acquire exclusive rights over natural resources. I believe that there is no good answer, within the standard libertarian framework, to this problem, but before I state my case, there is one common objection to the orthodox view that can, I think, be answered. Some criticize the orthodox view because it favors first appropriators over latecomers—those who get there first get the "good stuff." Thus the Lockean proviso that "enough and as good" be left for others is always violated. David Schmidtz provides the answer to this objection:

> Philosophers who write on the subject of original appropriation tend to speak as if people who arrive first, and thus do all the appropriating, are much luckier than those who come later. The truth is, first appropriators begin the process of resource creation while latecomers like ourselves get most of the benefits. Consider the Jamestown colony of 1607. Exactly what was it, we should ask, that made their situation so much better than ours? Of course, they never had to worry about being overcharged for car repairs. They were never awakened in the middle of the night by noisy refrigerators, or leaky faucets, or flushing toilets. They never had to agonize over the choice of long-distance telephone companies. Are those the things that make us wish we had gotten there first?[9]

Schmidtz uses the phrase "resource creation." This phrase reminds us that raw materials, such as oil and sand, are resources only for persons who know how to use them. The process of wealth creation begins with original appropriation, and thus it is a positive-sum game. The problems with the orthodox view lie elsewhere.

Suppose a first appropriator is using some land for farming. He has incorporated this resource into his projects, and this gives us a reason for not interfering. The standard libertarian view is that he is now the owner of the land, and as such his rights are far-reaching. He may continue to use it or sell it. He may even abandon it, and the land would still be his because "first use" establishes his ownership rights. First use also establishes a bequeathable property right, and thus he can determine who becomes the owner of the land after his death. Obviously there is a huge jump from thinking that we should not interfere with an agent's ongoing use of some land to the conclusion that the agent has a permanent, bequeathable right to the land.

Farming is the standard example used by libertarians in explaining appropriation by first use. There are, however, many other uses of land, such as traveling, hunting, and aesthetic appreciation. Were the first persons who contemplated the scenic beauty of the Grand Canyon using this land? Should this use of land be the basis of ownership rights? Or consider the disputes between European settlers and Native Americans. European settlers farmed land that Native Americans had been using for hunting. Does hunting count as "first use," and were the property rights of Native Americans therefore violated? How does one acquire property rights over lakes and rivers? Does the first person to travel on a river become its owner? Does the first person to drink from a lake acquire permanent, bequeathable property rights to the lake?

Even if libertarians can produce a plausible account of property rights that answers the questions I have posed, there would still be a crucial objection to the standard view. Whatever story is told about how persons could have acquired permanent, bequeathable rights over natural resources, no one can prove that present holdings are the result of legitimate transfers traceable back to the original appropriators. Thus libertarians who defend the orthodox view must answer the charge of historical irrelevancy. Why should we think that a story about how things could have happened is relevant to our present situation?

My main concern in this section has been to establish that there are legitimate sources of revenue (leasing natural resources and resource taxes) that can be used to pay for the public goods of national defense and law enforcement. My solution to the public goods problem requires rejecting the orthodox libertarian view concerning the ownership of natural resources. Specifically, I have rejected the view that first use establishes permanent, bequeathable property rights over natural resources. This is one part of my answer to the theoretical problem of showing that it is possible to have a government that does not violate libertarian rights. In the next section, I turn to punishment and examine the conditions under which the punishment of lawbreakers does not violate rights.

8. Justice

Any treatment of justice faces the problem that the words 'just' and 'unjust' as used in ordinary language have wide application. Persons, rules, laws, governments, and societies can all be called just or unjust. As Joel Feinberg notes, "There is a great variety of kinds of human activity in which questions of justice can arise: distributions of goods and evils, requitals of desert, compensation for loss, appraisals of worth, judgments of criticism, administration and enforcement of rules and regulations, games of amusement, settlements of disputes (by bargaining, voting, flipping coins), contracting, buying, selling, and more."[10] In the face of this complexity, a theorist must focus his inquiry, and in the process he cannot treat every topic that might be relevant to the idea of justice. My focus is on political justice, that is, on what makes a state just or unjust.

Justice requires that we render to persons that which they are due. For a rights-based moral theory, what persons are "due" is determined by their rights. This leaves us with the Millean problem—to distinguish the demands of justice from moral requirements in general. Following Mill, I appeal to the idea of enforcement to make the distinction.[11] Justice is concerned with the moral requirements that we think should also be legal requirements. For example, keeping a promise is usually a moral requirement, but a government that tried to enforce promise-keeping in most cases would be excessively intrusive. Some moral requirements should be enforced by law, and some should not. The former requirements supply the content to my conception of justice. Thus, justice is concerned with the legal rights persons should have and the procedures and penalties appropriate in enforcing rights.

Under what conditions may the state enforce rights by punishing lawbreakers? Let us begin, as in Section 2, with the simple case in which A attacks B and B has done nothing to provoke the attack. If B injures A while using force to defend himself, he would not violate A's rights because A has no right to attack B. In defending himself against A's attack, B is not claiming a superior right to be free; he is defending his equal right to be free by ending an interaction to which he did not consent. Self-defense differs from punishment because (by definition) only the interference necessary to defend oneself is used; in cases of punishment, the offender is penalized for his transgression. Why does the state have the right to punish an offender *after* the offense has been committed? Let us assume that the society in which A and B live has a law prohibiting assault and A is arrested and punished for violating this law. Furthermore, the law is well publicized, and A knows that he is running the risk of punishment when he chooses to attack B. In this case, A brings the punishment on himself by choosing to do what he has no right, legally and morally, to do.

Our simple example suggests that punishment does not violate the freedom principle when (1) the law prohibits acts that violate the freedom principle (which means the offender had no right to perform the act) and (2) the offender could have avoided punishment by choosing not to break the law. In other words, the state has the right to punish when the offender could have avoided punishment by choosing not to do what he had no right to do. Condition (2) entails the recognition of excuses—when a lawbreaker has no real choice, he should be excused. An excuse is grounds for thinking that a wrongdoer should not be held responsible for wrongdoing. Let us review some common excuses along with some examples. Harm caused by accident is often excusable. An example is a driver who loses control of his vehicle because of a heart attack and injures a pedestrian. Coercion can also be an excuse for wrongdoing. While stopped at a red light, a bank robber armed with a gun jumps in your car and orders you to drive to a location where he can escape from the police. Helping a robber to avoid apprehension would normally be a crime, but in this case you have an excuse. In some cases, ignorance is an excuse. Sam rings a doorbell that has been rigged to a bomb that kills someone. If we assume that Sam had no reason to believe that ringing the doorbell would trigger the bomb, he should not be held responsible for the victim's death. Age can be an excuse. If a three-year-old finds a loaded gun and shoots someone, we do not hold the child responsible. In general, what we are looking for when we hold persons responsible for wrongdoing is knowledge and control: Did the person understand what he was doing, and was he in control of his behavior?

The first step in the libertarian theory of punishment is to establish the right to punish. Establishing the right to punish, however, does not show that the state should exercise this right; there may be, after all, good reasons for not doing what we have a right to do. What we need at this point (the second step) is the reasons for exercising the right to punish. One might think that the reason for punishing lawbreakers is obvious, namely to reduce crime. This is, I think, the correct response, but some theorists have proposed alternatives to punishment. Thus, we need to show that punishment is preferable to the alternatives. I shall examine two alternatives: treatment and restitution.

Karl Menninger was the most prominent advocate of the therapeutic approach to lawbreakers.

> If we were to follow scientific methods, the convicted offender would be detained indefinitely pending a decision as to whether and how and when to reintroduce him successfully into society. All the skill and knowledge of modern behavioral science would be used to examine his personality assets, his liabilities and potentialities, the environment from which he came, its effects upon him, and his effects upon it.
>
> Having arrived at some diagnostic grasp of the offender's personality, those in charge can decide whether there is a chance that he can be redirected into a mutually satisfactory adaptation to the world. If so, the most suitable techniques in education, industrial training, group administration, and psychotherapy should be selectively applied.[12]

The indefinite sentence is a crucial part of the Menninger proposal: Lawbreakers are released from custody if and when the psychiatrists determine that they are no longer a danger to themselves or others. Trustworthy offenders may receive treatment without being confined to an institution.

What should we say about replacing our punishment system with treatment? First off, it seems clearly inappropriate for some crimes, such as cases involving civil disobedience. The civil disobedient has a moral motive for breaking a law. Suppose that when the civil disobedient is examined by the psychiatrists, he continues to exhibit antisocial tendencies due to his moral beliefs. What is the cure for this kind of offense, and what training makes psychiatrists competent to judge the motivation of these offenders? In the former Soviet Union, political dissidents were often confined to mental hospitals. This is a practice that a free society should not emulate.

Treatment also seems inappropriate for many ordinary crimes. Consider the case of the burglar who steals primarily because he can make more money by stealing than by working at the legitimate jobs for which he is qualified. He also finds ordinary jobs to be boring; he has had several different jobs, but he has always gone back to burglary, in part because he missed the excitement. What is the cure? Should the government find him a high-paying, exciting job at taxpayers' expense? If not, suppose that there is only one known "cure"—psychosurgery, which will result in a very passive and dependent individual. In a treatment system, the psychiatrist who can cure an offender only by using extreme measures such as psychosurgery faces a dilemma. The method used to cure the offender is objectionable, but the offender who is not cured must be detained indefinitely.

The tendency in a treatment system will be to continue the confinement of offenders even when a large percentage could be safely released. If a former "patient" commits a serious crime, the mistake will be widely publicized. The opposite mistake (confining a patient who could have been released) will usually go unnoticed. In this case, the politics of the system will affect decisions. In general, the system gives far too much discretionary power to psychiatrists—there is too much latitude for racism, evil, and stupidity. For example, a lawbreaker may not "recover" because he is given the wrong treatment, and since he has not been cured, he must be detained indefinitely. This raises a problem concerning justice: Persons committing the same crimes may receive very different treatments. One armed robber may be quickly released and another confined for many years.

Clever lawbreakers will quickly learn how to exploit the system. They will determine what responses will lead to their release, and they will fake cooperation. In general, treatment is more likely to be successful when it is voluntary, that is, when the patient seeks help. In cases where feigned cooperation is not a problem, offenders may object to psychiatrists reconstructing their personalities. They may see the system as a challenge to their dignity and individuality. Menninger tells us to ignore their objections: "In the psychiatrist's mind nothing should be done in the name of punishment, though he is well aware that the offender may regard either the diagnostic procedure or the treatment or the detention incident to the treatment as punitive. But this is in his mind, not in the psychiatrist's mind. And in our opinion it should not be in the public's mind, because it is an illusion."[13] It doesn't matter what the "patients" think; they are objects to be manipulated by the anointed elite. A free society must reject this annihilation of individual freedom and personal responsibility.

In his classic article "Restitution: A New Paradigm of Criminal Justice," Randy E. Barnett states that the idea of restitution "views crime as an offense by one individual against the rights of another. The victim has suffered a loss. Justice consists of a culpable offender making good the loss he has caused."[14] In a restitution system, the state would not punish an offender for his transgression; instead, the state would require the offender to compensate his victim. The lawbreaker's debt is to his victim, not to society. As Barnett puts it, "The armed robber did not rob society, he robbed the victim."[15]

There are a number of crimes where it is not clear how the restitution paradigm should be applied. When an offender commits a murder, for example, there is no victim left to compensate. How would attempted murder be dealt with? Jones puts a bomb in Smith's car, but the bomb fails to detonate. In this case, perhaps we could say that Smith has suffered a loss because his life was endangered. Another problematic crime is driving while intoxicated. We can say that the drunk driver endangers other motorists, but it would be very difficult to identify the persons who are harmed. Who are the victims in counterfeiting cases? Suppose the counterfeiters are apprehended before the "money" is used. In general, the restitution paradigm is most plausible where there is an identifiable victim who suffers a compensable loss. Where these conditions do not hold, application of the paradigm is problematic.

Another difficulty is that many offenders will not have regular jobs, and thus they will lack a normal source of income from which compensation can be paid. As a result, they may commit further crimes to acquire the money. Barnett recommends that unemployed offenders who cannot pay compensation be assigned to employment projects.[16] However, if these lawbreakers are not institutionalized, they may commit further crimes. If they are institutionalized, the cost of maintaining security plus the cost of room and board may well exceed the income that the offender *earns*. In this case, there would be no excess income from which the offender could pay compensation.

Barnett tells us that the "level of security at each employment project would vary according to the behavior of the offenders."[17] In this regard, he exhibits some concern for the goal of reducing crime—and not simply doing justice to the victim. Perhaps the most important objection to restitution (as an alternative to punishment) is that the penalties imposed may have little or no deterrent effect. The clearest example is the wealthy person who can easily compensate the victims of his crimes. Lack of deterrence will also be a problem in many cases involving ordinary criminals. Suppose that Jones is an incompetent car thief who is caught on average once every 10 times he steals a car. What is the penalty? He obviously has to return the car. Suppose he is ordered to pay the victim $1,000 for the victim's inconvenience and mental distress. Let us also assume that he must pay court costs, so he pleads guilty to keep the costs down and he pays an additional $1,000. To summarize, the price of getting caught is $2,000. However, since he steals without being caught 9 times out of 10, the thief can treat the $2,000 as a business expense that he can cover by stealing another car.

Most crimes are not solved, and thus most victims will not be compensated under a restitution system. Furthermore, it is not just the immediate victims who are hurt by crime. We all pay avoidance costs. We pay for police protection. People buy locks, burglar alarms, guard dogs, and so on. Businesses hire security personnel, and the cost is passed on to the consumer. Many persons buy insurance to protect themselves from financial loss due to crime, and many persons restrict their activities because of crime. The rapist, for example, harms other persons besides his immediate victims; the woman who stays home at night because she fears being attacked is also harmed. Crime can have a very divisive influence on society, and if the crime rate becomes excessive, social living is impossible. Thus, the state punishes lawbreakers to protect society from crime. Barnett's proposal, in contrast, collapses the distinction between criminal law and civil law (between crimes and torts).

A defender of restitution might argue that the lack-of-deterrence problem can be dealt with by more severe penalties. However, this solution goes beyond the restitution paradigm: Restitution (as an alternative to punishment) is based on the view that the victim should be compensated by the offender. Whether this causes the offender to suffer or whether it deters anyone else is irrelevant. Restitution is concerned only with doing justice to the victim; it is not concerned with the suppression of crime. If deterrence is a consideration in determining penalties, then we have a punishment system—not a restitution system.

It is time to take stock. I have argued that the state has the right to punish lawbreakers when the offender could have avoided punishment by choosing not to do what he had no right (legally and morally) to do. Unlike the (Kantian) retributive theory, the libertarian theory does not hold that we have a duty to punish lawbreakers. Instead, the state should exercise the right to punish because the alternatives, treatment and restitution, are unacceptable. I am not claiming that treatment and restitution are never appropriate; what I am claiming is that punishment should not be replaced by *systems* of treatment or restitution.

The purpose of punishment is to reduce crime. Can this purpose be the basis for assigning penalties to various crimes? Punishment can reduce crime in at least three ways: (1) punishment plays an important role in moral education by giving dramatic expression to society's disapproval of certain activities, (2) the fear of punishment can deter potential lawbreakers, and (3) punishment can remove known lawbreakers from society. If suppression of crime were our only concern, then we would usually impose severe penalties on lawbreakers. For example, thousands of persons are killed and injured in the United States every year by drunk drivers. This carnage could probably be reduced by executing persons convicted of driving while intoxicated (DWI). Suppose we test this hypothesis by trying it experimentally in New York State. In the year prior to making DWI a capital offense, suppose that 1,000 persons were killed and many more injured by drunk drivers. In the year in which the state begins imposing the death penalty, 100 persons are executed for DWI. The next year, the number of persons killed by drunk drivers declines dramatically, say to 500. Apparently, the execution of drunk drivers in the first year convinced some motorists that driving while intoxicated wasn't worth the risk. Fifty persons are executed in the second year, and the deaths and injuries caused by drunk drivers continue to decline. From a utilitarian point of view, the experiment is a success. However, I assume that few of us think that capital punishment is the appropriate penalty for driving a car while one's blood alcohol level is above a certain number.

The libertarian theory of punishment needs an additional principle of justice, namely that punishment should fit the crime. We should not execute shoplifters even if doing so would save billions of dollars. Determining the proper punishment for a crime involves weighing two values: crime reduction and the principle of justice. For serious crimes, both values recommend severe penalties. Since there is less urgency to reducing minor crimes, the principle of justice is the ruling precept in these cases. In other words, there should be a correspondence between the seriousness of the crime and the severity of the punishment. These general guidelines leave room for reasonable persons to disagree, both in the ranking of crimes (how serious they are) and in the importance they assign to crime reduction. Such indeterminacy is unavoidable, and lawmakers will simply have to make the practical decisions that need to be made.

Let us look for firmer ground by turning our attention to the topic of victimless crimes. The freedom principle entails that victimless crimes, suitably defined, should be abolished. What is a victimless crime? Victimless crimes cannot be characterized by a lack of harm. Illegal gambling is often said to be a victimless crime, but clearly persons are often harmed by this activity. The same can be said about prostitution and the sale and use of illicit drugs. We know, however, that there is a difference between prostitution and rape: Prostitution is a consensual crime and rape is not. Let us recognize this difference by stipulating that we have a victimless crime when an activity is illegal but there is no interference, that is, no one causes another person to behave involuntarily by using force, a threat, or deception. One of the conditions of justified punishment is that the law prohibits acts that violate the freedom principle. Consensual behavior does not violate the freedom principle, and thus the state does not have the right to punish persons who participate in victimless crimes. The consequences of abolishing victimless crimes will be discussed in "Liberty and Economics" and "Liberty and Reality."

The category of victimless crimes is much larger than is generally recognized; it includes many economic activities that are illegal in the United States. For example, if Jill pays Jack $3 an hour for his labor, they violate the minimum-wage law. Since this law prohibits consensual activity, it would be abolished in a libertarian society. In many cases, violations of licensing laws are victimless crimes. If Jill is a dental hygienist who establishes her own independent business, this would be a victimless crime in states where dental hygienists are required to work under the supervision of licensed dentists. This example assumes that Jill does not deceive her customers, that is, she does not claim qualifications she does not have. Violations of foreign trade restrictions, such as tariffs and import quotas, are also victimless crimes. Unsurprisingly, a free society would have a free market economy: Voluntary exchanges of goods and services (capitalistic acts among consenting agents) would not be prohibited.

The distribution of goods and services in a free society will not fit a pattern. In a given year, Jane has an income of $100,000 and Joe's income is $10,000. If we believe that incomes should be equal, then we could say, straightaway, that the distribution is unjust. If we believe that no one's income should be more than five times as large as anyone else's, we could also declare this distribution unjust. For the libertarian, however, whether this distribution is just depends on whether anyone's rights have been violated. Suppose Jane is a popular rock singer who makes the $100,000 by giving one concert, and Joe is a folk singer who earns $10,000 by singing in bars on weekends. They acquire their money by voluntary economic exchanges, and thus no one's rights are violated. Thus the libertarian conception of economic justice is historical: We cannot know whether a distribution is just until we know how it came about. If Joe stole the $10,000, for example, the distribution would be unjust.

Economic justice and political justice are closely related. The voluntary exchange of goods and services depends on property rights. A libertarian government must establish who has the right to use natural resources. Where persons have exclusive rights, protected by the military and police power of government, they should pay for these rights by leasing natural resources or paying a resource tax. The second principle of property rights is that persons have ownership rights over their own labor and over what they produce using resources they have the right to use. A libertarian government should protect, and not violate, these rights. With property rights established, persons can voluntarily exchange goods and services. Justice consists in rendering to persons that which they are due. What persons are due is determined by their rights. Respect for property rights is a crucial aspect of political and economic justice.

I shall conclude this section with an analysis of Mill's views concerning economic justice and the proper role of government in the good society. It can certainly be questioned whether Mill had a coherent utilitarian view, but whatever we make of his professed utilitarianism, the following statement must be at the heart of it: "It is proper to state that I forego any advantage which could be derived to my argument from the idea of abstract right as a thing independent of utility. I regard utility as the ultimate appeal on all ethical questions, but it must be utility in the largest sense, grounded on the permanent interests of man as a progressive being."[18] The key phrase in this quotation is "progressive being." Mill's utilitarianism is not a static view that says, Take human beings as they are and maximize their pleasure. Instead, he was concerned with what policies would have the best consequences for human beings in the long run. Furthermore, we cannot interpret Mill as a coherent theorist if we read him as a hedonist. It is better to be Socrates dissatisfied than a satisfied fool, even if the fool experiences more pleasure.[19] Brink has dubbed Mill's ultimate value the deliberative conception of happiness. For Mill, happiness "consists in large part in the exercise of those higher capacities that distinguish us from other animals. Our higher capacities include our rational capacities, especially our capacities for rational deliberation."[20]

Mill's opposition to big government flows easily from his deliberative conception of happiness. In *On Liberty*, Mill states,

> Though individuals may not do the particular thing so well, on the average, as the officers of government, it is nevertheless desirable that it should be done by them, rather than by the government, as a means to their mental education—a mode of strengthening their active faculties, exercising their judgment, and giving them a familiar knowledge of the subjects with which they are thus left to deal.[21]

Mill complains that government programs stifle individuality and diversity: "Government programs tend to be everywhere alike. With individuals and voluntary associations, on the contrary, there are varied experiments and endless diversity of experience."[22] A recurrent theme in *On Liberty* is that "different experiments in living" are the key to human progress.[23]

Mill's most systematic treatment of this subject is found in *Principles of Political Economy*. Mill assumes that there are certain "ordinary functions" of government, such as protection of persons and property by suppressing force and fraud, that everyone will agree to. He then asks whether government intervention is useful in other cases, and he notes the strong reasons in favor of a narrow interpretation of the proper role of government. His purpose is to establish who has the burden of proof, namely those who favor government intervention. Mill again emphasizes the importance of individuality and diversity:

> And the present civilization tends so strongly to make the power of persons acting in masses the only substantial power in society, that there never was more necessity for surrounding individual independence of thought, speech, and conduct, with the most powerful defenses, in order to maintain that originality of mind and individuality of character, which are the only source of real progress, and of most of the qualities which make the human race much superior to any herd of animals. Hence it is no less important in a democratic than in any other government, that all tendency on the part of public authorities to stretch their interference, and assume a power of any sort which can be easily dispensed with, should be regarded with unremitting jealousy.[24]

Mill continues in a contemporary-sounding vein by noting the wide dispersal of knowledge and the importance of competition: "... it is evident that government, by excluding or even by superseding individual agency, either substitutes a less qualified instrumentality for a better qualified, or at any rate substitutes its own mode of accomplishing the work, for all the variety of modes which would be tried by equally qualified persons aiming at the same end; a competition by many degrees more propitious to the progress of improvement, than uniformity of system."[25] These considerations establish who has the burden of proof:

> The preceding are the principal reasons, of a general character, in favour of restricting to the narrowest compass the intervention of a public authority in the business of the community: and few will dispute the more than sufficiency of these reasons, to throw, in every instance, the burden of making out a strong case, not on those who resist, but on those who recommend government interference. Laissez-faire, in short, should be the general practice: every departure from it, unless required by some great good, is a certain evil.[26]

Having established a strong presumption against government intervention, Mill proceeds to argue that this presumption can be rebutted in several cases. For our purposes, the most important are education and aid to the poor.[27]

Those who think that Mill is a strong supporter of public education should read him with more care. In *On Liberty* he states: "That the whole or any large part of the education of the people should be in the State hands, I go as far as anyone in deprecating. All that has been said of the importance of individuality of character, and diversity in opinions and modes of conduct, involves, as of the same unspeakable importance, diversity of education."[28] Mill does recognize a legitimate state interest in setting minimum educational standards. Both paternalism (legitimate in this case because it is directed at children) and social utility support this policy.

> The instrument for enforcing the law could be no other than public examinations, extending to all children and beginning at an early age. An age might be fixed at which every child must be examined, to ascertain if he (or she) is able to read. If a child proves unable, the father, unless he has some sufficient ground for excuse, might be subjected to a moderate fine, to be worked out, if necessary, by his labor, and the child might be put to school at his expense. Once in every year the examination should be renewed, with a gradually extended range of subjects, so as to make the universal acquisition and, what is more, retention of a certain minimum of general knowledge virtually compulsory. Beyond that minimum there should be voluntary examinations on all subjects, at which all who come up to a certain standard of proficiency might claim a certificate. To prevent the State from exercising, through these arrangements an improper influence over opinion, the knowledge required for passing an examination (beyond the merely instrumental parts of knowledge, such as languages and their use) should, even in the higher classes of examinations, be confined to facts and positive science exclusively.[29]

In *Principles of Political Economy*, Mill takes up the issue of funding an education requirement. He states that in "England, and most European countries, elementary instruction cannot be paid for, at its full cost, from the common wages of unskilled labor... ."[30] Low-income families will need help, either from government or private charities. "It is, of course, not desirable, that anything should be done by funds derived from compulsory taxation, which is already sufficiently well done by individual liberality. How far this is the case with school instruction, is, in each particular instance, a question of fact."[31] Whether the state should be involved in the funding of education depends on social circumstances such as the poverty rate and the cost of a minimally decent education. Mill expresses his opinion that charitable contributions in England in the middle of the nineteenth century would be insufficient, and thus he recommends a government role in funding education. Nothing that he says on this topic, however, requires the direct government funding of schools. In fact, everything that he says about the importance of diversity and experimentation favors limiting government control. Tuition vouchers given to the parents of school-age children would answer most, if not all, of Mill's concerns. Tuition vouchers would give poor parents the means to send their children to school while preserving the independence of the schools. Mill states that the government "would be justified in requiring from all people that they possess instruction in certain things, but not in prescribing to them how or from whom they shall obtain it."[32] Mill emphatically rejects government control of education through the licensing of teachers, and this (inter alia) leads me to believe that he would have been sympathetic to tuition vouchers.[33]

A libertarian will reject the coercive funding of schools on principle, whether it be done directly or indirectly through tuition vouchers. However, I should note that in societies where voluntary assistance to poor families would be adequate, Mill and the libertarian reach the same practical conclusion: Government funding of schools is illegitimate. Mill recommended government assistance to poor families in England in the middle of the nineteenth century. It is not clear that he would make the same recommendation concerning the United States today.

In his analysis of Poor Laws (welfare programs), Mill states that the crucial issue is whether "energy and self-dependence" are increased or decreased by the laws:

> When the condition of any one is so disastrous that his energies are paralyzed by discouragement, assistance is a tonic, not a sedative: always provided that the assistance is not such as to dispense with self-help, by substituting itself for the person's own labour, skill, and prudence, but is limited to affording him a better hope of attaining success by those legitimate means. This accordingly is a test to which all plans of philanthropy and benevolence should be brought, whether intended for the benefit of individuals or of classes, and whether conducted on the voluntary or on the government principle.[34]

Welfare programs should guarantee against "absolute want" while not decreasing the incentive of recipients to take care of themselves. Mill claims that the Poor Law in England passes this test.

For Mill, it is a factual question whether a particular welfare system does more harm than good. This will depend on both the nature of the system and the social conditions in which it is applied. "… in all cases of helping, there are two sets of consequences to be considered; the consequences of the assistance, and the consequences of relying on assistance. The former are generally beneficial, but the latter, for the most part, injurious; so much so, in many cases, as greatly to outweigh the value of the benefit."[35] The libertarian will reject welfare systems funded by coercive taxes on principle, but once again Mill and the libertarian may come to the same practical conclusion, that is, a given society should not have a government-funded welfare system. I shall argue in Section 12 that this is true of the United States today.

9. The Constitution

In this section I turn to the practical aspect of the constitutional problem, namely identifying the political institutions that are most likely to protect individual rights. I focus on the Constitution of the United States. When the Constitution is interpreted according to the political philosophy of the Founding Fathers, it provides an adequate grounding for a free society.

The Declaration of Independence states: "We hold these truths to be self-evident, that all men are created equal, that they are endowed by their Creator with certain unalienable Rights, that among these are Life, Liberty, and the pursuit of Happiness. That to secure these rights, Governments are instituted among Men, deriving their just powers from the consent of the governed. ... " According to Jefferson, our fundamental rights include the equal rights to life, liberty, and the pursuit of happiness. If these rights are interpreted as negative, they are covered by the freedom principle. As a negative right, the right to life is the right not to be killed. Killing someone is the most obvious and extreme case of interfering with a person's freedom. The equal right to liberty limits our freedom by requiring respect for the equal right of others to be free. The pursuit of happiness can be interpreted as what people do when they have the freedom (noninterference) to pursue their own good in their own way. The upshot is that if these rights are negative, Jefferson's formulation of them, although rhetorically effective, is philosophically redundant. Jefferson did not need three inalienable rights because the other two are included in the equal right to liberty.

Jefferson did not explicitly distinguish positive and negative rights, and thus it would be presumptuous to proclaim him a libertarian. We can, however, make some general observations. The founders believed in individual rights, and they held that the primary concern of government should be the protection of these rights. Furthermore, Jefferson and Madison did not envision a federal government that would be heavily involved in promoting health, education, and welfare. They were very aware of the danger that government poses to our liberties. Their ideal was a small, limited government, not the bloated monster we have today. The libertarian view that I am defending is compatible with these general observations; there are other views, currently popular, that are not.

Individual rights are under assault from both liberals and conservatives. Let us consider some examples. The Fourth Amendment states: "The right of the people to be secure in their persons, houses, papers, and effects, against unreasonable searches and seizures, shall not be violated, and no Warrants shall issue, but upon probable cause, supported by Oath or affirmation, and particularly describing the place to be searched, and the persons or things to be seized." In *United States vs. Leon* (1984), the Supreme Court approved a "good faith" exception to the exclusionary rule.[36] The exclusionary rule requires the suppression of evidence that is obtained illegally. The officers in this case thought that they had a valid warrant when they seized illegal drugs. It was determined by lower courts that probable cause was lacking because the warrant was based upon stale information (too old) whose reliability had not been established. The Supreme Court did not dispute the lack of probable cause, yet the Court reversed because the officers had acted in good faith.[37]

There are (at least) two *different* justifications for the exclusionary rule: (1) it is necessary to prevent police misconduct, and (2) respect for individual rights requires suppression of illegally obtained evidence. The good-faith exception is compatible with (1) but not (2). If the exclusionary rule is justified as a (utilitarian) device for preventing police misconduct, then the good-faith exception makes sense: The police would not have been deterred in the *Leon* case because they had followed the appropriate procedures and they believed that they had a valid warrant. However, since the warrant was issued without probable cause, the search should not have taken place. A constitutional right of the defendant was violated. To respect the defendant's right, the Court must behave as if this illegal search and seizure did not take place. In other words, the evidence must be suppressed. Rights set limits on the pursuit of ends. Whatever utilitarian benefits might be gained by upholding such convictions, they should take a back seat to the protection of individual rights.

Property rights have been under attack from liberals for many decades. Before I examine some cases, I should note that the protection of property rights is a crucial feature of the founders' political philosophy. Perhaps the best evidence for this is Madison's essay *Federalist* no. 10, which deals with the danger of factions. "By a faction I understand a number of citizens, whether amounting to a majority or minority of the whole, who are united and actuated by some common impulse of passion, or of interest, adverse to the rights of other citizens, or to the permanent and aggregate interests of the community."

A major cause of factions is differences in talents and abilities that give rise to different interests.

> The diversity of faculties of men from which the rights of property originate, is not less an insuperable obstacle to the uniformity of interests. The protection of these faculties is the first object of Government. From the protection of different and unequal faculties of acquiring property, the possession of different degrees and kinds of property immediately results: and from the influence of these on the sentiments and views of the respective proprietors ensues a division of the society into different interests and parties.

Madison states that "the most common and durable source of factions, has been the various and unequal distribution of property." He notes that the levying of taxes will often be a temptation to mischief: "The apportionment of taxes on the various descriptions of property, is an act which seems to require the most exact impartiality; yet, there is perhaps no legislative act in which greater opportunity and temptation are given to a predominant party, to trample on the rules of justice. Every shilling with which they over-burden the inferior number, is a shilling saved to their own pockets." Madison states that there is no realistic hope of controlling factions in a pure democracy: "... such Democracies have ever been spectacles of turbulence and contention; have ever been found incompatible with personal security, or the rights of property: and have in general been as short in their lives, as they have been violent in their deaths." Madison recommends a "scheme of representation" where elected legislators are less likely to be moved by mob psychology. He also recommends a division of powers between national, state, and local legislatures. "Factious leaders" may gain power in particular states, but the dispersal of powers makes them less dangerous to the nation as a whole. "... a rage for paper money, for an abolition of debts, for an equal division of property, or for any other improper or wicked project, will be less apt to pervade the whole body of the Union, than a particular member of it; in the same proportion as such a malady is more likely to taint a particular county or district, than an entire State."

In *Federalist* no. 63, Madison sees the Senate as the legislative body at the federal level that will be most resistant to proposals by which some persons seek advantage by violating the rights of others.

> ... such an institution may sometimes be necessary as a defence to the people against their own temporary errors and delusions. As the cool and deliberate sense of the community ought, in all governments, and actually will in free governments, ultimately prevail over the views of its rulers; so there are particular moments in public affairs when the people, stimulated by some irregular passion, or some illicit advantage, or misled by the artful misrepresentations of interested men, may call for measures which they themselves will afterwards be the most ready to lament and condemn.

Madison's support for property rights was based in part on his belief in the efficiency of free markets. In an address to the First Congress, he states: "I own myself the friend to a very free system of commerce, and hold it as a truth, that commercial shackles are generally unjust, oppressive, and impolitic; it is also a truth, that if industry and labor are left to take their own course, they will generally be directed to those objects which are most productive, and this in a more certain and direct manner than the wisdom of the most enlightened Legislature could point out."[38]

In the Constitution, property rights are protected by the takings clause of the Fifth Amendment, which states, "Nor shall private property be taken for public use, without just compensation." Obviously the takings clause does not afford absolute protection to property rights, but it does require the government to provide an equivalent for what is lost. Libertarians favor a broad interpretation that applies to any taking of property, including taxation. This interpretation rules out all schemes designed to redistribute wealth and, in the words of Richard Epstein, "stops the New Deal in its tracks."[39] According to this view, the government may tax only when the taxpayer receives a benefit of equal value. The proposal for government finance that I have offered—user fees, leasing natural resources, and resource taxes—satisfies Epstein's interpretation of the takings clause. The taxpayer who pays a resource tax is paying for the right to use a natural resource, a right protected by the military and police power of government. If the taxpayer believes that the protected right to use a resource is not worth the cost, she can choose not to pay. She forfeits the right to use the resource, but she is the one who decides whether she is getting equal value for her money.

In addition to broadly interpreting the takings clause, libertarians favor a narrow interpretation of the phrase "the general welfare." The relevant section of Article 1 reads: "The Congress shall have the Power to lay and collect Taxes, Duties, Imposts, and Excises, to pay the Debts and provide for the common Defense and general Welfare of the United States; but all Duties, Imposts, and Excises shall be uniform throughout the United States." If the phrase "the general welfare" is interpreted so that it does not include transfer payments to particular individuals, then the welfare state is unconstitutional. In other words, libertarians insist that promoting the *general* welfare refers to public goods, such as the maintenance of peace and order, that benefit everyone. Libertarians also favor a narrow interpretation of the commerce clause in which "commerce" does not include the manufacture of goods or the production of food. The relevant section of Article 1 grants Congress the power "to regulate Commerce with foreign Nations, among the several States, and with the Indian Tribes." The natural reading of this section is that it refers to the trade of goods and services, not to their production. Finally, libertarians regret the passage of the Sixteenth Amendment, ratified in 1913, which gives Congress the power to tax incomes: "The Congress shall have the power to lay and collect taxes on incomes, from whatever source derived, without apportionment among the several States, and without regard to any census or enumeration." Given the supermajority needed to repeal this amendment, there is no realistic hope of repeal in the foreseeable future.

The radical changes that libertarians prefer run up against the very real problem of conservative justice. Past practice creates expectations; a sudden reversal of direction causes persons to behave involuntarily because they have made choices based on those expectations. This is one reason that *stare decisis* is an important legal principle. There is a strong presumption that judges should be bound by the reasoning used in deciding similar cases. This gives the law continuity and predictability, so that agents can know what is required of them. It is also a requirement of the formal principle of justice that like cases be treated alike. The presumption in favor of following legal precedent can be rebutted; past errors can be corrected, but the burden of proof on those advocating change is justifiably heavy.

I should mention that at this point I am speaking of reversing policies by means of judicial review. The battle for libertarian ideals can also be fought in the legislative and executive branches of government. It is often better to make changes gradually, by legislative action, so that persons can adjust their behavior in anticipation of the changes. The institutional structure of the Court (lifetime tenure for judges) also makes radical changes in direction unlikely. One realistic hope is that the present Court will begin to take property rights and economic liberties more seriously. Since the New Deal, violations of economic liberty have usually received the lowest scrutiny, which in practice has often amounted to no scrutiny at all. An example is *Lee Optical*:[40]

> *Lee Optical* contested an Oklahoma bill that required a prescription from an optometrist or ophthalmologist before having lenses replaced or even fitted in new frames by opticians. The law gave every appearance of being a victory of the interest of optometrists and ophthalmologists over opticians and consumers. The law was unsupported by any legislative reasons linking that added income of eye doctors with the general good of the state. Justice Douglas admitted the apparent 'needless' and 'wasteful' character of the Oklahoma law, but then proceeded to invent hypothetical reasons, one might say a rationalization, for the legislature.[41]

Restrictions on economic liberties should be scrutinized because persons often seek through government regulation private advantage that they cannot win in the marketplace. In addition, protection of these liberties has a deeper significance. For many persons, the choice of an occupation or career is one of the most important decisions they make—it is at the heart of their identity and conception of their own worth. Tolerance of diversity is no less important in this area than it is in freedom of speech and religion. Furthermore, the existence of a thriving private sector has often made the difference in people's access to religious, artistic, and intellectual freedoms. It is no accident, for example, that freedom of the press has always been limited in socialist countries. Vocational choice affects where persons can live, what they can do for members of their family, and the avocations they can pursue. If the pursuit of happiness is important, economic liberties and the protection of property rights are important.

I have proposed that the Constitution should be interpreted in light of the political philosophy of the Founding Fathers. I have not claimed that when we interpret vague phrases like "freedom of speech" or "equal protection" we must divine the original intent of the framers. In many cases, the Constitution is deliberately vague and open-ended. For example, the Ninth Amendment states, "The enumeration in the Constitution of certain rights, shall not be construed to deny or disparage others retained by the people." Thus, I reject the view that the Constitution has no meaning unless it is fixed by the original intent of the framers. The meaning and practical significance of the Constitution could be shaped by contemporary ideologies through the decisions of the different branches of government (and not just the Supreme Court). We do not face a choice between discovering original intent and intellectual chaos. Why, then, should we be bound by the political outlook of the white men who created the Constitution over 200 years ago? At the heart of the political philosophy of the founders was a belief in individual rights and a profound distrust of government. This political philosophy will shape our interpretation of the Constitution only if we understand it and accept it. The best reason for accepting the founders' political outlook is that it is better than its competitors.

Part of the genius of the Constitution is its implicit understanding of human psychology. The underlying psychological insights are stated explicitly in *The Federalist*, most notably *Federalist* no. 50. In this essay, Madison focuses on the importance of the separation of powers:

> But the great security against a gradual concentration of the several powers in the same department consists in giving to those who administer each department the necessary constitutional means and personal motives to resist encroachment of the others. The provision for defense must in this, as in all other cases, be made commensurate to the danger of attack. Ambition must be made to counteract ambition. The interest of the man must be connected with the constitutional rights of the place. It may be a reflection on human nature that such devices should be necessary to control the abuses of government. But what is government itself, but the greatest of all reflections of human nature?

Each branch of government, legislative, executive, and judicial, is given the means to check the excesses of the other branches. The president can veto legislation, but presidential vetoes can be overridden by a two-thirds vote of both branches of Congress. The power to impeach a president is given to the Senate, and a two-thirds vote is necessary for conviction. The president has the power to make treaties provided two-thirds of the Senate concur. The president appoints members of the Supreme Court with the advice and consent of the Senate. The president is the commander in chief of the army and navy, but Congress is granted the power to declare war. The Supreme Court is granted the power to decide constitutional issues. To preserve their independence, the members of the Court have lifetime tenure, and their compensation cannot be diminished.

In *Federalist* no. 51 Madison states, "In Republican government, the legislative authority necessarily predominates." Thus, special attention was given to the control of legislative power. Legislation must be passed by both branches of Congress and signed by the president. According to *Federalist* no. 63, the Senate was expected to express "the cool and deliberate sense of the community." Thus, senators were granted six-year terms and they were chosen by state legislators, not popularly elected, a practice not changed until 1913. Noting the dangers of popular government, Madison states, "How salutary will be the interference of some temperate and respectable body of citizens, in order to check the misguided career and to suspend the blow mediated by the people against themselves, until reason, justice, and truth can regain their authority over the public mind?"

The Supreme Court was expected to play an important role in controlling legislative excesses. This view is expressed by Alexander Hamilton in *Federalist* no. 78:

> This independence of the judges is equally requisite to guard the Constitution and the rights of individuals from the effects of those ill humors, which the arts of designing men, or the influence of particular conjunctures, sometimes disseminate among the people themselves, and which, though they speedily give place to better information, and more deliberate reflection, have a tendency, in the meantime, to occasion dangerous innovations in the government, and serious oppressions of the minor party in the community. ...

The founders also sought to control legislative excesses by the enumeration of legislative powers in Article 1, Section 8, of the Constitution. There limited taxing powers are granted along with limited military powers. Congress is granted limited powers to regulate commerce, along with the power to coin money, to borrow money, and to punish counterfeiters. Congress is also granted the power "to establish Post Offices and Post Roads" and "to promote the Progress of Science and useful Arts, by securing for limited Times to Authors and Inventors the exclusive Right to their respective Writings and Discoveries." It should be noted that Congress is given only "all legislative Powers herein granted" (Article 1, Section 1). The significance of this limitation is made clear by the Tenth Amendment: "The powers not delegated to the United States by the Constitution, nor prohibited by it to the States, are reserved to the States respectively, or to the people." In *Federalist* no. 45, Madison comments on the limitation of legislative power:

> The powers delegated by the proposed Constitution to the federal government are few and defined. Those which are to remain with the State governments are numerous and indefinite. The former will be exercised principally on external objects, as war, peace, negotiation, and foreign commerce: with which last the power of taxation will, for the most part, be connected. The powers reserved to the several States will extend to all the objects which, in the ordinary course of affairs, concern the lives, liberties, and properties of the people, and the internal order, improvements and prosperity of the State.[42]

There was much debate over whether the Constitution needed a bill of rights. Some thought that the enumeration of limited powers provided sufficient protection, and Madison worried that a bill of rights would be construed too narrowly. This problem was dealt with by the inclusion of the Ninth Amendment: "The enumeration in the Constitution, of certain rights, shall not be construed to deny or disparage others retained by the people."

What should we say about the Second Amendment? Is it an embarrassing anachronism that should be ignored? Its original significance must be understood in the context of the heated debate over whether the federal government would have a standing army; many feared that a standing army would be a threat to the independence of the states. In a debate during the Virginia Convention, Madison stated, "A standing army is one of the greatest mischiefs that can possibly happen."[43] The Second Amendment states: "A well regulated Militia, being necessary to the security of a free State, the right of the people to keep and bear Arms, shall not be infringed." In *Federalist* no. 45, Madison writes:

> The only refuge left for those who prophesy the downfall of the State governments is the visionary supposition that the federal government may previously accumulate a military force for the projects of ambition. The reasonings contained in these papers must have been employed to little purpose, indeed, if it could be necessary now to disprove the reality of this danger. That the people and the States should, for a sufficient period of time, elect an uninterrupted succession of men ready to betray both; that the traitors should, throughout this period, uniformly and systematically pursue some fixed plan for the extension of the military establishment; that the governments and the people of the States should silently and patiently behold the gathering storm, and continue to supply the materials, until it should be prepared to burst on their own heads—must appear to everyone more like the incoherent dreams of a delirious jealousy, or the misjudged exaggerations of a counterfeit zeal, than like the sober apprehensions of genuine patriotism.

This issue was dealt with in the body of the Constitution in the enumerated powers of Congress as stated in Article 1, Section 8: "To raise and support Armies, but no Appropriation of Money to that Use shall be for a longer Term than two Years." No similar qualification was attached to the power of Congress to maintain a navy. Section 8 simply states, "To provide and maintain a Navy." In place of a standing army, Congress was granted the power to "call forth" state militia to "suppress insurrections and repel invasions." Still, critics of federalism wanted additional assurance, and that assurance was provided by the Second Amendment.

The clear intent of the Second Amendment is to protect the independence of the states by prohibiting the federal government from regulating access to firearms. The amendment, however, does not prohibit state and local regulation. This is not a case where it can be said that the framers were deliberately vague; no matter how popular federal gun control may be, it is simply unconstitutional. Those who think that the Second Amendment is an anachronism should face up to the constitutional responsibility of amending the Constitution. Libertarians will oppose this (amending the Constitution) because individuals have the right of self-defense, and preventing law-abiding citizens from owning guns (while criminals continue to be armed) violates this right. Also, the state has no right to punish persons for the mere possession of a firearm.

As a final point on this subject, some proponents of federal gun control claim that the phrase "the people" should be interpreted as the people collectively, not as individuals, and thus the amendment does not grant a right to individuals to bear arms. This interpretation should be rejected because the same phrase is used in the Fourth Amendment: "The right of the people to be secure in their persons, houses, papers, and effects …" No one seriously disputes that the right against illegal searches and seizures is a right possessed by individuals.

Antimajoritarian features are at the very heart of the Constitution. They include the Bill of Rights, enumerated powers, judicial review, geographic representation in the Senate, the electoral college, the impeachment process, and the amendment process. If democracy means majority rule, the Constitution is antidemocratic. There is, however, a better way to understand democracy, which is to contrast it with its opposite, a dictatorship. In other words, how does a democracy differ from a regime that we would call a dictatorship? In a democratic regime, those who hold positions of significant political power are elected, or they are appointed by elected officials. There are regularly scheduled elections so that the persons who hold political power can be removed from office. All (noncriminal) adults have the right to vote and to run for elective office. Finally, persons have the protected right to criticize political officials and offer alternative policies (freedom of speech). In a dictatorship, some or all of these features are lacking.

In a constitutional democracy, there is an inevitable tension between the goal of protecting individual rights and the desire of politicians to please voters. It is a measure of how difficult the constitutional problem is that we have strayed so far from the limited government conceived by the founders. We have gone astray primarily because two features of the Constitution, the enumeration of legislative powers and the protection of property rights, have simply been ignored. This result would not have surprised Madison. His study of history led him to conclude: "Since the general civilization of mankind, I believe there are more instances of the abridgment of the freedom of the people, by gradual and silent encroachments of those in power, than by violent and sudden usurpations."[44] Fortunately, our constitutional democracy provides the means, through elections, to begin dismantling the Leviathan we have created.

Serious thought should also be given to additional constitutional protections. One of the weaknesses of majoritarian democracy is that it encourages what economists call rent-seeking. Rent-seeking refers to "actions taken by individuals and groups to alter public policy in order to gain personal advantage at the expense of others."[45] This was also anticipated by Madison: "It remains to be enquired whether a majority having any common interest, or feeling any common passion, will find sufficient motives to restrain them from oppressing the minority.... If two individuals are under the bias of interest or enmity against a third, the rights of the latter could never be safely referred to the majority of the three. Will two thousand individuals be less apt to oppress one thousand or two hundred thousand one hundred thousand?"[46] Rent-seeking is disallowed when public spending must promote the *general* welfare, and not the welfare of some at the expense of others. This constitutional protection, however, has proven to be ineffective.

Requiring a supermajority for the passage of legislation would make rent-seeking more difficult.[47] Assume that we have a legislature composed of 100 legislators who represent the interests of their constituents. If a majority vote is sufficient to pass legislation, a coalition of 51 legislators can implement policies that favor most of their constituents by making the minority fund those policies. If passage of legislation requires a 60 percent majority, exploitation is less likely. And a higher percentage will make exploitation even less likely—except for one problem. Holdouts may bargain for special gains by refusing to support legislation that would benefit almost everyone. Another issue is whether a supermajority requirement should apply to some legislative matters and not to others. Such a requirement may have been a good idea 200 years ago. It is not clear that it is a good idea today when the need is to dismantle government programs. These are some of the issues that must be studied before any serious recommendations can be made.[48]

Madison's experience in government, as a member of Congress, secretary of state, and president, confirmed his belief in the importance of limiting the powers of the federal government. In the last year of his presidency, he vetoed a bill that contained federal funding for public works and "internal improvements."

> I am not unaware of the great importance of roads and canals and the improved navigation of water courses, and that a power to the National Legislature to provide them might be exercised with signal advantage to the general posterity. But seeing that such a power is not expressly given by the Constitution, and believing that it cannot be deduced from any part of it without an inadmissible latitude of construction and a reliance on insufficient precedents; believing also that the permanent success of the Constitution depends on a definite partition of powers between the General and the State Governments, and that no adequate landmarks would be left by the constructive extension of the powers of Congress as proposed by the bill, I have no option but to withhold my signature from it. ...[49]

Jefferson wrote that the bill was "negatived by the President, on constitutional, and I believe, sound grounds; that instrument not having placed this among the enumerated objects to which they are authorized to apply the public contributions."[50] It is both interesting and sobering to think about how radical the views of Madison and Jefferson sound today.

10. Summary

A libertarian government could provide the following goods and services:

> National defense
> Law enforcement
> _____
> Water and sewer services
> Streets and roads
> Parks
> Student loans
> Certification

National defense and law enforcement, in their most general and purest forms, are public goods, that is, benefits that cannot be given to some individuals and withheld from others (see Section 7). They should be funded by leasing natural resources and by resource taxes. The other goods and services (below the line) should be funded by user fees. A brief examination of each governmental function follows:

National Defense

There are a number of questions concerning the scope of this governmental function. For example, should U.S. national defense be limited to protecting the territory of the United States? Or should it also include protecting American citizens in other countries? Or the protection of ships carrying cargo to and from the United States? The United States has large oceans on two sides and friendly neighbors north and south. The only realistic threat to U.S. territory is from missiles and bombers. The rationale for the huge military establishment in the United States was the threat of international communism. The spread of communism to Western Europe and Asia would have left the United States isolated in a hostile world, or so it was claimed. An assessment of this claim requires an understanding of both the intentions and the capabilities of communist leaders, an assessment that is beyond the scope of this book. In any case, the threat of international communism no longer exists. Requiring American taxpayers to pay for the defense of Western Europe, Japan, and South Korea violates the injunction against using some as mere means to benefit others. As for the issue of protecting American citizens in other countries, as a general rule, citizens who choose to travel to or reside in other countries should assume the risks involved in their decisions. Exceptions could be made in cases where citizens are involved in official government business. When the United States is threatened by hostile countries, the protection of shipping is a public good. This rationale has less force during more peaceful times. The cost of protecting shipping could be defrayed by requiring owners of ships who seek protection to register their ships in the United States and pay a substantial registration fee.

Law Enforcement

Law enforcement obviously involves the protection of person and property.[51] It includes protection of property in ideas and inventions through copyrights and patents. It includes prohibiting deceptive advertising, since deception is a means of causing others to behave involuntarily. It does not include victimless (consensual) crimes. Laws prohibiting (inter alia) prostitution, gambling, and the sale and use of illicit drugs would be abolished in a libertarian society. This was discussed in Section 8, and I take up these matters again in Section 18. Law enforcement also includes protecting the environment. The libertarian theory of punishment establishes the right to punish, not the duty to punish. Thus, the government can be selective in this area. For example, backyard barbecues can violate the rights of others, since the pollution will usually drift to adjacent property. However, we can decide that the harm is not sufficient to warrant police action.

Water and Sewer Services

These services are perhaps the clearest example of natural monopolies: The water is delivered in a pipe and it is carried away in a pipe. And it does not make economic sense to have competing firms laying different sets of pipes in the same neighborhood. As Milton Friedman has pointed out, there are three ways to deal with natural monopolies: (1) private firms can supply the services and set their own prices, (2) government can regulate the prices charged by private firms, or (3) government can supply the services.[52] Each solution has its disadvantages: (1) can produce price gouging and (2) and (3) can discourage technological innovation and the development of substitutes. Since the provision of water and sewer services is not a high-tech activity, government provision of the services appears to be the best option. Due to its tremendous carrying capacity, fiber-optic cable is an interesting example of a natural monopoly. In return for granting the rights of way necessary for laying the cable, the government could require that it be a common carrier. Government then could regulate access (including prices) to the "information superhighway."

Streets and Roads

The users of streets and roads should pay for their construction and maintenance. Where there is limited access, tolls could be charged; however, it would not be practical to establish tollgates on each city street. One option would be to install electronic sensors that would allow the government to monitor how many miles motorists were driving. This option has a serious privacy problem, since the government would know both where drivers were and where they had been. A lower-tech solution would be to require purchase of a license and then assess further fees depending on the weight of the vehicle and how many miles it is driven. An even less disruptive option would be to continue to pay for the construction and maintenance of roads with revenue from the gasoline tax. Given our present technology (where almost all vehicles are gasoline powered), the gasoline tax is a reasonable user fee.

Parks

The construction and maintenance of parks should also be paid for by those who use the parks. Where there is limited access, this can be done by charging an entrance fee. In other cases, the users of parks could be required to purchase a "park permit." This procedure would be similar to the common practice of requiring fishermen to purchase a license to fish on public lakes and streams. Seeking voluntary contributions is still another possibility.

Student Loans

Loans could be offered to students who are old enough to assume the requisite responsibility. The government could sell bonds to acquire the initial capital, and payment schedules could be set so that the program is self-financing. Provided the beneficiaries are charged the market rate for their loans (i.e., the loans are not subsidized by taxpayers), libertarian rights would not be violated. Why should the government provide this service when private institutions, such as banks, can make student loans? Initially, it was argued that given the mobility of Americans, the federal government would be in a better position to collect. In fact, the federal student loan programs have been poorly managed, and default rates have been extremely high.[53] Milton Friedman has recommended income-contingent loans where recipients would agree to pay a percentage of their future income.[54] So long as the United States has an income tax, this would make collection easier. For the hard-core libertarian, however, this would be a temporary solution.

Certification

Licensure, insofar as it prohibits voluntary exchanges, violates the freedom principle. Instead, the government could certify that doctors, lawyers, accountants, restaurant owners, and others have met specified standards. For example, the conditions in which food is stored and prepared in restaurants could be inspected and certified as sanitary by an agency of the government. If customers preferred to go to certified establishments, it would be financially advantageous for restaurant owners to seek certification. Those who wished to be certified would be required to pay the administrative costs of the certification programs. In a libertarian society, private organizations could also provide certification services, and these organizations might acquire better reputations than the governmental agencies with which they competed.

In cases where persons want a specific government service they are willing to pay for, there is no theoretical limit to the services a libertarian government could provide. What is most noteworthy about a libertarian society, however, is what government would not do. For example, there would be no welfare programs, public schools, or Social Security. These government programs are illegitimate because they are funded by coercive taxes. However, there are, in each case, deeper problems that I should note.

In Section 3, I introduced the moral theory called dualism. In addition to the fundamental right of libertarianism (the equal right to be free), dualism specifies the equal right to basic goods. I noted that one can be a dualist in theory and a libertarian in practice. In fact, the ideal solution to poverty, according to dualism, is voluntary programs to help the poor. Since the ideal programs are voluntary, the burden of proof is on those who advocate coercive programs. They must prove that there are tax-funded programs that will produce a greater reduction in poverty than voluntary ones. It is one thing to talk in general terms about the value of reducing poverty; it is another matter entirely to propose real programs that will actually produce this result. I discuss just how heavy this burden of proof is in Section 12. I should also note that it is hard to meet this burden of proof while maintaining a recognizable conception of moral equality. The natural way to meet the burden of proof is to argue that normal persons cannot be trusted to make the right choices about whether to help others or how to care for themselves. The elitism that underlies this line of argument is obvious. If you believe that others must be prevented from making the wrong choices, then you must believe that some persons (presumably the best and the brightest) have the right to determine what others shall do.

Loren Lomasky employs an instructive analogy to illustrate the deeper problems with public schools:

> Suppose that individuals were free to join and worship in the church of their choice, but that, alongside the various private religious denominations, there was one officially recognized by the state as the Public Church System (perhaps justified on the grounds that its services, unlike the others, be made available equally to rich and poor at no direct cost). All are taxed to erect Public Church buildings in every community, pay the salaries of Public Church ministers, deacons, janitors, groundkeepers, and accountants, purchase vestments, provide bus transportation to daily services, sponsor Public Church softball teams and Theological Disputation clubs, buy picnic tables for Public Church socials, and otherwise endow various Public Church programs. Those of other religious persuasions may provide alternative religious services, but they will have to do so with the resources that remain to them after paying their full share to fund the Public Church.[55]

The taxpayers in a society with public churches would not enjoy religious freedom. Likewise, a society with tax-funded public schools does not have educational freedom.

Lomasky points out that bureaucratic control of public schools leads inevitably to the promotion of a political agenda.[56] We can be fairly certain, for example, that students in American history classes will not be taught that the welfare state (including federal support for public schools) is unconstitutional according to the political philosophy of the Founding Fathers. Instead, whatever is currently fashionable with the educational elites, such as multiculturalism with its emphasis on racism, sexism, and classism, will shape the educational offerings of public schools. Taxpayers who do not want to fund a curriculum that they believe undermines American values are out of luck.

Equality of opportunity is often cited as the value that requires public schools. What does the phrase 'equality of opportunity' mean? Suppose we say that it means getting an equal start in life. If we took this ideal seriously, we would have to do something about genetic differences. This could involve serious eugenics programs, including the future use of cloning. Given our present technology, it could also mean "leveling down." If our goal is equality, children who are above average are as much a problem as those who are below average. Thus, children who are especially bright could be given brain operations that would reduce their intellectual potential. We could remove some of the muscles of children who are physically gifted, and so on. I assume, however, that this is not what the proponents of equal opportunity have in mind.

Another interpretation is that persons should have an equal chance to develop their talents and abilities. This differs from the first one because genetic differences are accepted as a given. However, if we take it seriously, its implications are still quite radical. Given the wide variance in parental interest and aptitude, we could not claim that this value is satisfied if parents are allowed to raise their own children. More modest goals might be attainable: The competitive position of some children, for example, could be improved by requiring their participation in Head Start programs.[57] But these programs fall far short of providing every person with an equal chance to develop his or her talents and abilities.

Lomasky challenges the metaphor that often gives form to this debate:

> "Everyone should have an equal place on the starting line!" Yes—if it's a race that's being run. But the metaphor is thoroughly inapposite. A race features a course that all competitors must run and is zero-sum: if A wins, then B does not. Liberal rights theory *denies* that there is any one Grand Racetrack on which we are all necessarily bidden to run, *denies* that there is a Social Referee duly authorized to place all the participants in their proper starting positions, *denies* that outcomes are zero-sum. Rather, individuals assume for themselves the course they elect to run and take charge of providing for themselves the resources they require. Because projects are infinitely various, A's success does not necessarily entail B's failure. Both may succeed on their own terms—or both may fail.[58]

Any serious attempt at producing equality of opportunity will require massive interference with the choices of parents and their children. I assume that such interference is politically impossible (short of a police state) and morally unacceptable. The answer to these problems is to reject the terms on which this debate has usually been framed.[59]

The deeper problems of Social Security require an understanding of the paternalistic nature of this program. Social Security (at least the major part of it) is not a welfare program. There is no means test for eligibility for benefits, and many recipients are well off. Social Security is a retirement program. Its rationale appears to be paternalism—too many persons will make the wrong choices if they are given the freedom to decide whether and how to save for their own retirement. Joel Feinberg has challenged this view, claiming that Social Security is a "dubious example" of paternalism: "I suspect that the assumption behind the legislation, however, was that few citizens would be compelled to save against their will, so that the law functions less to compel the unwilling than to enable the vast majority to do what they desperately want to do (make their old age and that of their parents and loved ones secure), and cannot otherwise do efficiently."[60] Suppose Feinberg is right and the vast majority, say 90 percent, do want to participate in the Social Security system. Why must the remaining 10 percent be compelled to do so? Is it because there wouldn't be enough money without their participation? This seems doubtful, since the 10 percent who chose not to participate wouldn't receive any benefits. Would it be administratively too inefficient to exempt the 10 percent? In the age of computers, this isn't plausible. In any case, for a philosopher who has written eloquently on the importance of rights, Feinberg's appeal to administrative efficiency is surprising.[61] How can Feinberg know that my life will be better if I am compelled to participate in Social Security? And what gives Feinberg the right to make this decision for me? How to extricate ourselves from the Social Security quagmire will be discussed in Section 18.

If persons have a social objective (a program to help the poor, more public libraries, more classical music, etc.) that they would like to achieve through government, there is an obvious question to ask: Why can't this be done voluntarily—by people agreeing to do it? Why is coercion necessary? If the answer is that government programs are more efficient (which is often dubious), there is another obvious question to ask: Why is efficiency morally relevant?

I shall conclude this section with some comments about the libertarian rejection of welfare rights. Suppose that we grant that persons have objective needs, including needs for food, shelter, and clothing. What conclusions regarding government policies follow from this admission? Compare the following claims:

(1) The objective needs of all citizens should be met.
(2) The government should ensure that the objective needs of all citizens are met.

The first thing to note is that these are *distinct* claims; a person can accept (1) without accepting (2). One might believe, as I shall argue, that programs to help

Summary

the needy should be administered by private charities because governmental programs are ill conceived and poorly managed.[62] The libertarian will reject (2) on principle, but one does not have to be a libertarian to reject it. No libertarians, to my knowledge, reject (1).[63] In "Liberty and Economics," I marshal the evidence for the claim that objective needs would be met in a libertarian society. In doing so, I am not retreating from my earlier claim that for those who accept a dualist viewpoint, the burden of proof lies with the advocates of tax-funded programs. There is a presumption against coercion, and thus it requires justification. Opponents of the libertarian solution to poverty must prove that objective needs can be met only by government programs.

THREE

Liberty and Economics

... it is also a truth, that if industry and labor are left to take their own course, they will generally be directed to those objects which are most productive, and this in a more certain manner than the wisdom of the most enlightened Legislature could point out.

James Madison, Address to the First Congress, 1789[1]

11. General Observations

When we discuss economic issues, it is easy to miss the forest by looking at the trees. I begin, therefore, with some general observations concerning the economy of the United States. Living standards have improved dramatically since the Great Depression. There is no universally accepted way to define and measure standards of living, but one of the best measures is a statistic published by the Department of Commerce: personal income, on a per capita basis, after taxes, and adjusted for inflation. This statistic is commonly called per capita disposable income. Personal income, by this measure, more than doubled (a 112 percent increase) in the 30-year period from 1939 to 1969.[2] If we take a more recent time period that excludes World War II, personal income rose by more than 120 percent in the 40 years from 1950 to 1990.[3] These are impressive numbers, but they actually understate the buying power of consumers because the inflation adjustment does not take into account improvements in the quality of products. Are televisions, tires, and razor blades cheaper or more expensive than they were 20 years ago? Given improvements in quality, there is no easy way to answer this question. There is also no way to account for the availability of new products. To what degree has our standard of living improved due to compact-disc players, personal computers, cellular phones, and dishwashers?

The dramatic rise in living standards is often downplayed by those who have forgotten, if they ever knew, what life was like for many Americans in 1940. Robert Samuelson provides us with a sobering reminder:

> Any nostalgia for prewar America is mostly misplaced. The country was poorer, and life was harder. In 1940, more than a fifth of the population still lived on farms, less than a third of the farms had electric lights and only a tenth had a flush toilet. Among all Americans, 56 percent were renters. More than half of the households didn't have a refrigerator, and 58 percent lacked central heating. Nearly half the labor force worked at grueling farm, factory, mining, or construction jobs. Home life was demanding. The famous study by sociologists Robert and Helen Lynd of "Middletown" (Muncie, Ind.) in the 1920's found that wives in working-class families (about 70 percent of the total) were typically up by 6 a.m. to start cooking; 40 percent rose by 5 a.m.[4]

Along with the rise in living standards, the life expectancy of Americans increased from 63 years in 1940 to 76 years today.[5]

The growth in personal income since World War II has been uneven. It grew at a 2.3 percent annual rate from 1950 to 1970, but at a 1.8 percent rate from 1970 to 1990.[6] There was very little growth in the nine years from 1974 to 1983.[7] Much of the growth in personal income during the second 20 years was concentrated in "the seven fat years" that began in the first quarter of 1983 and ended with the recession that started in the third quarter of 1990. During this period, gross domestic product (GDP) increased by 31 percent. Civilian employment rose by 19.5

percent as the economy added 18.4 million jobs.[8] The benefits of economic growth "trickled down" as the number of persons classified as poor by the Census Bureau fell from 15.2 percent in 1983 to 12.8 percent in 1989, a decline of 3.8 million.[9] During the "energy crisis" of the 1970s, many experts foresaw, at best, a stagnant economy or, at worst, another depression. These pundits and prognosticators failed to appreciate an elemental fact of economics: It is normal for capitalistic economies to grow. The primary reason for growth is competition, which forces producers to provide goods and services more efficiently. Greater efficiency is achieved primarily through the use of new technologies that allow workers to be more productive.

Although growth is normal in capitalistic economies, governments often suppress this natural tendency. Economic growth can be retarded by high taxes, inflation, government deficits, and excessive regulations. A brief examination of each factor follows:

High Taxes

Competition is the engine of capitalism, and savings are its fuel. Growth is achieved primarily by investment in new technologies, and persons must save (i.e., forgo immediate consumption) to provide the capital for investment. Taxes reduce both the ability to save (since taxpayers have less money) and the incentive to save. Since deficit spending must be covered by borrowing, the best measure of the tax burden is government spending. Total spending by federal, state, and local governments increased from 24 percent of GDP in 1950 to 34 percent in 1994,[10] which means that the government directly controlled one-third of the economy by determining how taxpayers' money was spent. It is no accident that economic growth has declined while spending by government has increased. Let us consider an example to illustrate these general remarks. T. J. Rodgers founded Cypress Semiconductor in 1983. Rodgers is one of the entrepreneurs who, in President Clinton's words, "profited most from the uneven prosperity of the last decade."[11] Cypress makes data-communication chips, memory chips for supercomputers, and microprocessor modules for "massively parallel" computers. In 1993, Rodgers testified before Congress in opposition to the increase in the corporate income tax. He stated that in its first 10 years Cypress had "generated more than $1 billion in cumulative revenue; made over $160 million in profits, on which we paid $60 million in taxes, and created 1500 jobs that paid cumulative salaries of nearly $500 million, on which employees paid further taxes of $150 million."[12] Rodgers noted how the increase in the corporate income tax would affect Cypress: "Suppose, as a result of the [Clinton] plan, that Cypress's corporate taxes increase by $1 million next year. As CEO, I can only take the money directly out of R&D— the lifeblood of the organization. Again, let's be clear about the logic: A tax increase of $1 million means that Cypress will employ ten fewer Ph.D. technologists who would be working on high-performance chips for the data superhighways and supercomputers."[13] Rodgers also testified against the Clinton plan to funnel government money into high-tech companies:

> I own shares in Silicon Graphics. It exists because hundreds of institutions and individuals like me—excesses of the 80s—put their money into the company through venture capital. Washington cannot create more companies like Silicon Graphics. The way to create more Silicon Graphics is to allow knowledgeable investors, steering their money through world-class venture capitalists, to try to fund just the right companies with just the right technology at just the right time. Even these venture experts are not right all the time. But surely they are right more often than Washington.[14]

As George Gilder points out, "An economy can continue to grow only if its profits are joined with entrepreneurial knowledge."[15]

The capital gains tax cut in 1978 helped set the stage for the seven fat years.

> After the capital gains tax cut of 1978, all the indices of the entrepreneurial economy moved massively up, as a long backlog of innovations at last found significant funding. By the end of the year, new commitments to venture capital funds had risen almost fifteenfold, from $39 million in 1977 to $570 million in 1978. By 1981, actual venture outlays had tripled to some $1.4 billion and the total venture capital pool had doubled to $5.8 billion. The tax cut of 1981, dropping the maximum rate on long-term capital gains to 20 percent, spurred a new surge of investments. By the end of 1983, the pool of venture funds soared to $11.5 billion. During the severe recession of 1982, while many economists spoke of a new great depression, actual venture capital outlays rose to $1.8 billion, more than the five-year total during the slump of the mid–1970s, and in 1983, these outlays approached $3 billion.[16]

In 1986, the capital-gains tax rate for most investors was raised from 20 percent to 28 percent. The Congressional Budget Office (CBO) predicted that capital-asset sales would exceed $250 billion by 1992. Actual sales were just over $100 billion, a result that produced far less revenue than the CBO had predicted.[17]

To appreciate the damage that the capital-gains tax does, we must understand the "lock-in effect." Suppose that you buy 1,000 shares of XYZ in 1978 for $10,000 and you sell the shares for $30,000 in 1994. You report a $20,000 capital gain and pay the tax of $5,600. However, during the 16 years in which you owned the shares, prices (in general) have doubled, and thus inflation has wiped out half of your $20,000 profit. Thus, your real after-tax gain is just $4,400, an annual increase of less than 3 percent a year. To change the case, if you sold the shares for $20,000, you would be required to pay a capital gains tax of $2,800 even though your real profit (after inflation) is zero. Many investors are understandably reluctant to pay taxes on phantom profits, and thus they hold onto investments when the money could be put to better use in other parts of the economy. It is estimated that the amount of locked-in capital exceeds $1 trillion.[18] Taxes, in general, reduce the amount of money available to individuals for savings. The capital-gains tax penalizes savings directly. Abolition of this tax would provide a tremendous stimulus to the American economy.

Inflation

I have noted that savings fuel economic growth by providing the capital for investment in new technologies. Inflation (along with high taxes) reduces the incentive to save. Suppose that you purchase a $1,000 bond that pays 10 percent interest. You receive $100 in interest income after one year. Inflation is 5 percent and your marginal income tax rate is 50 percent (you live in New York). In this case, your real after tax return is zero. When inflation exceeds 13 percent, as it did when Reagan became president in 1981, it is very hard to make a profit by investing in financial assets. While inflation raged in the 1970s, investors poured money into tangible assets such as gold, jewelry, paintings, and real estate. Half the new multimillionaires listed by *Fortune* in 1978 made their fortunes in real estate.[19] Tax laws also encouraged excessive investment in real estate by allowing investors to depreciate properties that were actually increasing in value. These policies helped set the stage for the savings and loan debacle, which I shall discuss shortly.

During periods of high inflation, it is good to be a borrower because you repay your loan with cheaper dollars. The flipside is that savers are penalized. In addition to discouraging saving, inflation harms the economy by distorting price signals and creating uncertainty. Market economies function efficiently when prices give businesses undistorted information about changes in consumer preferences. Inflation makes it difficult to distinguish changes in relative prices from changes in the general price level. The frequent result is misallocation of resources. Uncertainty concerning the future level of prices makes it difficult for producers to predict what their profits (if any) will be. Inflation even makes it difficult for businesses to determine what their present profits are. The value of inventories may increase, but how much will it cost to replace them? Producers will also question whether they are taking adequate depreciation on their plants and equipment, for they cannot be certain what the replacement costs will be. During an inflationary period, businesses often report profits when they are really using up their capital. Finally, businesses will be concerned about what action the government may take to control inflation. Will there be a recession or a depression? These uncertainties decrease the willingness of businesses to take risks by investing in long-term projects.

Unstable monetary policies can cause recessions and depressions. The severe recession that started in the fourth quarter of 1981 and lasted through 1982 was caused by the Federal Reserve Board slamming on the monetary brakes to control inflation.[20] Milton Friedman has argued persuasively that the Great Depression was caused in large part by a dramatic decrease in the quantity of money:

All told, from July 1929 to March 1933, the money stock in the United States fell by one-third. ... Had the money stock been kept from declining, as it clearly could and should have been, the contraction would have been both shorter and far milder. It might still have been relatively severe by historical standards. But it is literally inconceivable that money income could have declined by over one-half and prices by over one-third in the course of four years if there had been no decline in the stock of money. I know of no severe depression in any country or any time that was not accompanied by a sharp decline in the stock of money and equally no sharp decline in the stock of money that was not accompanied by a severe depression.[21]

Many have assumed that the Great Depression demonstrated the failure of free market capitalism. In reality, it was caused primarily by the mistakes of a few men who controlled the monetary system.

How to achieve price stability is a complicated matter. There is considerable evidence that the Federal Reserve Board is following a price rule rather than targeting money supply aggregates.[22] These are technical matters that I leave to the experts to sort out.

Government Deficits

The federal government has run a deficit every year since 1969. The accumulated deficits, before and after 1969, are called the national debt, which is approaching $5 trillion. The federal government must borrow to cover its deficits, and interest payments on the national debt are now about $200 billion a year, the third largest item in the federal budget behind Social Security and defense spending.[23] At present, interest payments on the national debt are roughly equal to current deficits.[24] In other words, revenues cover expenditures on programs and services, and thus the current deficit is caused by past deficits.

Critics of deficit spending often claim that debt-financing permits us to live beyond our means today while we send the bill to our children and grandchildren. There is some truth to this charge, but its significance can be overblown. Whereas there is some foreign investment in government debt, most of the bonds are held by Americans. Our children and grandchildren will have to pay higher taxes to meet interest payments on the national debt, but most of the interest income will go to Americans. As James Gwartney and Richard Stroup point out, "Debt-financing influences future generations primarily through its potential impact on savings and capital formation. If the current generation leaves lots of factories, machines, houses, knowledge, and other productive assets to its children, then the productive potential of the next generation will be high."[25] The money the government borrows could be used for investments. If the government invests in productive assets such as roads and new technologies, future generations will benefit. However, most of the money (53 percent) goes for transfer payments that benefit some individuals at the expense of others without adding to the capital stock of the country.[26] Thus, future generations will have a lower standard of living because debt-financing by government reduces the stock of tools, machines, factories, houses, and so on.

The allure of debt-financing is not hard to understand. In general, voters want more government services and lower taxes, and debt-financing is the means of satisfying these incompatible desires in the short run. If the scheme of government finance that I have recommended had been followed—user fees for private goods and funding for law enforcement and national defense provided by resource taxes and the leasing of natural resources—there would be no national debt and the country would be far wealthier.

Excessive Regulations

George Bush will be remembered as the president who broke his "no new taxes" pledge. In the long run, the regulations that were passed during his tenure will be more costly than new taxes to American citizens.[27] They include an increase in the minimum wage, the Americans with Disabilities Act, a new Civil Rights Act, and the Clean Air Act. With the exception of the Clean Air Act, these regulatory measures are designed to prohibit voluntary exchanges or to force people to interact. In other words, they violate the principle of freedom of association. I discuss these measures in Sections 12 and 16.

The United States has too many laws and too many lawsuits. Not surprisingly, the country also has too many lawyers. For many years prior to 1970, the number of lawyers per 100,000 Americans remained fairly constant at about 120. That number more than doubled by 1992 to over 300.[28] Regulations often provide a bonanza for lawyers as litigants fight over the distribution of existing wealth rather than expending their energies in producing new wealth. Legal fees rose from 0.9 percent of GDP in 1972 to 1.7 percent in 1990.[29] With the increased willingness of government to impose costly regulations on businesses, the United States has experienced a dramatic increase in lobbying. In 1960, there were 365 lobbyists registered with the Senate. There were over 40,000 by 1994, or (roughly) 400 per senator.[30] Lobbyists have not succeeded in reducing the number of regulations. The number of pages in the Federal Register (which records new regulations and adds them to those still in existence) increased from a post-Carter low of 47,418 in 1986 to more than 67,000 in 1991.[31] The number of federal regulatory employees, which declined during the Reagan presidency, rose by 20 percent in the Bush years.[32] Bush claimed that he was the "education president," but he could more aptly be called the regulation president.

Although the total loss in productivity caused by regulations is quite large, the damage that any particular regulation causes is often small and hard to measure. However, since 1970 there have been two major regulatory failures that deserve special attention. These are the regulations that produced the "energy crisis" of the 1970s and the savings and loan disaster in the 1980s. During his bid for reelection in 1971, President Nixon, using the authority granted by Congress, imposed wage and price controls in order to reduce inflation. Price controls on domestic oil and natural gas remained in effect, in various forms, until January 1981 when Reagan became president.[33] Appreciation of the damage these policies caused requires an understanding of the role of prices in a market economy.

Prices convey information about the *changing relative scarcities* of different goods and services. Without this information, producers produce too much of some things and not enough of other things. In other words, price controls lead to shortages and surpluses. When a price is fixed below the free market price, production is discouraged while consumption is encouraged. An example is a housing shortage caused by rent control. When a price is fixed above the free market price, production is encouraged and consumption is discouraged. An example is a surplus of dairy products caused by a price support for milk. The baseline for comparison in both cases is what would have been produced in the absence of price controls.

In the early 1970s, many "experts" predicted a rapid decline in the availability of fossil fuels.[34] These prophesies were abetted by controls that limited increases in energy prices. Some sanity was restored to the debate over the wisdom of price controls by a small government agency, the Energy Research and Development Administration. The agency issued a report in 1977 that reached what should have been the unremarkable conclusion that a higher price for natural gas would lead to increased production.

> The Carter administration proposals would have put a ceiling on the price of natural gas at $1.75 per thousand cubic feet. But the MOPPS (Market Oriented Program Planning Study) study had estimated that a price of $2.25 would bring out "inferred reserves" of ordinary gas, as well as the Devonian shale deposits in Appalachia, the Western "tight sands" and coal-stream methane. The numbers attached to these deposits would leave the nation "awash in natural gas."[35]

Due to opposition to market solutions in the Carter administration, the policies that produced the energy crisis continued until the Reagan presidency. Subsequent developments have shown that this "crisis" was not the result of a shortage of carbon in the earth's crust.

A price control was also instrumental in producing the savings and loan debacle. The infamous Regulation Q prevented S&Ls from paying more than 5.5 percent interest on savings accounts. As inflation soared, many depositors moved their savings to money market funds. Regulations also limited the kinds of loans S&Ls could make—primarily mortgage loans. The thrifts were forced to borrow short and lend long, and inflation caused their long-term loans to be unprofitable. To avert the immediate collapse of the S&L industry, the Depository Institutions Deregulation and Monetary Control Act was passed in 1980. Regulation Q was phased out, and S&Ls were given more freedom to make higher yielding, and hence more risky, investments. In addition, the fateful decision was made to increase federal deposit insurance from $40,000 per account to $100,000.[36] Protected by government-backed insurance, depositors could simply look for the highest interest rate without worrying about the financial condition of the institution in which they placed their savings.

In the 1980s, political interference prevented the prompt closing of many insolvent thrifts. Speaker of the House Jim Wright stalled a recapitalization bill that would have allowed the closing of money-losing thrifts while he pressured regulators to go easy on Texas banks.[37] The "Keating Five" (Senators Alan Cranston, Dennis DeConcini, John Glenn, John McCain, and Don Reigle) urged regulators not to close Lincoln Savings and Loan. Lincoln was finally shut down at a cost of $2.5 billion to taxpayers.[38] S&Ls are also regulated by state governments, and more than one-half of the failed thrifts were located in Texas and California. Arkansas, under the leadership of Governor Clinton, had the worst regulatory record. Over 80 percent of the state-chartered S&Ls in Arkansas failed.[39] The S&L bailout has cost taxpayers about $170 billion.[40] This debacle is not an example of "market failure." Looting, theft, and political chicanery amplified the disaster, but its initial causes were inflation, Regulation Q, and federal deposit insurance.

I have argued that economic growth has been retarded by high taxes, inflation, government deficits, and excessive regulations. In spite of these policies, which seem to assume that economic growth occurs automatically no matter what government does to discourage it, Americans still enjoy the highest standard of living in the world. The World Bank and the International Monetary Fund estimate the relative size of economies using purchasing-power parities instead of market exchange rates. This procedure is based on what money actually buys in each country. By this measure, the United States has by far the largest gross domestic product (more than twice as large as Japan's) and also the largest GDP per head.[41]

The *Economist* has noted that American businesses are well positioned for future growth: "America leads in most of the young industries likely to grow fastest in the future—from multimedia and all things digital to biotechnology and all things scientific. American firms have lost their lead in the manufacture of commodity chips and computers, but enhanced it in more profitable areas such as microprocessors and software. They have slipped in consumer electronics but strengthened their dominance in entertainment."[42] Future growth could be derailed by ill-advised policies, but businesses in other countries must also deal with governments. Government spending, as a percentage of GDP, is lower in the United States than in the other "industrialized" nations, with the exception of Japan. Whereas government spending accounts for one-third of American GDP, it exceeds 40 percent in Canada, England, France, and Germany.[43] Government deficits are also larger in most countries. The Organization for Economic Cooperation and Development (the OECD) forecasts that Norway will be the only OECD country to have a smaller 1995 deficit (as a percentage of GDP) than the United States. Japan's deficit is forecast at 4.1 percent of GDP compared to 2.3 percent for the United States.[44]

The United States has other comparative advantages. It has the most open market to foreign trade. Trade restrictions and government subsidies, which are more common in Europe and Japan, protect inefficient businesses. The American economy has also benefited from deregulation of the trucking industry, the airlines, and phone services. The Brookings Institution has estimated that deregulation saved American air travelers $100 billion in the first ten years.[45] Operating costs at Europe's airlines are much higher (48 percent in 1993) than at America's.[46] Since the breakup of AT&T, long distance prices have dropped 40 percent on average.[47] Subsidies to American farmers cost consumers an average of $360 a year in 1993, but this was less than in Europe and Japan, where consumers paid an extra $450 and $600, respectively.[48] Food processing is the largest manufacturing industry in both the United States and Japan, and it is primarily responsible for the solid lead the United States holds in overall manufacturing productivity. American workers produce three times the volume of food as their Japanese counterparts.[49]

The United States has outperformed Europe by a wide margin in creating new jobs. Since 1960, the American labor force has expanded by over 80 percent; European employment has risen by a paltry 6 percent. Unemployment rates in Europe climbed from 2.4 percent in 1970 to 6 percent in 1980 to almost 12 percent in 1994.[50] Europe's doleful performance can be attributed to some of the factors already mentioned: high taxes, inflation, and government deficits. Excessive regulations and government benefits have also hurt: The minimum-wage and unemployment benefits are much higher in most European countries. Employment-protection rules and high unionization have produced inflexible labor markets.[51] Only 13 percent of American workers in the private sector are unionized; the comparative figures in England and Germany are 28 percent and 30 percent, respectively.[52] It is becoming harder to fire workers in the United States, but it is more difficult to do so in Europe. Employers are reluctant to take on new workers if they cannot be removed from the payroll when market conditions change.

The American record on job creation is much better than Europe's, but the unemployment rate in the United States is still too high. In its attempt to find a government solution to a government-created problem, the Clinton administration wants to spend more on job training. However, training people for nonexistent jobs will not help. Abolition of the capital-gains tax would be a far more effective remedy.[53] Since government-funded training programs must be paid for by taxes, there is no reason to expect any net gain in jobs. And training accomplished by government mandates ignores the reason that many employers open their own businesses—so that they can be the boss without government, or anyone else, telling them what they must do.

The training remedy appeals to interventionists such as Robert Reich (presently labor secretary) because it preserves a role for government activism.

Reich is attracted to the German model, which has produced the most expensive workforce in the world. By contrast, without extensive training programs, American workers are far more productive.[54] One reason training is often counterproductive is that it increases labor market inflexibility by providing persons with job-specific skills. Governments have had a sorry record in predicting the specific skills that workers will need. Furthermore, it is worth noting that many jobs do not require high skills. There are 1.5 times as many janitors in the United States as lawyers, accountants, investment bankers, stockbrokers, and computer programmers.[55] Millions more are employed in the food industry as clerks, waiters, cooks, bartenders, and so on. What *is* needed is a major reform of the American educational system: A good general education is often the best preparation for being a productive worker. I discuss these matters in Section 15.

Japan has had the fastest-growing economy of the industrialized countries since World War II. George Gilder argues, persuasively in my opinion, that this is due primarily to resourceful entrepreneurs and to a tax system that does not discourage savings and investment.[56] Income derived from savings accounts is not taxed, and Japan did not have a capital-gains tax until 1990. Securities transactions are now taxed at a maximum rate of 5 percent.[57] Some observers have credited MITI (Ministry of International Trade and Industry) with Japan's success. Until recently, evidence for and against this claim was largely anecdotal. Supporters pointed to targeted industries that did well, and opponents noted that MITI tried to discourage Sony from producing transistor radios and Honda from making cars. A study by Professors Richard Beason (University of Alberta) and David Weinstein (Harvard University) supports the critics. Their principal finding is that Japanese industrial policy did not pick winners. They looked at cheap loans, net transfers, trade protection, and tax relief for 18 sectors of the Japanese economy. Calculating the correlation between growth in each sector and the support provided by the various industrial policies, they found a negative correlation in every case. In other words, more support was given to slow-growth industries.[58] Furthermore, Japan's industrial policies have produced an enormous imbalance of exports over imports. This has led to an overvalued yen, making it more difficult to pursue the strategy of export-led growth. Japan has had a stagnant economy since 1991.[59]

American success in high-definition television has heartened those who oppose government intervention. Once again, MITI backed a loser, spending over $1 billion supporting the development of an analog system. European governments did the same. American companies, without government support, developed a digital system that has made the Japanese and European versions obsolete.[60]

I shall conclude this section with some observations concerning the failure of socialism. Many critics have noted that without the information supplied by market-determined prices, socialist planners cannot make good economic decisions. In addition, there is a deeper reason that capitalism has proven to be the superior economic system. Consider the following question: What new ideas will produce economic progress in the next 40 years? Is this a difficult question to answer, or is it a question that can't be answered? Suppose we say that a new idea is one that has not been thought of yet. By this definition, it is clear that the question can't be answered. Human beings have been creative in the past, and there is no reason to expect that creativity will cease. We cannot know what technological breakthroughs will be driving the economy 40 years from now, or even 10 years from now.

Bureaucracies have never been known for innovation. Central planning is easier when producers do what they have done in the past. Thus, creativity is stifled under socialism. Free market capitalism rewards creativity and, more important, allows it. Bill Gates and T. J. Rodgers did not need the government's permission to start their own companies. Gilder notes that the crucial role of the entrepreneur is often ignored in the standard academic treatments of economics: "The prevailing theory of capitalism suffers from one central disabling flaw: a profound distrust and incomprehension of capitalists. With its circular flows of purchasing power, its invisible-handed markets, its intricate interplays of goods and moneys, all modern economics, in fact, resembles a vast mathematical drama, on an elaborate stage of theory, without a protagonist to animate the play."[61] What is missing from too much of economic analysis is the spirit of enterprise, the willingness of creative people to take risks, which has made the United States and Japan the economic leaders of the world.

12. Poverty

For those who seek a government solution to poverty, the basic problem is to devise a welfare system that helps the poor without encouraging the behavior that produces poverty. Unfortunately, this has proven to be the social policy equivalent of squaring the circle. Thus, the beginning of wisdom in this area is to recognize that there is no good welfare system. Then we can face the fact that we have a choice of evils, and we can ask which policy (or, more accurately, which group of policies) is the lesser evil.

What would a good welfare system look like? I shall assume that most persons would agree that a good welfare system should satisfy the following precepts:

(1) *Help should be given only to the needy*. This precept may seem too obvious to mention, but a surprising number of proposals have violated it. Of course, reasonable persons can disagree about what counts as real need, but let us charitably assume that legislators can reach practical compromises. We must also be willing to tolerate some welfare fraud. Any time the government hands out money, there will be some unworthy persons who take advantage of it.

(2) *Help should be sufficient for the needy to lead a decent life*. Once again, reasonable persons can disagree about what counts as a "decent life," but we should be able to reach a consensus that avoids the extremes.

(3) *Assistance should not remove the incentive to work*. One reason for accepting this precept is that when a welfare system violates it, persons who could support themselves will stay on the welfare rolls, which is unfair to taxpayers. Furthermore, welfare recipients are harmed by a system that removes work incentives: A class of dependent persons is created with all the social pathologies that accompany welfare dependency.

(4) *A good welfare system should be affordable*. By this I mean that it should not be so expensive that it does serious damage to the overall economy. Only an affluent society can afford a good welfare system. In a poor country, a serious attempt to "share the wealth" would simply result in universal poverty.

It is obvious that it is very difficult (if not impossible) to satisfy both (2) and (3). If welfare benefits are sufficient to lead a decent life, why should recipients seek employment? It is generally acknowledged that the American system violates (3). In most cases, if a recipient goes to work, he loses benefits, and since welfare benefits are often comparable to take-home pay, the recipient usually has no financial incentive to seek employment.[62]

Milton Friedman proposes a welfare system that appears to satisfy (3):

> In 1978 allowances amounted to $7200 for a family of four, none above age sixty-five. Suppose a negative income tax had been in existence with a subsidy rate of 50 percent of unused allowances. In that case, a family of four that had no income would

have qualified for a subsidy of $3600. If members of the family had found jobs and earned an income, the amount of the subsidy would have gone down, but the family's total income—subsidy plus earnings—would have gone up. If earnings had been $1000, the subsidy would have gone down to $3100 and total income up to $4100.[63]

To bring these numbers up-to-date, suppose we say that the guaranteed income for a family of four should be $10,000, which is still well below the poverty line and thus many will complain that it is insufficient to satisfy (2). To preserve the work incentive, every family of four with an income below $20,000 would receive a subsidy. If the income floor were raised to just below the poverty line, say to $14,000, the number would jump to $28,000. At this level of support, the program would violate (4). Furthermore, since the 7.65 percent Social Security tax is paid on every dollar earned, the work incentive would be diminished. The welfare recipient would face a marginal tax rate of almost 58 percent, and this does not include the additional expenses incurred by going to work (transportation costs, new clothes, etc.).

Suppose that the guaranteed income for a single person is $5,000. In this case four unmarried persons could share an apartment and collect $20,000 from taxpayers. Any guaranteed-income scheme in which employable persons choose not to work violates (1). Since their eligibility for the guaranteed income depends on reported income, if they want additional income, they can work "off the books" in the underground economy. To Friedman's credit, he does not offer his proposal as a final solution to the welfare problem. He says that his proposal would "ease the transition from where we are to where we would like to be."[64]

In order to satisfy (2) and (3), some have recommended that welfare be replaced by "workfare" for most recipients.[65] In a typical workfare program, a welfare recipient is given a specified period of time (for example, Clinton's two years and out) to find a regular job. If she cannot find a regular job, she must accept a public service job to continue receiving benefits. Some welfare recipients, such as those with health problems, would be exempt from the work requirement.

Is workfare affordable? This depends on whether workfare jobs are real jobs. Real jobs are expensive because of capital, training, and supervisory costs. To cite a simple example, if a welfare recipient is given a job as a secretary, she must be provided with a place to work, a desk, a phone, a computer, and so on. Since she has not been able to find a regular job, it is unlikely that she is a highly skilled employee, so she must be trained and someone must monitor her work to see that she is performing assigned tasks effectively. How expensive are real jobs? If past experience in government job creation is any guide, they are very costly. The major jobs program of the 1970s, the Comprehensive Employment and Training Act (CETA), was widely criticized for its do-nothing jobs, yet the jobs were very costly to taxpayers. CETA sponsored (in round numbers) 750,000 jobs at a cost of $60 billion.[66] This comes to $80,000 per job. With a rough inflation adjustment, a CETA job cost, on average, over $200,000 in 1995 dollars.

How many welfare recipients would be affected by a work requirement? Over 5 million families receive AFDC (Aid to Families with Dependent Children) benefits.[67] In addition, many states have welfare programs for childless adults, such as Home Relief in New York. Since some welfare recipients would be exempt from the work requirement, let us assume that jobs must be found for 4 million.[68] If I make what I think is a *very* optimistic assumption that a workfare job will cost, on average, $50,000 per year, the yearly cost to taxpayers would be $200 billion.

If "ending welfare as we know it" turns out to be very costly, this will not be popular with taxpayers. Money can be saved if the ideal of providing real jobs is sacrificed, but then workfare will be both costly (although less so) and counterproductive. When asked what jobs workfare employees would do, Mickey Kaus gave the following examples: "But just looking around us, we can see there are playgrounds that are overgrown by weeds. There are basketball hoops without nets. There is visible filth on urban streets. There are streets with potholes. There are bridges that need painting. There are schools that need painting."[69] Apparently Kaus has not thought about what to do with workfare employees in the winter. What happens when employees are assigned to make-work jobs? Both employees and supervisors will eventually become cynical. It will make little difference whether employees show up on time or complete assigned tasks. The General Accounting Office noted in 1969 that some people hired for summer jobs "regressed in their conception of what should reasonably be required in return for wages."[70] Make-work jobs do not provide the skills or instill the self-discipline that welfare recipients need to become productive workers. Will supervisors fire uncooperative employees? If not, workfare employees will get a very distorted picture of what real work involves.

Workfare programs founder on the following dilemma: (1) if workfare jobs are real jobs, the program will be too expensive, or (2) the program will be counterproductive. Furthermore, each dollar spent on a nonproductive workfare job is a net drain on the economy. When taxes are raised to pay for workfare jobs, employers will have less money to fund private-sector jobs. The result could be a massive increase in jobs in the public sector with no net gain in employment.

The optimism of the 1960s regarding the ending of poverty has given way to cynicism and despair. President Kennedy promised a new approach in his welfare message to Congress in 1962: "The goals of our public welfare program must be positive and constructive. ... [The welfare program] must stress the integrity and preservation of the family unit. It must contribute to the attack on dependency, juvenile delinquency, family breakdown, illegitimacy, ill health, and disability. It must reduce the incidence of these problems, prevent their occurrence and recurrence, and strengthen and protect the vulnerable in a highly competitive world."[71] No one believes that changes made in the 1960s achieved the objectives that Kennedy outlined. For example, the illegitimacy rate rose from 5.3 percent of infants in 1960 to 10.7 percent in 1970 to 18.4 percent in 1980 to 33 percent in 1992.[72] In his influential article "The Coming White Underclass," Charles Murray notes that the white illegitimacy rate is 22 percent, just 3 percent below the black illegitimacy rate in 1965 when Senator Moynihan gave his prescient warning:[73] "A community that allows a large number of young men to grow up in broken families, dominated by women, never acquiring any stable relationship to male authority, never acquiring any set of rational expectations about the future, that community asks for and gets chaos."[74] Murray states that "the trend lines on black crime, dropout from the labor force, and illegitimacy all shifted sharply upward as the overall black illegitimacy rate passed 25 percent."[75]

I agree with Murray's analysis of our social problems: "My proposition is that illegitimacy is the single most important problem of our time—more important than crime, drugs, poverty, illiteracy, welfare or homelessness because it drives everything else. Doing something about it is not just one more item on the American policy agenda, but should be at the top."[76] The problems of children (especially males) who have been raised by single mothers are well documented. For example, children living in single-parent families are twice as likely to drop out of high school. Barbara Whitehead notes that "even after controlling for race, income, and religion, scholars find significant differences in educational attainment between children who grow up in intact families and children who do not."[77] Seventy percent of juvenile court cases involve children from single-parent families, and more than 70 percent of juveniles in state reform institutions come from fatherless homes.[78] One study concludes that the relationship between crime and one-parent families is "so strong that controlling for family configuration erases the relationship between race and crime and between low income and crime."[79]

I also agree with Murray's solution to the illegitimacy problem: Stop subsidizing illegitimacy by ending all government support to single mothers.[80] This approach does have a serious moral drawback due to conservative justice. Persons have made choices based on current welfare programs, and the sudden abolition of these programs would cause, in many cases, these choices to be involuntary. Hence, I would phase out AFDC over a 16-year period. The first step would be to state unequivocally that there will be no AFDC payments for children born nine months from now. A single mother receiving AFDC prior to the cutoff point would continue to receive welfare benefits. Benefits would end when the child reaches 16.

What should be done when women choose to have children even though they lack the means to take care of them? States have laws prohibiting child neglect, and neglected children can be taken from their mothers. Murray calls for liberalization of adoption laws so that most of these children can be quickly placed in good homes. Children who are not adopted can be cared for in orphanages. "Some small proportion of infants and larger proportion of older children will not be adopted. For them, the government should spend lavishly on orphanages. I am not recommending Dickensian barracks. In 1993, we know a lot about how to provide a warm, nurturing environment for children, and getting rid of the welfare system frees up lots of money to do it."[81] Libertarians will maintain that orphanages should be funded by voluntary contributions, not taxes.

Public policy should try to ensure that the overwhelming majority of births occur within marriage. As a legal institution, marriage has two primary goals: to protect children and to provide for a just distribution of property if the marriage ends in divorce. Feminists insist, correctly I believe, that the choice to continue a pregnancy belongs with the woman. With this choice comes the responsibility to take care of the child if she is unmarried. To restore the value of marriage, policy should dictate that persons may not enjoy its legal benefits without getting married. A woman should know that she has a legal claim against the father of her child only if she is married to the father. And fathers should know that they have legal rights to the children they sire only if they are married.

So far we have focused on the failures of welfare. If welfare isn't the answer to poverty, what is? The libertarian solution to poverty has two components: a growing economy and voluntary assistance to the needy. A growing economy will provide more jobs so that more persons can take care of their own needs. If real per capita income grows at 3 percent a year, incomes will double in 23 years and poverty will diminish. Furthermore, with much lower taxes, persons living in a libertarian society will have more discretionary income to contribute to worthy causes.

The most quoted poverty statistic, the number of individuals and families with incomes below the poverty line, gives a distorted picture of the nature of poverty. For example, persons with substantial wealth are "poor" if they happen to have a low income in the relevant year. In a recent report, nearly 40 percent of the individuals and families identified as poor by the Census Bureau owned their own homes. More than 750,000 owned homes worth more than $100,000, and 71,000 owned homes worth more than $300,000. Sixty-four percent of poor households owned a car, and 15 percent owned two or more cars.[82] Many young adults who are poor do not remain so for long. For example, graduate students with low incomes are classified as poor even though their life prospects are generally good.

> The Treasury Department's Office of Tax Analysis analyzed a random sample of people who filed tax returns during the decade of 1979 to 1989. Only 14 percent of those in the bottom quintile in 1979 remained there 10 years later; everyone else had moved up the income ladder as they got older. Indeed, more of them (15 percent) made it all the way to the highest quintile than remained at the bottom.[83]

The real problem of poverty is the underclass—the persons who are poor for long periods of time, and in some cases, from one generation to the next. The best way to attack this problem is to stop subsidizing unwed mothers.[84]

We have noted that economic growth is normal in capitalistic economies because competition forces producers to produce goods and services more efficiently. Growth can be retarded by high taxes, government deficits, inflation, and excessive regulations. The regulation of wages is particularly relevant to the problem of poverty. For each potential worker who has enough interest and skills to be productive, there is a market clearing price, a price at which the worker will probably find employment. For some workers, especially those who are young and unskilled, the price is quite low. When government, through minimum-wage legislation, does not permit prices to fall to market clearing levels, there will be fewer jobs for those who are marginally productive. Although this may not seem like an important loss (because of the low productivity of these workers), it is important nevertheless because low-paying jobs provide persons with the opportunity to acquire work experience and job skills that will lead to more productive (and higher paying) work in the future. When this rung on the economic ladder is removed by government regulation, the damage to individuals and society is significant.

At present, the employer's contribution to Social Security and Medicare taxes is 7.65 cents of every dollar paid to low-wage employees. When payroll taxes are raised, as they inevitably must be unless radical changes are made in the Social Security and Medicare programs (see Section 18), this will produce a further increase in the cost of labor. Labor markets can adjust to higher payroll taxes by reducing wages, but this is not possible for workers who are already making the legal minimum. In addition to federal taxes, there are state mandates that require employers to pay for unemployment and disability insurance. In many cases, these mandates add more than 4 percent to the price of labor.[85] Employers must also bear the burden of paperwork that they must complete to comply with government regulations and to pay taxes. In a libertarian society, these impediments to employment would be removed.

Many persons who support minimum-wage legislation do not understand labor markets. Suppose that Jack is paid $4 an hour, but his labor is actually worth $6 an hour. In a competitive labor market, there would be an employer who would pay Jack $5 an hour. If I can hire Jack for $5 an hour and his labor is worth $6 an hour, I will make a dollar for every hour he works for me. Likewise, there would be an employer who would pay him $5.50 an hour. If Jill can hire him for $5.50 an hour, she will make 50 cents for every hour Jack works for her. The tendency in free labor markets is for the price of labor to be bid up to the contribution that labor makes to the production of goods and services. This is why over 95 percent of American workers make more than the minimum wage.[86] Like other prices, wages are determined by supply and demand, and employers must pay market wages to attract qualified workers.

Another common (but erroneous) belief is that capitalist economies will not produce enough low-cost housing. The argument is that the need for low-cost housing does not register in the marketplace because of the lack of effective demand. The reality is that zoning laws often prohibit low-cost housing. For example, many low-income families live in mobile homes that are often moved to trailer parks and not moved again. Capitalism (as an economic system) should not be blamed for zoning laws that exclude this type of housing. The most common way in which capitalism provides low-cost housing is to build middle-class homes and apartments that clearly are profitable. How does this help low-income families? The family that moves into a new home moves from somewhere. In most cases, it vacates a less expensive house or apartment. And the family that moves into this house or apartment usually vacates a less expensive dwelling. Thus, the need for low-cost housing is met by building *new* housing, which does not have to be low cost.

I believe that attempts by government to do something about poverty have been counterproductive. Welfare, public housing, and minimum-wage laws have increased poverty, not lessened it. A growing economy is the best antipoverty program, but government spending and regulations have decreased economic growth. In addition, welfare programs have subsidized the behavior that produces poverty. Those who believe that government programs to alleviate poverty do more good than harm have the burden of proof. Since coercion requires justification, they must prove that tax-funded programs are better than the libertarian solution to poverty. Given the abysmal record of the past thirty years, this is a very heavy burden of proof.

13. The Taxpayer's Dilemma

The title of this section was inspired by the classic problem of game theory, the Prisoner's Dilemma. Peter and Paula are arrested for a crime. The district attorney offers both prisoners a deal to get them to testify against each other. Peter is told that his punishment depends on whether he does testify *and* on whether Paula agrees to testify against him. If he refuses to testify and Paula testifies against him, he will get a 10-year prison sentence. If both testify against each other, they will get 5-year prison sentences. If both refuse to testify, they will each get a 1-year sentence. If Peter testifies and Paula doesn't, Peter will not be punished. If Peter is self-interested and his interests lie in the shortest prison sentence, he should testify against Paula. Testifying is his dominant strategy because it is at least as good as, and sometimes better than, any other strategy *regardless* of what Paula does. The same analysis applies to Paula. But if both testify, they will get longer sentences (5 years) than if both remain silent (1 year). The "rational" strategy does not produce the best result.

We can imagine a similar situation involving taxpayers. Suppose that a society called Transferland has 100 taxpaying citizens (T1, T2, T3 ...). The government of Transferland provides benefits inefficiently: Taxes must be raised by $200 to provide $100 in benefits. T1 lobbies successfully for a subsidy worth $100. Taxes are raised by $2 to pay for T1's subsidy, and his after-tax benefit is $98. If each taxpayer follows T1's example, taxpayers will receive benefits worth $10,000, but will pay $20,000 in increased taxes. Thus, although it is rational for each citizen (as an individual) to seek a subsidy, the collective result is not rational.

All of us at least vaguely understand that real governments cannot transfer resources without some loss along the way. In other words, transfers are not frictionless: It costs money to collect money from Peter to give it to Paula. How much friction is there? In his book *Costly Returns,* James Payne estimates that for every dollar the Internal Revenue Service collects, Americans pay 65 cents more in additional costs.[87] I shall examine the factors underlying Payne's estimate shortly, but as long as transfers are not frictionless, the basic dilemma remains: It is rational to seek subsidies, but if everyone succeeds, everyone will be worse off. There can be winners in this game only if some can exploit others. The winners must see to it that they get the subsidies (or at least most of them) while other taxpayers do not.

In the 1992 presidential campaign, Ross Perot, speaking to voters, accused the major parties of trying to "buy your votes with your own money."[88] This would not be irrational if the government provided one dollar in benefits for each dollar of taxes, but government benefits are far more costly. Let us begin with the cost of collecting the money. The federal government has pushed most of the compliance costs onto private individuals and businesses. They must learn about the requirements, keep records, and do the actual tax computations. All of this takes time, and there are often capital costs as well. James Payne uses a study by the accounting firm of Arthur B. Little to estimate compliance costs. The Little study was commissioned by the Internal Revenue Service to comply with the Paper Reduction Act of 1980. According to the study, the total compliance burden for 1985 was 5.427 billion hours. This was broken down to 3.614 billion hours for businesses and 1.813 billion hours for individuals.[89]

To make a monetary estimate of the compliance burden, Payne must convert the hours into dollars. He notes, "If we take the total IRS costs for 1985 and divide by the total employee hours, the average cost was $21.14 per hour."[90] Payne thinks that this number is too low because it does not include the capital costs that private businesses must pay. The IRS number is much lower, for example, than the $35.47 per hour costs of Arthur Anderson, Inc., the largest accounting firm in the industry.[91] Payne splits the difference and uses $28.31 as the hourly tax-compliance cost for businesses. Thus, he concludes that the tax-compliance cost for businesses was $102.31 billion in 1985. Payne uses the same number ($28.31 per hour) to calculate the compliance costs for individuals who prepared their own tax forms. He argues that "when the government confiscates an asset or conscripts labor, the appropriate payment should be the market-determined price for that asset or labor."[92] He concludes that the tax-compliance cost for such individual taxpayers was $51.33 billion. Payne uses a study by economists Joel Slemrod and Nikki Sorum to estimate the total cost to individuals who hired paid preparers to do their taxes. A total of 45.22 million individuals paid an average of $127.81 to have their taxes done by tax preparers.[93] Paid-preparer costs come to $5.78 billion. To summarize, the total cost of tax compliance in 1985 was almost $160 billion. Federal revenue was $652.56 billion, and thus the total is more than 24 percent of the revenue collected.[94]

The largest component of Payne's estimate is the disincentive costs of the tax system. Taxes on labor and investments reduce the incentives to work and invest. We have already noted that high taxes reduce economic growth, but the question is, By how much? Different studies have reached different conclusions, so Payne adopts a conclusion from a study that avoids the extremes. This study, by Charles L. Ballard, John B. Shoven, and John Whalley, estimates that the disincentive cost of federal taxes is 33.2 percent.[95] This is the marginal cost of additional revenue. For example, if federal taxes are raised to produce $1 million in additional revenue, this will reduce output by $332,000.

When other costs are factored in, such as the costs of responding to IRS inquiries and audits, Payne reaches his conclusion that the costs associated with raising revenue are equal to 65 percent of the revenue collected.[96] *Costly Returns* is the first systematic attempt to estimate the total cost of the federal tax system. Since it is a pathbreaking book, we should expect that in the future methods will be refined and numbers will be revised. It will be very surprising, however, if future studies fail to confirm Payne's essential conclusion: The American tax system is a tremendous economic burden.

Members of Congress get reelected by bringing home the "pork." If this merely involved shuffling money around among the districts, it would perhaps be foolish but not irrational. However, the government cannot transfer resources without causing significant losses. In pork-barrel politics, there are very few, if any, winners, and thus the collective result is not rational. There is a remedy, and as we have seen, it is already in the Constitution. One of the enumerated powers granted to Congress in Article 1, Section 8, is the power to collect revenue to provide for the common defense and the general welfare of the United States. The general welfare does not include building a dam in Congressman Smith's district. The phrase 'the general welfare' refers to public goods, such as preserving peace and order, that benefit everyone. If the Constitution were interpreted correctly, pork-barrel politics would be unconstitutional.

The scheme for funding government that I have proposed also eliminates the problem. Private goods (i.e., benefits that can be given to some individuals and withheld from others) are funded by user fees. The public goods of national defense and law enforcement are funded by leasing natural resources and resource taxes. Other taxes violate the freedom principle.

The American tax code is a costly mess. It is too complicated, and it punishes savings and investments. The ideal tax is fair, easy to collect, hard to evade, and it does not discourage production. The resource tax is fair because the person who pays the tax receives a corresponding benefit—the protected right to use the resource. Tax assessments are public information, so taxpayers can know what others are paying. The resource tax is both easy to collect and hard to evade. The owner of a resource must identify himself and pay the tax, or he will lose the right to use the resource. Production is not discouraged because improving one's property does not result in a higher assessment. For example, a vacant lot would be taxed at the same rate as a lot in the same neighborhood with a house on it.

What would happen if all taxes except resource taxes were eliminated? Billions of dollars that are now "locked in" because of the capital-gains tax would be released to fund more profitable (and thus more productive) businesses. The tax code would no longer favor large corporations (because of the deductibility of interest payments) over small businesses.[97] Capital would move freely to its most productive uses. Savings and investments would no longer be discouraged by high taxes. Thousands of lobbyists, bureaucrats, tax lawyers, and accountants would lose their jobs. These talented people would be employed producing new wealth. Living standards would rise more rapidly and poverty would diminish. Voluntary funding for worthy causes (charities, the arts, education, etc.) would increase.

Finally, a tremendous burden would be removed from the backs of the American people. Big Brother is here, and He is the Internal Revenue Service.

> The Internal Revenue Service does indeed monitor U.S. citizens from the cradle to the grave. It forces employers, financial institutions, and a multitude of other payers to report virtually every significant financial transaction of every person. This infor-

mation is mastered by IRS central computers, which collate the data and merge it with information from other state and federal data banks to detect transgressions. The citizen is then punished by computer-generated letters demanding payment, or by computer-generated seizures of funds. The electronic system is supplemented by an informants program, which induces citizens to spy on each other in exchange for government cash rewards. This comprehensive system of surveillance and control, presumptuous yet highly error-prone, frightens and frustrates large numbers of Americans.[98]

In a congressional subcommittee hearing, Representative Charles Rangel stated: "It is clear to me ... that what makes a voluntary system work is the fear of sanctions and penalties."[99] The Orwellian nature of Rangel's admission is so blatant that it is amusing. What is not amusing is the morally unacceptable invasion of privacy that is an essential feature of our present tax system.

14. Health Care

Prices provide both information and incentives. They provide information concerning the trade-offs buyers and sellers are willing to make. Since trade-offs are based on subjective preferences, this information can be gotten only through the actual choices of buyers and sellers. The trade-offs that individuals are willing to make vary according to available options, mood, the preferences of other persons, and other factors. For example, I cannot predict whether I will want to go to a movie, play bridge, or stay home and read next Friday night. This simple example is reiterated billions of times every day as consumers decide what to buy and what to forgo. In making these decisions, they are influenced by the relative prices of various options. They will buy more when prices decline and less when prices rise. When demand (at a particular price) for a good or service exceeds supply, producers can raise their prices. When supply exceeds demand, they must lower prices to clear the market. Producers respond to higher prices (other things being equal) by producing more and to lower prices by producing less. Given the subjective nature of consumer preferences, the information and incentives provided by market prices cannot be duplicated by any other procedure.[100]

Trade-offs are a fact of life. We can have more of one thing only if we have less of something else, and thus the cost of something is what we forgo, what we could have had (or done) instead. Economics is often defined as the study of the allocation of scarce resources that have alternative uses. The basic economic problem is that there is not enough of the things that people want to satisfy everyone's desires. Economic systems decide who gets what, and thus they ration goods and services. In contrast, there is no need to allocate the air we breathe; it is literally abundant, and thus there is no market for it. These simple truisms are widely acknowledged, and at the same time they are often ignored. In some cases they are ignored because people do not want to face the fact that goods and services such as health care must be rationed. They want health care, like the air we breathe, to be abundant. But since it isn't, we can have more health care only if we have less of other things. Confusion has been engendered in this area by the claim that health care is a right. What does this claim mean? Does it mean that we should make health care as abundant as air, so that persons can have as much of it as they might want? Since this is unrealistic, the right to health care, if there is such a thing, must be a right to *some* health care. How much? Should the government decide? There is an alternative: We could assume that health care is like other goods and services and let consumers decide how much they value it in comparison to other things. Since there is no reason to think that one size fits all, there is at least a strong presumption in favor of the free market solution.

The study of economic systems is the study of different ways of allocating goods and services. All economic systems ration goods and services. If you believe in socialized medicine, you hold that government should decide how health care is to be rationed. In other words, government should have the power to decide what care you will get or not get. In extreme cases, this means ceding to government the power to make life and death decisions concerning whether you will have access to health care. For example, a study by the Brookings Institution estimated the number of British patients denied treatment in a year, based on U.S. levels of treatment. About 9,000 patients with kidney disease did not receive dialysis or a kidney transplant, and 15,000 cancer patients and 17,000 heart patients did not receive the treatment that modern medicine can provide.[101] Serious illnesses are treated aggressively in the United States; this is often not true in countries with socialized medicine.[102] The political incentives behind these decisions are worth considering. Under socialized medicine, the government has a limited amount of money to spend on health care. In a democracy, politicians have an incentive to provide health services that please the majority of voters, and a small percentage of voters are seriously ill or injured. In contrast, politicians will want to ensure that those who have minor ailments can see a doctor. If we realized that we had to choose between having access to physicians for minor ailments and access to aggressive treatment for life-threatening conditions, most of us (I assume) would choose the latter. Sprained ankles, sore backs, and hemorrhoids can be tolerated. When we need open-heart surgery, we want to know that the treatment is available. However, the political incentives do not work this way; politicians get elected by pleasing the majority of voters. The answer to this problem is to not grant government the power to make these decisions.

No one thinks that we should spend unlimited amounts of money on medical care. The crucial question thus becomes, Who will decide how much to spend? The common assumption underlying most policy proposals is that government must decide how health care will be rationed. The libertarian view is that persons (with some exceptions) have the right to control their own lives, including deciding how much to spend on health care. Does the right to control one's own life include the right to be uninsured, to choose not to have health insurance? Adults have the right to do risky things, including driving race cars, playing football, climbing mountains, and smoking cigarettes. Unless we cede to government a general power to regulate risky behavior, why should we think that the decision not to buy health insurance is an unacceptable risk? I think that the feeling that health insurance is different stems in part from a misunderstanding concerning what real insurance is.

What risks are Americans who choose not to buy health insurance taking? The primary reason to buy insurance is to protect one's assets: The cost of medical care for a major illness or a serious injury can wipe out a family's savings. About half of uninsured adults are under 30.[103] Since young adults are usually healthy and many have few assets, the decision not to purchase health insurance is not obviously irrational. But aren't the voluntarily uninsured running the risk that they will be denied medical care? In most cases, the answer is no. Hospitals that treat

Medicare patients must accept all patients with emergency health problems. In addition, many states have laws that require hospitals to treat uninsured patients: "... 47 states require state, county, and/or city governments to provide care for the indigent and uninsured, and numerous court decisions have upheld the right of hospitals to sue state and local governments for reimbursement for such care."[104] Admittedly these laws are not the solution to this problem that libertarians would prefer. Voluntary means of providing health care for the indigent will be discussed later. What is relevant at this point is that the risk that uninsured individuals will be denied medical care is usually quite small. Thus, when a person says that he can't afford health insurance, he often means that he prefers to spend his money on other things, and for some persons, this choice is, at the very least, not unreasonable.

Given that the need for health insurance is not transparently obvious to many young adults, they are likely to be very price conscious. Like all consumers they will purchase health insurance only if they believe that the benefit outweighs the loss from forgoing other purchases. If they have to choose, for example, between buying health insurance and a vacation in Europe, they may prefer the vacation. Regulations that increase the cost of insurance will "price" many of them out of the market. If they are unable (because of government regulations) to buy health insurance that is tailored to their individual needs and that accurately reflects their low health risk, young adults are more likely to choose to be uninsured. State mandates often achieve this perverse result. For instance, persons who don't use drugs and who practice safe sex may see no need for coverage that pays for drug-abuse treatment or for the treatment of AIDS. When states mandate that policies include this coverage, they are "insuring" that more persons will choose not to buy insurance. Another problem with state mandates is that their effects are regressive. They raise the cost of health insurance, and thus the greatest impact falls on persons with low incomes. This is most obvious when a person decides that health insurance is too expensive. But even for low-income families who continue to purchase insurance, price increases are a greater burden.

What many people think of as health insurance is actually prepayment for medical care. Such programs do share a common feature with ordinary insurance: They create a pool for sharing risk. Ordinary insurance protects against unforeseen loss. You buy fire insurance in order to protect the money you have invested in your home. You have a similar reason to buy health insurance, which protects your assets from major medical expenses. Ordinary insurance is often the most efficient way to protect oneself from risky events, but some regulations actually prohibit the sale of real insurance. An obvious example is prohibiting insurance companies from testing prospective buyers for the HIV virus. If sellers must sell "insurance" to those who have already experienced the risky event, this regulation prevents the sale of real insurance. Furthermore, why should one disease get special treatment? If insurance must be sold to persons who are already sick, then there would be no reason to buy real insurance. This practice is analogous to saying that homeowners can buy fire insurance after their house burns down, and the insurance company must pay for the loss. Persons should have the freedom to buy policies that are really prepayment for medical care. This is one way to create a risk pool that protects members against major medical expenses. Persons should also have the option of purchasing less costly insurance that is tailored to their individual needs.

State mandates require insurers to overcharge low-risk buyers so that high-risk individuals can buy insurance at subsidized prices. Since this spreads the cost of insuring against risk over more buyers, this may seem like a beneficial result. However, state mandates can easily lead to spiraling price increases. When mandated coverage increases the price of insurance, more low-risk individuals choose to be uninsured. Since the insurance pool then contains a higher percentage of high-risk buyers, premiums must be raised to cover increased costs. This causes more low-risk buyers to opt out. According to Elizabeth McCaughey, "The 1980s—the first decade ever to see an increase in the percentage of the population that is uninsured—was also the decade in which state lawmakers doubled the number of benefits that customers are compelled to buy, whether or not they want them or can afford them."[105] The only way to ensure stability in a voluntary insurance system is to charge high-risk buyers more for coverage that is, in fact, more expensive. Otherwise, high-risk buyers will seek coverage at the artificially low price, and low-risk persons will look for other options. This produces an unstable system that cannot continue for long.[106]

Those who prefer government solutions will note that this analysis holds for voluntary insurance schemes. One answer is to require that everyone buy insurance so that low-risk individuals cannot opt out. This proposal is a classic example of government creating a problem that, supposedly, only more government can solve. The best answer is to eliminate the regulations that created the problem.

If real insurance is often the most efficient way to protect against risky events, why don't more Americans buy real insurance? The main reason is that our tax system encourages the overconsumption of health insurance, and this is a major cause of our spiraling health care costs. Suppose that my employer provides health insurance, a comprehensive family policy that is really prepayment for medical care and costs $5,000. I ask my employer to pay me the $5,000. I will use $2,000 to buy insurance coverage with a large deductible, say $3,000. This would save me money because my family's normal medical expenses are $1,000 a year. I would now be paying for routine care out-of-pocket; this would save money by reducing paperwork that is generated by filing insurance claims. From my employer's point of view, the cost of employing me is the same whether the $5,000 goes to me or to an insurance company. This arrangement is clearly rational: I would be better off and my employer would be no worse off. However, under present tax laws, I have no monetary incentive to do what otherwise would be both good for me and good for society in the sense of reducing the waste of unnecessary paperwork. When my employer spends $5,000 to provide health insurance for my family, the $5,000 is not taxed. If my employer increases my income by $5,000, the additional income is taxed and my marginal tax rate is 51 percent (28 percent federal income tax, 15.3 percent Social Security and Medicare tax, and 7.8 percent state income tax). Given these perverse incentives, there is usually no financial reason for individuals to do what they would normally do to reduce health care costs.

Suppose that automobile insurance could be purchased by employers with pre-tax dollars. This would give employees a strong incentive to ask for auto coverage in lieu of a raise in pay, and it would encourage the overconsumption of insurance because as many employees would opt for policies that cover every scratch and dent. This would be a boon to auto shops, just as it has been to doctors, because consumers would not make the trade-offs they would otherwise make. In normal markets, the benefits of wise decisions often "spill over" and benefit others; the losses from bad choices usually fall primarily on the agents who make mistakes. Thus, when you buy health insurance with a large deductible, this saves you money and it also reduces the cost of medical care. The money that you save can be invested or spent on things that are more valuable than unnecessary paperwork. When markets produce irrational results, normal incentives have usually been skewed by government regulations and taxes.

Representative Jim McDermott, an advocate of the "single-payer" system, blames rising health care costs on the free market: "We have had almost totally uncontrolled free enterprise in the medical-industrial complex since the Second World War, and an outrageous cost explosion has been going on for at least 20 years. The forces of the free market have not worked at all."[107] One wonders whether the congressman lives in a different world. About half of medical bills are paid by the federal and state governments.[108] In addition, by subsidizing the purchase of low-deductible, high-cost insurance, the government has created a health care system where more than three-fourths of all medical bills are paid by third parties.[109] Many other cost increases can be attributed to government regulations. We have already looked at some of the regulations affecting the insurance industry. The regulatory hurdles of the Food and Drug Administration increase the cost of drugs.[110] Licensing laws limit competition by prohibiting consumers from receiving medical care directly from nurses, midwives, and dental hygienists. Laws prohibit consumers from buying many drugs directly from pharmacists even though pharmacists often know more about the drugs than the doctors who must write the prescriptions. Contrary to Representative McDermott's view, the American health care system bears only a faint resemblance to a free market.

Senator Bob Kerrey's diagnosis is closer to the mark: "… for 50 years or more, the government has been intervening in the health care system, always saying we want to make it easier for people to get the care they need. Every time, we have increased the demand for health services, and often, we have restricted the supply of service-givers. And then we're shocked—shocked—when prices go up."[111] Is it an accident that health costs began to soar after Medicare and Medicaid were passed?[112] Significant funding of these programs began in 1967, when spending on health care was 6.33 percent of GDP.[113] Spending in 1994 exceeded 14 percent.[114] In addition to government programs and policies, many other factors have contributed to the rise in expenditures, such as an older population and the availability of new procedures and technologies. In 1967, no one "needed" bypass surgery or coronary angioplasty because these procedures were unavailable. George Will reminds us that increased expenditures have bought better health care: "Health care cost 5 percent of GDP in 1960. All in favor of spending at 1960 levels signify by saying let's do without bypass operations (300,000 this year), CAT and PETT scans, MRIs, endoscopes and other diagnostic technologies, laser microsurgery and all the other capabilities that have come with increased costs."[115] There is no "correct" percentage of GDP that the government should be aiming for. Persons should have the right to spend as much of their own money on medical care as they wish. What libertarians do object to are the subsidies and regulations that prevent persons from making the choices they would normally make to reduce expenditures.

Why are so many people willing to let the government, through taxes, determine how much they will spend on health care? Only the most die-hard socialists want the government to determine how much we will spend on shoes. Why is health care different? Shoes are more clearly "necessities" than many medical procedures. Perhaps part of the answer to this puzzle lies in the belief that there are medical experts but there are no "shoe experts." The experts know what kind of health care we should have. This brings us back to the problem of rationing. If the United States had something like the British National Health Service or the Canadian system, the government would pay for some medical procedures and the availability of others would depend on market conditions. Political battles would be waged over which procedures would get government funding. It is quickly apparent that these decisions cannot be based simply on "medical expertise."

Consider the contentious issue of abortion. In my opinion, taxpayers who are morally opposed to abortions should not be forced to pay for them. If we had socialized medicine, heated battles would be fought over government funding of abortions. What should be done for women who want to become pregnant but haven't succeeded? Like pregnancy, infertility is neither an injury nor a disease, so why should it be covered at all? If it is covered, what should be the liability of taxpayers? If the government pays for in vitro fertilization, for example, how many procedures should a woman be entitled to? Is three a reasonable number?

Cosmetic surgery is an easy target, and I would expect strong opposition to government funding for breast implants, face lifts, and nose jobs (rhinoplasty). But many persons would want cosmetic surgery if they were seriously burned or disfigured in an accident. Once again, deciding which procedures "deserve" government funding requires more than medical expertise.

What should be done for persons who are injured while taking extreme risks? Should taxpayers pay for the medical care of race-car drivers who are injured in crashes? Should wealthy football players be entitled to government-funded care for their injuries? Bruce Smith needs a knee operation if he wants to be a pro-bowl football player. He wouldn't need the operation if he wanted to sell insurance or work as a stockbroker.

There is a widespread tendency to talk about health care as if it were some monolithic good that can be given or withheld from individuals. When we stop to think about it, however, we quickly realize that what is commonly called "health care" includes a vast array of different treatments, therapies, tests, and procedures. Under a very broad interpretation, health care includes anything that affects our physical and mental well-being, in other words, almost everything—from gun control to driving cars to what we eat to what we watch on television and so on.

Many illnesses are self-inflicted due to lifestyle choices, lung cancer being the most widely publicized example. Under socialized medicine, smokers would be acting immorally, since they would have no right to "inflict" their medical costs on others. The same can be said of persons who consume too much cholesterol or drive motorcycles. One of the problems with socialized medicine is that the realm of privacy (self-regarding acts, as Mill called them) would continuously shrink. People already argue that motorcyclists must wear helmets because "society" has to pay for their injuries. How can the donut lover be so selfish when she knows that any self-induced illness will be another expense for taxpayers? Socialized medicine would encourage the lifestyle police to demand that all of us be risk averse. Dullness would be a virtue.

All of this is unnecessary. Most Americans can afford insurance that covers major illness, and almost everyone could afford it if taxes were lower and the medical market were deregulated—if we truly had free market medicine. Furthermore, if persons want to spend their money on other things besides health insurance, they should have the right to do so. People have the right to take risks. They should have the right to smoke cigarettes, play football, and go rock climbing. And they should have the right not to buy health insurance. Medical care is one good among many, and some persons may prefer to spend their money on other things.

What about the desperately poor who really can't afford medical care—the persons who don't have the luxury of choosing between buying cigarettes (or whatever) and paying for health care? One thing I cannot do is to prescribe what persons will voluntarily do in a libertarian society to help the indigent. What I can do is mention some things that could be done. One example is Cleveland's Free Clinic, "where volunteer physicians, dentists, nurses, and other therapists provide free care to some 15,000 patients a year... "[116] Charitable organizations like the Red Cross could run clinics to serve the poor. In rural areas, doctors could return to the practice, common many years ago, of charging patients according to their ability to pay. Other doctors might prefer to set a reasonable limit on their pro bono work by seeing nonpaying patients one day a week. Regular patients would be told that they must pay (by cash, check, or credit card) for medical services when they receive them. There is an obvious advantage to this procedure: Paperwork and bill collecting would consume less of the physician's time. Many doctors now see Medicaid patients for free because they don't want the hassle of trying to collect from the government.[117]

Voluntary programs to help the needy face the same problem as government programs: how to help the poor without encouraging the behavior that produces poverty. I believe that private individuals and charities are more likely than government bureaucracies to find creative solutions to this problem. Unlike the government, which gets its money from coercive taxes, charitable organizations must compete for voluntary contributions. In this area, like so many others, experimentation and competition are usually the keys to progress.

Physicians who fear being sued by nonpaying patients will be less inclined to provide pro bono care. Since some care is usually better than no care, serious thought should be given to tort reform that would reduce physicians' liability in cases involving nonpaying patients. I am not qualified to say exactly what these reforms should be, but one possibility would be to limit awards to actual economic loss (i.e., the cost of future treatment and loss of income). This would eliminate punitive judgments and awards for pain and suffering, both of which are highly subjective.

Many supporters of socialized medicine are egalitarians who think that everyone should get the same medical care. When we consider what this means in the long run, they favor leveling down. Advances in medicine are more likely to occur in a free market than in a government-controlled health care system. Earlier I asked the question, What new ideas will produce economic progress in the next 40 years? I noted that if a "new idea" is one that has not been thought of yet, this question cannot be answered. Creativity is unpredictable: It cannot be controlled or planned, and thus bureaucracies are not known for innovation. If the egalitarians have their way, everyone will have equal access to inferior medical care. New goods and services that are initially available only to the wealthy usually become common consumer items eventually. This has been as true for medicine as it has been for other areas of the economy. As paradoxical as it may sound, we can predict that under socialized medicine more persons will be sick and more persons will die because medical advances will not be made.

I shall conclude this section with part of a letter, signed by 562 economists, that was sent to President Clinton.

Dear President Clinton:

Price controls produce shortages, black markets and reduced quality. This has been the universal experience in the 4,000 years that governments have tried to artificially hold prices down using regulations.

You insist that your health care plan avoids price controls. We respectfully disagree. Your plan sets the fees charged by doctors and hospitals, caps annual spending on health care, limits insurance premiums, and imposes price limitations on new and existing drugs.

In countries that have imposed these types of regulations, patients face delays of months and years for surgery, government bureaucrats decide treatment options instead of doctors or patients, and innovations in medical techniques and pharmaceuticals are dramatically reduced. Here in America, the threat of price controls on medicines has already decreased research and development at drug companies, which will lead to reduced discoveries and loss of life in the future.[118]

15. Education

Can we buy better education by spending more money? The evidence so far suggests that more money is not the solution to our educational problems. A judicially imposed social experiment in Kansas City, Missouri, provides a test of the claim that higher spending can improve student performance. In 1986, Judge Russell Clark ruled that the concentration of black students in Kansas City's public schools (75 percent as opposed to 30 percent of the city's population) was unconstitutional. By 1993 the state of Missouri had spent more than $1.3 billion over and above the normal school budget to create 56 magnet schools. According to the *Economist*, "That is an extra $36,111 for each of the system's 36,000 places."[119] The results have been disappointing. There has been no improvement in scores on standardized tests in reading and mathematics. On reading tests, black students in the regular elementary schools have outperformed pupils in the more generously funded magnet schools. Moreover, the dropout rate, which had been falling, increased every year between 1986 and 1993.[120]

In his study of excellent black schools, Thomas Sowell also failed to find any relationship between spending more money and getting better results.[121] The schools did have some common characteristics. They were "quiet and orderly" with few disciplinary problems. Respect for teachers was generally reinforced by parents. Ability-grouping was a common feature of excellent schools, and all schools had strong leadership from dedicated principals. Sowell did not find that any special methods or programs were necessary to "reach" black children.[122]

> Teaching methods used in the schools studied varied enormously from school to school, and even in the particular schools the variation from teacher to teacher has been so great as to defy general characterization. Everything from religious principles to corporal punishment has been used to maintain order. The buildings have ranged from the most dilapidated wrecks to a sparkling plate-glass palace. The teachers and principles have been black and white, religious and secular, authoritarian and gentle, community leaders and visitors from another social world. Some have had a warm "human touch" and others would have failed Public Relations 1. Their only common denominators have been dedication to education, commitment to the children, and faith in what it was possible to achieve.[123]

If spending more money were the answer, the United States would have one of the best educational systems in the world. American taxpayers have been generous, and per pupil expenditures in the United States are higher than every other country except Switzerland.[124] This generosity has not been repaid with high test scores. On international tests, the reading scores for American 13- to 14-year-olds are mediocre, and the math scores are abysmal. For example, American 13-year-olds ranked thirteenth among the 14 nations surveyed in 1991.[125]

Not only does the "lack of funds" hypothesis fail when comparisons are made with other countries, it also fails when we look at what has happened in the

United States since 1960. Combined average scores on the Scholastic Aptitude Test have fallen by more than 70 points. Whereas test scores dropped, spending more than tripled, rising from $1,700 per student in 1960 to $5,400 per student in 1994 (in 1993 dollars).[126] Defenders of the American educational system point out that a higher percentage of students take the SAT today than in 1960. This reply ignores the decline in the number of high scores.

> ... SAT scores declined at the top, not because there were more low scores averaged in. More than 116,000 students scored above 600 on the verbal SAT in 1972 and fewer than 71,000 scored that high ten years later. Between the early 1960s and the early 1980s, median SAT scores dropped at colleges coast to coast, including the most prestigious institutions. Both verbal and quantitative SAT scores declined at Yale, Princeton, Cal Tech, the University of Chicago, Oberlin, Rice, Brandeis, Carleton, Pomona, Reed, Whitman, and Davidson, for example.[127]

Since 1981, the number of students scoring above 700 on the math portion of the SAT has more than doubled, but the verbal scores of top students have not improved.[128]

In *Politics, Markets, and Public Schools*, published by the liberal think tank the Brookings Institution, John E. Chubb and Terry M. Moe recommend a radical restructuring of American public education. They do not recommend major increases in funding:

> In fact, the relationship between resources and performance has been studied to death by social scientists, and their consistent conclusion has been that resources do not matter much, except perhaps in cases of extreme deprivation or gross abundance .... Money is not what makes some schools more effective than others. To this we should add that private schools—which outperform public schools, on average—also tend to spend less than the public schools do in educating their students. They get better schools for less money.[129]

One thing that the public school establishment does not want to hear is that private schools generally do a better job of educating our children. Apologists point out that private schools can be, and often are, more selective than public schools. Chubb and Moe take this factor into account by controlling for socioeconomic status (SES) and student aptitude. Students in private schools generally do better than their counterparts in public schools with the same SES and aptitude.[130]

Why are private schools more effective? Chubb and Moe distinguish between democratic control of schools and market control. Democratic control imposes policies and standards "from above" through political and administrative superiors. The major players—members of school boards, superintendents, and state and federal officials—are (supposedly) ultimately accountable to the electorate. This method of governance produces a school system that is excessively bureaucratic. The members of the political hierarchy are removed from the classroom (and even the schools) where their policies are to be implemented. This creates a serious monitoring problem. The dominant strategy in this institutional setting is to specify what teachers must do and impose reporting requirements on the schools.[131] This process generates the rules, regulations, and paperwork that bureaucracies are famous for, and it stifles creativity and experimentation. "The incentives to bureaucratize are built into the system. The institutions of democratic control ensure that, in the politics and governance of public education, bureaucracy is almost everyone's dominant strategy when the key decisions actually get made. People may genuinely believe in autonomy and professionalism. But what they do—quite rationally, given their institutional setting—is bureaucratize."[132]

Chubb and Moe point out that "effective schools have the kinds of organizational characteristics that the mainstream literature would lead one to expect: strong leadership, clear and ambitious goals, strong academic programs, teacher professionalism, shared influence, and staff harmony, among other things."[133] These are in large part the same characteristics that Sowell found in excellent black schools. However, the method of governing public schools, which breeds bureaucracy and undermines autonomy, ensures that effectively organized schools will be lucky exceptions.

> The key to understanding why America's public schools are failing is to be found in a deeper understanding of how its traditional institutions of democratic control actually work. The nation is experiencing a crisis in public education not because these democratic institutions have functioned perversely or improperly or unwisely, but because they have functioned quite normally. Democratic control normally produces ineffective schools. This is how it works.[134]

Market control is very different. It is decentralized: Decisions are made by parents, students, teachers, and principals, not by political authorities.

> In private sector education, the people who run each school decide what they will teach, how they will teach it, who will do the teaching, how much to charge for their services, and virtually everything else about how education will be organized and supplied. Students and parents assess the offerings, reputations, and costs of the various schools and make their own choices about which to attend. No one makes decisions for society. All participants make decisions for themselves.[135]

Competition makes bureaucratic methods of governance unlikely because they generally do not produce schools that parents want to send their children to. "Because education is based on personal relationships and interactions, on continual feedback, and on the knowledge, skills, and experience of teachers, most of the necessary technology and resources are inherently present in the school itself, and thus are at the bottom of the organizational hierarchy (if there is one). Higher-level administrative units have little to contribute that is not already there."[136] In a decentralized market, schools can have clear missions and bold agendas because they do not have to please everyone or make compromises. It is sufficient for schools to find their market niche, that is, to please the parents and students who want what they have to offer.

To reform public schools, Chubb and Moe recommend a modified voucher system. Since "voucher" is a fighting word to the public school establishment, they call the money that is designated for a child's education a "scholarship." Schools become "public schools" by agreeing to accept the scholarship as total payment for each student's schooling. Thus, unlike with Milton Friedman's vouchers, parents cannot supplement the scholarship by making additional tuition payments.[137] Chubb and Moe also impose a nondiscrimination requirement, namely that public schools must accept students from all races, religions, and ethnic backgrounds. Within these guidelines, public schools would have the freedom to establish their own admissions criteria.

> Schools will make their own admissions decisions, subject only to nondiscrimination requirements. This is absolutely crucial. Schools must be able to define their own missions and build their own programs in their own ways, and they cannot do this if their student population is thrust upon them by outsiders. They must be free to admit as many or as few students as they want, based on whatever criteria they think is relevant—intelligence, interest, behavior, special needs—and they must be free to exercise their own, informal judgments about individual applicants.[138]

Chubb and Moe want to abolish state tenure laws so that each school can establish its own policies regarding the hiring and firing of teachers. They do recommend that a bachelor's degree be a minimum requirement for state certification. They oppose state mandated testing of students. In a market setting, schools will be monitored "from below, by parents and students who directly experience their services and are free to choose."[139]

Many persons have vested interests in our bureaucratic public school system. These persons make up the public school establishment to which I referred earlier. They oppose market-oriented reforms because they are a threat to their jobs. The persons with the most to lose are the teachers and administrators in the education departments of colleges and universities. Their power and influence depends in large measure on the state licensing laws, which require teachers to take their courses. The bureaucratic approach to ensuring teacher competence is to create more hurdles for prospective teachers to overcome. This emphasis on credentials has harmed public schools by keeping many talented people out of the teaching profession. Scientists and engineers, for example, cannot try teaching to see if it gives them more job satisfaction. Furthermore, teacher competence cannot be measured by taking courses and passing tests. Once again, the knowledge of who is competent and who is not is at the base of the pyramid in the schools. Colleagues and principals know who fits in and who doesn't, and they should have control over hiring and firing.

Teachers say that they want to be treated like professionals, but their unions line up solidly behind the bureaucratic system that removes discretion and burdens teachers with rules, regulations, and paperwork. Every serious attempt at market-oriented reforms has been opposed by the National Education Association (NEA) and the American Federation of Teachers (AFT). The NEA, with 2.1 million members, is the largest and most politically powerful union in the country. It endorsed Clinton in July 1992, and almost one in eight delegates to the Democratic National Convention were NEA members.[140]

The political power of teachers' unions is a recent phenomenon. In fact, no teachers were unionized in 1960, and 80 percent belonged to unions by 1990. Until 1961, it was generally believed that unionization of government employees was a dangerous idea. This changed when President Kennedy issued an executive order allowing collective bargaining for federal employees. Many states followed Kennedy's example, and New York City teachers were the first group to become unionized when AFT became their bargaining agent in 1961.[141] The much older NEA did not jump immediately on the bandwagon. Founded in 1857, its stated goal was to "elevate the character and advance the interests of the profession of teaching, and to promote the cause of public education in the United States."[142] In the early 1960s, many members continued to think of themselves as white-collar professionals who had little in common with blue-collar workers who belonged to labor unions. The organization changed from a professional association to a union when radical labor organizers from Michigan gained control in the late sixties.[143]

Unions thrive in noncompetitive environments. The Teamsters became the largest union when interstate trucking rates were set by the federal government, and they began to lose power as soon as the trucking industry was deregulated. Over 80 percent of public school teachers belong to unions; only 13 percent of private-sector employees are unionized.[144]

The unionization of most teachers coincided with declining student test scores. A correlation does not prove causation, but we can conclude that unionization did not prevent the decline. The same can be said for "better" credentials: "Back in the early 1960s, when student SAT scores peaked, fewer than one-fourth of all public school teachers had postgraduate degrees, and almost 15 percent lacked even a Bachelor's degree. But by 1981, when the test score decline hit bottom, just over half of all teachers had Master's degrees and less than one percent lacked a Bachelor's."[145] The educational establishment has gotten everything that it has asked for: more money, unionization of teachers, and licensing laws that require teachers to take more education courses. The result has been declining student performance.

Having lost the empirical argument, defenders of the status quo turn to their last refuge: egalitarianism. Public schools may be mediocre, but at least they level the playing field. This defense doesn't stand up to empirical scrutiny (a few public schools are good, some are mediocre, and many more are abysmal), but let us ignore this problem and examine its moral assumption. This view assumes that social engineers should pursue their egalitarian vision by leveling down. For many of us, this assumption loses whatever appeal it may have when we think of our own children: We don't want our children sacrificed to someone else's egalitarian ideal. Twenty-two percent of NEA members with school-age children follow the example of Bill Clinton and Al Gore—they send their children to private schools.[146]

16. Government Failure

Why does government regulation of markets so rarely achieve its intended consequences? When buyers and sellers agree to interact, they do so because they believe that they will benefit from the transactions. When government interferes with voluntary exchanges, at least one of the parties has an interest in circumventing the regulation. Consider, for example, attempts to shift costs from one group to another—some are charged more so that others can pay less. Those who are charged higher than market prices have an obvious reason to seek other arrangements, and alert entrepreneurs have an interest in satisfying their demand. A common response is to pass more laws to try to close these "loopholes," but these regulations usually have unintended, and frequently harmful, results. When prices do not reflect real costs, people often make poor decisions. When prices are artificially low, persons buy too much, and when prices are artificially high, they forgo purchases they would prefer to make at market prices. High prices can encourage imprudent behavior (such as choosing to be uninsured), and low prices encourage wasteful consumption.

Some laws, such as price controls and licensure, try to prevent buyers and sellers from dealing on mutually agreeable terms. Other laws try to force unwilling participants to interact. In the United States, for example, laws have been passed to "help" various groups achieve economic parity with white males. There are many reasons to think that these laws have been, and will continue to be, counterproductive.

There was much debate over whether the 1991 Civil Rights Act is a "quota bill." President Bush said that it is and Democrats said that it isn't, and Bush finally relented. It is a quota bill because that is the only practical way to enforce the law. The law seeks (inter alia) to prohibit racial discrimination in the hiring practices of private employers. Whether a particular employer discriminates depends on his motive for not hiring a minority applicant. If he thinks that a black worker is less qualified than the white worker he does hire, there is no discrimination. How can anyone determine what the employer's motive is? Motives are private—at least in the sense that we cannot see them. In fact, white males are often told that they do not know what their own motives are. A white employer may think that he isn't prejudiced, but some blacks and feminists believe that white males practice self-deception. They really are prejudiced, but they won't admit it, even to themselves. Given that we cannot know what an employer's motives are, discrimination can be inferred only from what the employer does. If you believe that employers often do discriminate, then you will assume that the failure to hire blacks, or a "proper" percentage of black workers, is evidence of discrimination. Thus, the logic of antidiscrimination laws leads to quotas because there is no other basis for enforcing the law. Whether an employer discriminates, as opposed to making an honest judgment that the white worker he hires is better qualified, cannot be determined. All we can know is how many minority workers the employer has hired.

The case of Daniel Lamp Company, which received national attention due to columnist Mike Royko, reveals how the Equal Employment Opportunity Commission (EEOC) enforces antidiscrimination laws.[147] Daniel Lamp, located in an Hispanic area of southwest Chicago, had 26 employees: 21 Hispanics and 5 blacks. The EEOC did not like owner Mike Welbel's hiring practices. He had established relationships with two local organizations: the Spanish Coalition and the Latino Youth Organization. He asked them for referrals when he needed a new worker. This was an efficient business practice because the referrals were, in effect, bonded by the referring organizations who wanted to be able to place workers in the future.

A disappointed black job applicant complained to the EEOC. The EEOC demanded that Daniel Lamp pay her $340 in back wages. In addition, Welbel was ordered to spend $10,000 on advertising to find blacks who had applied for work and not been hired so that he could pay them over $123,000. Welbel told Royko, "[The EEOC] wants me to spend $10,000 to find people who didn't work for me so I can pay them $123,991 for not working for me."[148]

The EEOC's decision was based in part on the racial composition of Chicago's southwest side. This procedure is probably less arbitrary than simply demanding that firms hire a certain percentage of minority workers based on their representation in the general population. However, this procedure sends a very unfortunate message to companies that might want to locate in areas with racially diverse populations. Businesses can avoid these difficulties by staying away from communities where they can expect large numbers of minority applicants. The result, of course, is to reduce the job opportunities for minorities.

According to the common-law doctrine of employment at will (EAW), employers may hire or fire for good reason, bad reason, or no reason at all. In other words, businesses do not have to justify their personnel decisions to anyone else. Under EAW, employers are more willing to hire marginal workers and give them a chance to prove that they can be productive employees. Reluctance to hire increases when it is more difficult to fire. For example, suppose you are an employer choosing between B and W. You think that the applicants have equal qualifications, but if you hire W and he doesn't work out (for whatever reason), you can fire him no questions asked. If you fire B, you run the risk of expensive litigation if he complains to the EEOC. In this case, the "rational strategy" is to hire W. Thus, the policies of the EEOC create a reluctance to hire black workers, the very reluctance they are designed to combat.

In a free labor market, businesses that practice racial discrimination pay a price: They place themselves at a competitive disadvantage by arbitrarily limiting their pool of qualified applicants. Unless racial discrimination is pervasive, it will not be a major problem: Blacks and other minorities can simply deal with businesses that do not discriminate. As Richard Epstein points out, from the individual's point of view it is the best offer that counts.[149] Consider a simple example where one-half of businesses refuse to hire black workers. Four businesses, E1, E2, E3, and E4, are hiring twelve workers (three workers for each business), and the odd-numbered firms (E1 and E3) practice racial discrimination. The twelve workers are ranked according to their qualifications as follows: W1, W2, B3, W4, W5, B6, W7, W8, B9, W10, W11, and B12. In this example, I am assuming the conditions that supposedly justify preferential treatment of black workers, namely that blacks (on average) are at a competitive disadvantage due to past discrimination. The workers are hired in order according to their ranking with two exceptions. Thus, E1 hires W1 and E2 hires W2, but E3 hires W4 instead of B3. The firms then continue to hire the top ranked worker until E1 hires W10 instead of B9. However, B3 is hired by E4 and B9 is hired by E2. In the real world, as the cream is skimmed from the pool of white workers, the comparative advantage in hiring black workers increases. To think that black workers will not be hired is to assume universal prejudice or universal stupidity or both. Competitive markets penalize stupidity, and not all employers are prejudiced.

Due to past discrimination, we would expect black wages (on average) to be lower than white wages. Another relevant factor is that the white population is older and workers with more seniority generally make more money. According to Census Bureau data, young black working couples living outside the South had achieved income parity with their white counterparts by 1971.[150] This was before preferential treatment programs for blacks could have had any appreciable impact. Thomas Sowell notes that "overall, the economic position of minorities has changed little since goals and timetables (quotas) became mandatory in December 1971."[151] This contrasts with the rapid rise in black incomes (as a percentage of white incomes) after passage of the 1964 Civil Rights Act.[152]

Blacks were helped by the general economic growth of the 1960s. In addition, the Civil Rights Act of 1964 mandated legal equality for blacks, and thus it struck the final blow to the Jim Crow laws of the South, which violated freedom of contract by requiring segregation. Occasionally we need to be reminded of just how evil these laws were, but also of how different they were from the voluntary segregation practiced by many whites and blacks today.[153] Consider the following law adopted by South Carolina in 1915:

> Criminal Code (167), 45. *Separation of Employees of Different Races in Cotton Textile Factories—Penalties*—That it shall be unlawful for any person, firm or corporation engaged in the business of cotton textile manufacturing in the State to allow or permit operatives, help and labor of different races to labor and work together within the same room, or to use the same doors of entrance and exit at the same time, or to use and occupy the same pay ticket windows or doors for paying off its operatives and laborers at the same time, or to use at any time the same lavatories, toilets, drinking water buckets, pails, cups, dippers or glasses: Provided, Equal accommoda-

tions shall be supplied and furnished to all persons employed by said person, firm or corporation engaged in the business of cotton textile manufacturing as aforesaid, without distinction to race, color or previous conditions.[154]

The qualification pertaining to "equal accommodations" reflects the "equal but separate" doctrine of *Plessy v. Ferguson*. Epstein points out that the only legal principle needed to disqualify such laws is freedom of contract. But then liberals would have to acknowledge that freedom of contract is also violated by laws that (try to) require employers to hire minority workers.

The threat of expensive litigation harms blacks by making employers reluctant to hire black workers. One might think that this impediment is overcome by the laws themselves, since employers will hire blacks to avoid lawsuits. However, employers must weigh the risk of refusing to hire against the risk of future litigation over their promotion and firing decisions. The likely result will be that employers will hire black workers who are clearly qualified but will shun blacks with marginal qualifications. If this is the common response, it is black workers who would do well in a free labor market who "benefit" from antidiscrimination laws.[155]

Antidiscrimination laws can have a similar impact on hiring decisions involving women. Again, imagine that you are an employer choosing between F and M and you believe that the applicants are equally qualified. If you hire M, you can fire him no questions asked if his performance is disappointing. If you fire F or even refuse to promote her, you run the risk of a lawsuit. The decision to treat sexual harassment cases not as common-law torts but as sex-discrimination cases under the jurisdiction of the EEOC has increased the problem. Consider the EEOC guidelines:

> Unwelcome sexual advances, requests for sexual favors, and other verbal or physical conduct of a sexual nature constitute sexual harassment when (1) submission to such conduct is made either explicitly or implicitly a term or condition of an individual's employment, (2) submission to or rejection of such conduct by an individual is used as the basis for employment decisions affecting such individual, or (3) such conduct has the purpose or effect of unreasonably interfering with an individual's work performance or creating an intimidating, hostile or offensive working environment.[156]

Under the broadest interpretation of these guidelines, verbal conduct (of a sexual nature) that creates an offensive working environment is grounds for a sexual harassment suit. Some persons are easily offended. Such suits may lose in court, but the threat of expensive litigation can affect hiring decisions.

Some interpretations of the Equal Pay Act (passed in 1963) can also place women at a competitive disadvantage. The idea of "equal pay for equal work" sounds simple, but in reality it raises many difficult issues. Worker compensation in the broad sense includes a number of factors such as wages, benefits, security, and job satisfaction. Of the quantifiable factors, benefits are generally worth more to females. I shall focus on two benefits: pensions and health insurance. In the case of pensions, females live longer than males. One way to deal with this sex difference is to provide pension benefits in a lump-sum payment upon retirement. However, the great majority of males and females prefer to receive their payments in the form of lifetime annuities.[157] Normal insurance practice accounts for this sex difference by reducing annuity payments to females. However, in *Los Angeles Department of Water and Power v. Manhart* (1978), the Supreme Court ruled that sex-based annuity payments violate Title VII of the 1964 Civil Rights Act. *Manhart* requires a significant transfer of wealth from males to females, and it could affect hiring decisions, since pension benefits will be higher for males if a company employs fewer females.

Health insurance benefits are also worth more to females since women have higher medical expenses. The Family Medical Leave Act (FMLA) is in theory gender neutral: It guarantees *all* workers in companies with 50 or more employees 12 weeks of unpaid annual leave following the birth or adoption of a child, to care for a seriously ill family member, or to recover from a serious injury or illness. In reality, since only females can give birth, it is likely that this benefit will be used more frequently by females. Although the leave is "unpaid," employers must continue to pay for other benefits such as medical insurance. Employers will also be concerned about possible lawsuits. FMLA appears to be a simple law, but the U.S. Department of Labor has issued 91 pages of regulations governing the rights and duties of employees and employers.[158] Interpreting these regulations is costly even when no legal action is threatened. For example, does a new mother have the right to stay home every Friday to catch up on household chores? The law could allow persons who prefer to work part time to get the benefits of full-time employees.

The general point of all this is that benefits (on average) are worth more to females than males. Thus, when the slogan "equal pay for equal work" is interpreted as requiring equal wages, total compensation (wages and benefits) is unequal. Feminists may be pleased with this result, but there is a downside for women. Once again, imagine that you are an employer choosing between F and M, and they appear to be equally qualified. However, it will cost you $30,000 per year (wages and benefits) to hire M, and it will cost $32,000 to hire F. From a strict business point of view, you would hire F only if she is clearly the superior applicant.

There is an alternative to government regulation, which is to allow adults to participate in capitalistic acts, that is, to freely contract on mutually agreeable terms. This is both economically superior and morally superior. From the moral point of view, it is the only approach that respects the equal right of each person to be free.

FOUR

Liberty and Reality

The essence of Government is power; and power, lodged as it must be in human hands, will ever be liable to abuse. In monarchies, the interests and happiness of all may be sacrificed to the caprice and passions of a despot. In aristocracies, the rights and welfare of the many may be sacrificed to the pride and cupidity of the few. In republics, the great danger is, that the majority may not sufficiently respect the rights of the minority.

James Madison, Address to the Virginia Convention of 1829[1]

17. Optimism and Pessimism

I have maintained that we can evaluate moral theories using four criteria: explanatory power, simplicity, coherence, and empirical content. The libertarian moral theory that I am defending has one fundamental right, the equal right to be free. In addition, I added a principle of retributive justice, that punishment should fit (correspond to the gravity of) the crime. Consequential values come into play for two reasons. First, our reason for adopting the moral point of view is that we are social beings and social living would be impossible if the basic moral rules were commonly violated. Second, consequential values can help us choose between alternatives that do not violate the freedom principle. I have argued that this libertarian view is simpler and more coherent than its chief rivals, namely various versions of utilitarianism and Rawlsian contract theories. I think that the most serious objections to libertarianism concern the libertarian's optimistic view of human nature, the belief that human beings can flourish without the direction and control that governments commonly provide. Critics charge that too much freedom will produce disastrous consequences.

A free society has a free market economy. Many liberals believe that we should not return to the "evils" of free market capitalism. The evils that the liberals point to were the result of poverty. The period of laissez-faire capitalism, roughly from 1800 to 1930, was characterized by rapid economic growth and rising living standards. Economic growth was uneven and life was hard for most Americans. Still, economic opportunity was an important attraction for millions of immigrants, many of whom worked long hours for low pay (by contemporary standards), and it was capitalism that allowed the vast majority to escape from poverty.

In 1928, spending by the federal government was about 3 percent of national income.[2] The Great Depression, the New Deal, World War II, and the Cold War changed the character of the federal government as Americans increasingly looked to Washington for solutions to national and international problems. Solutions to domestic problems have been elusive. The more than 60 years of state capitalism have given us (1) a welfare system that encourages single women to have babies and the fathers to disappear, (2) a Social Security system that is headed for bankruptcy, (3) a public school system that is an international embarrassment, (4) a war on drugs that has produced the highest incarceration rate in the world, and (5) an economy that is growing well below its potential.[3] Americans find themselves in the paradoxical position of knowing that the United States is the wealthiest country in the world while at the same time seeing that our social problems continue to fester or grow. I have maintained that the answer to these problems is less government, not more government.

In comparison to state capitalism, free market capitalism is characterized by lower taxes and less government regulation of the economy. On a deeper level, the values underlying free market capitalism are very different from state capitalism. This can be seen in the following comparisons:

Free Market Capitalism	State Capitalism
Individual freedom	Group entitlements
Personal responsibility	Society's responsibility
Spontaneous order	Government regulation
Competition	Leveling down
Personal excellence	Material equality
Toleration	Conformity

The underlying values of state capitalism are an uneasy combination of elitism and egalitarianism. The elitism is manifest in the unwillingness to trust ordinary people to make the right decisions about whether to help others or how to take care of themselves. Materialistic egalitarianism can be seen in the liberal notion of equal opportunity. This view assumes that persons want to be successful and that success is measured in economic (materialistic) terms. Having arbitrarily picked the race that persons are running, liberals proceed to tinker with the competitive conditions of the participants. This can be seen in the opposition to competition and to ability-grouping in schools. It is seen in support for public schools along with the denigration of market-based reforms of education. When "equal opportunity" fails to produce the desired results, liberals often favor quotas and set-asides to ensure that groups get their fair share.

In contrast, libertarians ask for toleration of the individual differences that produce economic inequality in a free market economy. They believe that competition is the engine of economic progress and that everyone benefits (even if unevenly) from the rising living standards that capitalism produces. Most important, libertarians reject the arrogance of the social engineers who want to ensure that everyone gets their "fair" share. This notion of fairness is based on an impoverished view of human aspirations. Fairness (according to this conception) is most manifest when we deal with values that can be quantified: Jack has 10 units, but Jane only has 5. Much of what matters in life, including love, friendship, and moral excellence, cannot be quantified. When we focus on units, percentages, and totals, we get a very distorted view of what is important. This includes not seeing the loss of freedom caused by social engineers who want their numbers to fit a particular pattern.

Let us consider an example to illustrate these general observations. Lawmakers established the Occupational Safety and Health Administration (OSHA) because they decided there were too many injuries, illnesses, and deaths caused by unsafe working conditions. If OSHA is serious about regulating risky occupations, it should not ignore professional football and stock-car racing. Football players could be required to wear far more protective equipment than they presently do, and the equipment could be deliberately designed to reduce the running speed of players so that collisions are less likely to cause injuries. The speed of stock cars could be regulated, and drivers who go too fast could be disqualified. Such regulations would help to make these occupations safer and, in addition, they would reduce the amount of money we spend on health care. In spite of these utilitarian benefits, many will complain that grown men should be allowed to run and drive as fast as they please. The libertarian agrees, but he also calls for the consistent application of this view to other occupations.

Grown-ups should be allowed to decide for themselves what risks they wish to take. What policies follow from this precept? First, employees should be informed of any unusual hazards in the workplace. The libertarian ideal of mutual consent requires that there be no deception. Beyond this, it requires that the parties know to what they are consenting. What incentives does an employer have to do his duty, to inform employees of unusual hazards? One incentive is lawsuits: Employers who practice deception or conceal information can be sued by their employees. In addition, there are a number of market incentives that make it costly for employers to ignore unsafe working conditions. Hiring and training replacements for workers who are injured is expensive. An employer who acquires a reputation for deception or for withholding information will have greater difficulty hiring qualified workers and retaining good employees. Mistreating employees, in most cases, is not good business practice. Most businesses carry liability insurance, and employers who are sued frequently will have to pay more for insurance or, in extreme cases, will be unable to buy it at all. Under free market capitalism, there is no free ride on safety.

One of the protections that a worker has is the option of taking another job. In other words, if a job is unsafe, the employee can quit. But his willingness to quit often depends on the availability of other jobs. The high taxes and excessive regulations of state capitalism reduce employment options by reducing economic growth. Once again, state capitalism makes it harder for persons to take care of themselves.

The stereotypical response of liberals is that under free market capitalism, ignorant workers will be exploited by greedy employers. This response illustrates both the elitism and pessimism of liberals. Ordinary people cannot be trusted to run their own lives, and only lawmakers and government bureaucrats have sufficient wisdom and virtue to determine what we should do. The optimistic libertarian counters by pointing out that lawmakers and bureaucrats do not have a monopoly on virtue, and most employers will try to provide safe working conditions simply because they are decent human beings. Those who are not virtuous face legal and market incentives that make it costly to mistreat workers.

One can be a liberal in theory and a libertarian in practice. For a liberal who believes that most persons can take care of their own needs and that the unfortunate few who can't will be helped by voluntary means, the libertarian society can be the ideal liberal society. This ideal society is characterized by affluence, compassion, and diversity. Economic growth will reduce poverty. With much lower taxes and higher incomes, persons will have more discretionary income to contribute to worthy causes. Experimentation will produce new solutions to social problems that seem intractable today.

This rosy scenario will be rejected by those who have little faith in the competence of ordinary people to run their own lives. If you believe, for example, that persons cannot be trusted to provide an education for their children or to save for their retirement years, then government paternalism will be an attractive option. One of the insidious things about paternalism, however, is that it feeds upon itself. When government treats adults like irresponsible children, many will behave like irresponsible children. Mill reminds us that good utilitarians take the long-range point of view, and in the long run, paternalism has bad consequences.

Rawlsian liberalism, with its focus on the worst-off members of society, can lead to pessimism. The least-advantaged members of society in terms of intellectual and physical abilities need the most help, either from government, family members, friends, or charities. According to Rawls, a society is unjust unless its least-advantaged members are as well off as they could possibly be. It is easy to assume that no matter how many resources are devoted to helping the worst off, more could be done. This perceived failure is exacerbated by policies that subsidize the behavior that produces dependence and poverty. Thus, the programs that are supposed to help the worst off are often counterproductive. But it is hard for persons who support these programs to see the need for change so long as they believe that society should be judged by the comparative standing of the least advantaged. The best answer to Rawlsian pessimism is to reject its normative foundation. We need not apologize for institutions and policies that work well for most persons. For example, suppose that 90 percent are better off when we have an economic system that rewards productive workers and the remaining 10 percent could be better off under some noncompetitive form of socialism. I have argued (Section 4) that it is reasonable to prefer the economic system where 90 percent are better off.

There is another ground for pessimism that, although it was more popular 20 years ago, is still influential, especially in academia. This is the view that we are headed for ecological and demographic disasters due to a shortage of natural resources. This view was popularized by Paul Ehrlich in *The Population Bomb*, and it was given respectability by *The Limits of Growth*, issued by the Club of Rome in 1972. Many acute thinkers, including the prominent philosopher Nicholas Rescher, were caught up in the pessimism:

A parting of the wave with the concept of progress will not come easy to us. It's going to take a lot of doing to accustom us to the idea that things are on balance to get worse or at any rate no better as concerns the quality of life in this nation. (And once we are persuaded of this, there may be vast social and political repercussions in terms of personal frustration and social unrest.) The conception of a deescalation of expectations, of settling for less than we've been accustomed to, is something Americans are not prepared for. We have had little preparatory background for accepting the realization that in some key aspects in the quality of life the best days may be behind us.[4]

A common thread running through these dismal predictions and sober warnings is the finitude of natural resources: It was commonly assumed that the fact that resources are finite has dark implications for the future of the human race. Fortunately for us, this pessimism is based on conceptual confusion and a faulty methodology.[5]

It is a conceptual truth that if there is a fixed amount of X, then X is not infinite. But it is not clear that this mathematical notion has any practical relevance when we think about whether X is, in some relevant sense, scarce. From the bare fact that a resource is finite, can we draw any interesting conclusions about scarcity? An examination of actual resources reveals that the answer is no. The amount of water on the planet is finite, but there is no danger that we will "run out" because what we use goes back into the ecosystem. Clean water is scarce in some countries, but this is because they have not adopted the technologies that are available for cleaning the water they have used. Water is also scarce in deserts, but this problem can be avoided by not living there.

Sand has been used for centuries to make glass. It is now used in making computer chips, and as such, it is one of the most important resources. The amount of sand in the world is finite, but there is no realistic rate of use at which sand would become scarce, that is, where there would be a shortage. This illustrates the general point that when a resource is adequate for any conceivable need, for practical purposes the resource is not relevantly finite (even though the amount of the substance is a fixed number).

What about living space? Isn't land scarce? If the United States (not including Alaska) were as densely populated as Holland, the American population would be, approximately, 2.8 billion instead of 260 million.[6] If living space is the concern, we can house more people by "building up." A 100-story apartment building can house 10,000 people on one acre of land. Ninety-five percent of the population could be easily housed on less than 1 percent of the land, leaving the rest (or most of it) for farming and recreational uses. As for population growth, birthrates in most industrialized countries have fallen below replacement levels, and there is concern about whether there will be enough young workers to pay for the generous pension benefits that governments have promised.[7]

Paul Ehrlich's prediction of mass starvation by the 1980s was based largely on the Malthusian assumption that agricultural productivity would not increase, at least not dramatically. However, grain production increased from 0.5 billion tons in 1971 to about 2 billion tons in 1991. China boosted wheat yields fivefold between 1961 and 1990, and farmers in India more than tripled wheat production in the same time period.[8] The World Bank estimates that the former communist countries, which were large importers of grain, will be grain exporters by 2010.[9] Ehrlich's failed prediction illustrates the crucial flaw in all doomsday scenarios: They assume that we are stuck in a technological rut. I previously asked: What new ideas will produce economic progress in the next 40 years? I noted that if a new idea is one that has not been thought of before, the question cannot be answered. We cannot know what technological innovations will make workers more productive in the future. What we do know is that all the trends are sharply up. This is perhaps the best reason for being optimistic about the future.

The analysis presented so far also applies to fossil fuels. For practical purposes, resource X is not scarce if another resource can be substituted for X. When the oil and natural gas that can be easily recovered run out, we will still have vast amounts of coal. Thus, we have hundreds of years to develop alternative sources of energy. If scientists learn how to produce electricity using hydrogen fusion, energy will be truly unlimited. I of course have maintained that we cannot predict such technological developments, but what we do know is that doomsday predictions, from Malthus to Ehrlich, have been proven wrong because of new technologies. One must be firmly committed to a pessimistic outlook to think that the future will be different.

There is one cloud on the horizon, the possibility of global warming caused by the burning of fossil fuels. On this issue, however, the evidence so far does not support the dire warnings of the radical environmentalists. In a recent Gallup survey of members of the American Geophysical Union and the American Meteorological Society, 49 percent of the scientists responding said that they did not believe humans had caused any global warming, 18 percent believed that they had, and 33 percent didn't know.[10] Al Gore notwithstanding, there is (at this time) insufficient proof that the very modest warming that has occurred in this century was caused by human activity. Politics, not science, often motivates the environmentalists. The environmental movement is one of the last refuges for socialists who want greater government control of the economy.

In 1980, Julian Simon bet Paul Ehrlich that the price of five natural resources, to be named by Ehrlich, would be lower in 1990. Ehrlich picked copper, chrome, nickel, tin, and tungsten. Ten years later, he sent Simon a check for $1,000.[11]

18. Strategies

The problem of conservative justice looms large for any political view that advocates radical changes. Persons have made choices based on expectations created by past practice. A sudden reversal of direction will cause many of these choices to be involuntary, that is, persons would have made different choices had they known that policies would be changed. This problem came up in my previous examination of welfare programs (Section 12). I proposed that AFDC benefits be phased out over a 16-year period, beginning with the announcement that there will be no further benefits for women who have babies nine months after a specified date. Benefits would continue for women who are presently receiving them until the youngest child (born prior to the cutoff date) reaches 16.

Libertarians also advocate abolition of the public school system and the Social Security system. Both policies have conservative-justice problems that should be addressed. Fortunately, an orderly transition to a private school system is not difficult to envision. The first step would be to give tuition vouchers to parents who want to send their children to private schools. Initially, vouchers could be some fraction (such as one-half) of what the government spends educating a child in a public school. This would encourage the expansion of existing private schools and the formation of new schools. The second step would be to end the direct funding of government-run schools. Instead, all parents of school-age children would receive tuition vouchers. Schools that were funded directly by the government would have to compete on an equal basis with "private" schools. Finally, the indirect funding of schools by government (through tuition vouchers) would end because tuition vouchers would be funded by taxes. In a libertarian society, parents would be responsible for providing an education for their own children. Scholarship programs to help the needy would raise money by voluntary means. It would probably be wise to coordinate these policy changes with the ending of AFDC. In this case, government funding of schools, direct and indirect, could be phased out over a 16-year period.

The Social Security system is facing major financial problems—not in the next few years, but early in the next century. The problems begin with the Hospital Insurance Trust Fund (HI), which pays the hospital-insurance portion of Medicare. As part of the 1990 budget deal, Congress more than doubled the taxable base for the trust fund—from $51,300 to $125,000—but this tax increase only pushed back the date of bankruptcy by about two years.[12] In 1994 the cap was eliminated, and all wages are now subject to the 2.9 percent Medicare tax. In spite of these changes, the fund will be insolvent by 2001 unless further tax increases are implemented.[13] Farther out, major financial problems loom as the baby boomers retire. The ratio of workers to retirees, which was 5 to 1 in 1960 and 3.2 to 1 in 1994, could shrink to 2 to 1 by 2030.[14] Some experts predict that a payroll tax of at least 25 percent will be needed to fund the baby boomers' retirement and Medicare benefits.[15]

By one estimate, Social Security will be insolvent by 2013.[16] When the revenues of a Social Security trust fund do not meet outlays, the fund sells government bonds. The Disability Insurance Trust Fund (DI) began to sell bonds in 1992, and it was merged with the Old Age and Sickness Insurance Trust Fund (OASI) in 1995.[17] HI will become a seller of bonds in 1996, and the combined funds will be net sellers by 1999. It is estimated that the selling of bonds will add $70 billion to the federal deficit in 1999, $130 billion in 2002, and $180 billion in 2004.[18] The upshot is that the winding down of the trust funds will create a fiscal crisis in less than 10 years, long before the funds are actually exhausted.

In addition to being in alarming financial condition, the Social Security system has serious moral problems. For libertarians, it is an example of unjustified paternalism (Section 10). Liberals should oppose the payroll tax because it is regressive. In addition, Social Security involves a massive transfer of wealth from those who are worse off to those who are better off. The fact that well-to-do retirees receive benefits has been widely publicized. For example, in 1990 nearly $8 billion in Social Security benefits were paid to families with incomes exceeding $100,000.[19] What has not been widely publicized is how the tax system treats middle-class families. Consider the example of two families, both with incomes of $30,000 in 1994. The first family is a married couple with two children, and the second family is a retired couple receiving $12,000 in Social Security benefits. The payroll tax on the young couple's income is $4,590 (15.3 percent of $30,000). The 1994 standard deduction is $6,350, and each exemption is worth $2,450. For the working couple, assuming that they do not itemize, their federal income tax liability is $2,078 (15 percent of $13,850). Thus, the total federal tax (not counting excise taxes) on their $30,000 income is $6,668.

The retired couple pays far less. In addition to their $12,000 in Social Security benefits (nontaxable), suppose that they have $12,000 in taxable pension income and $6,000 in interest and dividends that is taxable. They take the standard deduction, $7,850 for persons over 65, and their personal exemptions are worth $4,900. Thus, their taxable income is $5,250 ($18,000 minus $12,750), and their federal income tax is $788 (15 percent of $5,250). To summarize, the federal tax on the wages of the working couple with two children to take care of is $6,668, and the retired couple with the same income pays $788. If taxes should be based on need and ability to pay, as liberals maintain, they should be outraged by our Social Security system. Why should the federal tax liability of the working couple be over eight times what the retired couple pays?

There are good liberal and libertarian reasons for wishing that we did not have a Social Security system. Once started, however, a pay-as-you-go public pension system is very hard to stop. Workers who have paid Social Security taxes believe that they are entitled to benefits, but those benefits depend on the willingness of future taxpayers to fund them. Those taxpayers, in turn, will insist that their payments entitle them to benefits, which can only be funded by future taxpayers. The problem of conservative justice looms very large indeed.

How can we stop this Ponzi scheme in a way that is reasonably fair to both taxpayers and recipients? In a pay-as-you-go system, the first recipients receive benefits without paying taxes. Most retirees today receive benefits in excess of the actuarial value of their "contributions" (by both employer and employee).[20] Social Security is a good deal for early recipients, but it is a bad deal for later retirees. Younger workers would be better off if they were dropped from the system. Workers who contribute 10 percent of their earnings to a retirement fund can build a substantial nest egg. According to Gary Becker, "A 3 percent real rate return of savings for a period of 40 years will ensure a pension after retirement of almost two-thirds of annual real earnings for the subsequent 15 years."[21] This 10 percent contribution is less than two-thirds of the current Social Security tax. It is reasonable to ask younger workers to make the "sacrifice" of giving up any claim to future benefits. In return, they can expect to be beneficiaries of the economic growth that will result from lower taxes.

In light of this analysis, I offer the following proposal for abolishing Social Security:

(1) Abolish the payroll tax.
(2) Remove workers under 40 from the Social Security rolls.
(3) Credit persons over 40 with one year of benefits for each year of Social Security taxes paid after the age of 40 (with a 25-year limit).
(4) Fund Social Security benefits with a federal sales tax.

Under this proposal, Social Security would be phased out over a 25-year period. Consider the case of a 50-year-old who has paid Social Security taxes for 10 years after the age of 40. He would be entitled to ten years of benefits when he reaches 65. The 65-year-old who has paid Social Security taxes for 25 years (after the age of 40) would be entitled to 25 years of benefits. To keep the phaseout within the 25-year timeframe, he would have to start his benefits immediately, that is, he could not postpone receiving his benefits and still receive them for 25 years. However, there is no reason to insist that he stop working in order to receive his benefits.

Although my proposal for phasing out Social Security differs from Milton Friedman's, it would have the same beneficial consequences: "The winding down of Social Security would eliminate its present effect of discouraging employment and so would mean a larger national income currently. It would add to personal saving and so lead to a higher rate of capital formation and a more rapid growth of income. It would stimulate the development and expansion of private pension plans and so add to the security of many workers."[22] Abolishing the payroll tax and making workers responsible for their own retirement would be a tremendous stimulus to personal savings. This would fuel economic growth by providing more money for investments in research and new technologies.

During the transition to a libertarian society, revenue must be raised to fund welfare programs, Social Security benefits and tuition vouchers. The obvious strategy is to use the tax that is least objectionable, morally and economically. The payroll tax should be abolished because it is regressive and it reduces employment opportunities by raising the cost of labor. The income tax is morally unacceptable because it requires a massive invasion of privacy by the government. It is also costly to collect, and it discourages work and savings. The capital-gains tax is unfair because it taxes phantom profits that are the result of inflation. It is economically unsound because it directly discourages savings and investments. The corporate income tax does not raise enough revenue, and it reduces employment and investment. In comparison to these alternatives, the sales tax is the least evil. It is far easier to collect than the income tax. Since it is a consumption tax, it does not directly discourage work, savings, or investments. Unlike its rival, the value-added tax, it is plainly visible so that taxpayers will be aware of their tax burden. The main objection to the sales tax is that it is regressive, hitting low-income families the hardest. A partial answer to this problem is to not tax food. The larger answer is that many of the poor will benefit from the economic stimulus provided by a shift to a consumption tax—a growing economy is the best antipoverty program.

During the transition to a libertarian society, law enforcement and national defense should be funded by leasing natural resources and by the resource tax. The payroll tax should be replaced with a federal sales tax. The capital-gains tax should be abolished immediately because this would provide a tremendous stimulus to the economy. The dreaded income tax would have to be phased out gradually, since it provides so much revenue. However, the income-tax code could certainly be simplified, and the tax deduction for purchasing health insurance should be given to all individuals, not just to persons who receive employer-provided insurance.

Under my proposals, a libertarian society would be in place after 25 years except for one problem—the national debt. Dealing with this problem requires, first, an understanding of just how large the national debt is. As Friedman points out, "The figures usually cited for the debt are misleading because they include debt owed by federal agencies and the Federal Reserve System. For example, in June 1990, the gross debt was $3.233 trillion and the net debt $2.207 trillion, a third less."[23] When government bonds are held by a government agency such as the Federal Reserve, interest payments on the bonds are made by one government agency (usually the Treasury Department) to another government agency. Furthermore, the Fed must turn over its excess profits (which are substantial) to the Treasury.[24] Hence, it is misleading to include these bonds in the national debt. About 70 percent of the bonds issued by the federal government to cover deficit spending are publicly held. At present, the net public debt is about 44 percent of GDP. If the federal government had a balanced budget (on average) for 25 years and GDP doubled, the net public debt would shrink to 22 percent of GDP.

Assuming that the Federal Reserve Board expands the money supply during this period, there would be a further decline in publicly held debt. In a healthy (growing) economy, the Fed can increase the stock of money by 3 percent a year without causing significant inflation. The primary means by which the Fed expands the stock of money is to increase deposits in commercial banks by buying government bonds. When the Fed buys government bonds, it reduces the publicly held debt. When Social Security has been phased out after 25 years, the federal sales tax would still be in place to deal with the remaining national debt. Thus, the national debt is a serious problem, but not an intractable one. Economic growth is the key. The national debt exceeded GDP at the end of World War II, and although the nominal debt continued to grow, net public debt dropped to less than 25 percent of GDP by 1980.[25]

One more social policy needs to be addressed: the war on drugs. Millions of persons have been incarcerated for possession, use, or sale of drugs.[26] For libertarians, this is immorality on a massive scale, exceeded only by some of the most tyrannical regimes of history. The reason for this claim is simple: The state has no right to punish persons for consensual behavior. One of the conditions for justified punishment (see Sections 2 and 8) is that the law prohibits violations of the freedom principle. Mere possession, sale, or use of drugs does not violate the rights of others, and thus the state has no right to criminalize these behaviors.

In spite of the transparent immorality of the drug war (to libertarians at least), those who want to end drug prohibition face an uphill battle. Many supporters of prohibition, perhaps sensing the weakness of their views, don't want to talk about it. Without a serious dialogue on this topic, there is little hope for change. One strategy to get the dialogue started is to point out that reasonable people, such as William F. Buckley, Milton Friedman, and Thomas Sowell, have called for an end to drug prohibition. Sowell, for example, asks us what we are willing to give up to achieve the following:

(1) An end to drug-related murders of policemen and of innocent by-standers in neighborhoods where drug wars take place.
(2) A substantial reduction of the nation's prison population, relieving over-crowding and providing space to hold violent criminals.
(3) An end to drug-financed corruption of law enforcement officials, including judges, and of politicians here and in foreign countries.

Sowell states that these benefits are available if politicians are willing "to give up the attempt to run other people's lives."[27] Unfortunately, many persons hold the elitist view that ordinary people cannot be trusted to run their own lives. Once again, Mill provides the answer: Paternalism, in the long run, has bad consequences. When the government treats us like irresponsible children, more persons will behave like irresponsible children. This is especially true when the government has welfare programs to rescue people when they make bad choices. These programs may seem compassionate, but they produce welfare dependency and all the social pathologies, including drug use and crime, that go with it.

Another libertarian strategy in this debate is to point out that the drug war is another example of the failure of socialism. Many conservatives pay lip service to the idea of permitting capitalistic acts among consenting adults, but they draw the line when it comes to illicit drugs. As so often occurs, the effects of government intervention in markets are very different from what the proponents of intervention hope for. In the case of drugs, Friedman notes that the primary beneficiaries are the drug cartels: "Whose interests are served by the drug war? The U.S. government enforces a drug cartel. The major beneficiaries from drug prohibition are the drug lords, who can maintain a cartel that they would be unable to maintain without current government policy."[28] Our welfare system, public schools, and the war on drugs are all examples of the failure of socialism. The devastation that these policies have caused in our inner cities is one of the great tragedies of American history.

Liberals and conservatives worry about the loss of productivity due to drug use. Once again there is a free market solution to this problem, employment at will. In a free labor market, employers can fire unproductive workers. If a business has a policy of testing employees for drug usage, so it is known that this is one of the conditions of employment, the business can identify and fire workers who have drug problems. If drug abusers are protected by the Americans with Disabilities Act, the Civil Rights Act, or other government regulations, then worker productivity will suffer. If we want responsible behavior, the government should stop protecting persons who make irresponsible choices.

The silence of many liberals on the drug war exposes one of the inadequacies of the Rawlsian approach to justice—they have no theory of punishment. They can do their utilitarian calculations, like other commentators, but they have no grounds for taking a principled stand on whether the state has the right to punish persons for using drugs. If millions of persons have been incarcerated unjustly, then this is one of the great evils of the twentieth century.

A majority of Americans use caffeine, nicotine, or alcohol. In other words, most Americans use drugs to alter how they feel. In a free society, adults must decide what role drugs will play in their lives. The pessimists, both liberals and conservatives, say that persons cannot be trusted to make responsible decisions concerning the use of politically unpopular drugs. The optimistic libertarian says that we should treat adults as if they were responsible persons. If we do, more people will behave responsibly.

19. Change

In the ideal libertarian society, government provides national defense and law enforcement that are funded by leasing natural resources and by the resource tax. Government builds and maintains streets and roads and it provides water and sewer services, with both activities funded by user fees. User fees also fund other services such as certification and the construction and maintenance of parks. The only "coercive" tax is the resource tax, and this is analogous to a user fee, since the taxpayer receives a benefit, namely the protected right to use a natural resource.

The ideal libertarian society would not have a welfare system, a Social Security system, public schools, tariffs and import quotas, price supports for farm products, minimum-wage laws, rent control, the Food and Drug Administration, the Occupational Safety and Health Administration, and the Equal Employment Opportunity Commission. This is not a complete list, but it does indicate how American governments (federal, state, and local) would be fundamentally changed and how opportunities for rent-seeking (transferring existing wealth from one person to another) would disappear. Hundreds of thousands of lobbyists, lawyers, and accountants would have to find productive jobs. Many persons, including many politicians, have vested interests in the present system. Change will not come easily. It is important, however, to outline the ideal so that we know where we should be headed. In general, libertarians should support market solutions to social problems, and they should oppose policies that increase government control over our lives.

In this imperfect world, it is not wise to make the ideal the enemy of the good. In most cases, libertarians should support changes, no matter how small, that move us in the right direction. An example is abolition of the tax exemption for employer-provided health insurance. This single reform would go a long way toward reintroducing market control to this sector of the economy. We cannot have market control when what persons spend is disconnected from how they pay for it. Nearly 90 percent of Americans with health insurance get their policies from their employer, and 80 percent of medical expenses are paid by third parties.[29] The tax exemption for health insurance should be given to all taxpayers. The deduction should be small (for example, $2,000 for a family of four) to encourage the purchase of catastrophic coverage that would protect persons from large medical expenses. In 1960, when health care expenditures were 5 percent of GDP, almost 60 percent of spending was out-of-pocket.[30] The government should not be setting targets for expenditures, but we do know that people are far more prudent when they are spending their own money.

Opposition to new government programs and support for realistic reforms must be part of the libertarian agenda. In addition, we need to understand why the political system does not work as the founders hoped. Structural reform may be possible, but even if it is not, focusing attention on where the system is producing unwanted results could be salutary.

This chapter began with a quotation from Madison that recognizes the danger of majority tyranny. Madison also recognizes the danger posed by special-interest groups (factions):

> Every new regulation concerning commerce or revenue, or in any manner affecting the value of the different species of property, presents a new harvest to those who watch the change and can trace the consequences; a harvest reared not by themselves, but by the toils and cares of the great body of their fellow-citizens. This is a state of things, in which it may be said, with some truth, that laws are made for the *few*, not for the *many*. (*Federalist* no. 62)

In recent years there has been remarkable growth in what Jonathan Rauch calls the parasite class, aka professional lobbyists: "Parasites in nature force you to spend energy and resources fending them off. Transfer seekers are analogous, because they require their targets to fend them off. It takes a lobbyist to stop a lobbyist, and in a society where everyone can lobby, everyone needs Washington representation to defend against raids by everyone else's Washington representatives."[31] Some lobbyists seek the transfer of existing wealth (rent-seeking); others try to protect the status quo. Both groups benefit from a Congress that is willing and able to make changes. In other words, both groups thrive when there is a large and active government.

The founders tried to limit the scope and power of the federal government by means of the Bill of Rights and the enumerated powers of Congress in Article 1, Section 8.

> The powers delegated by the proposed constitution to the federal government are few and defined. Those which are to remain in the state governments, are numerous and indefinite. The former will be exercised principally on external objects, as war, peace, negotiation, and foreign commerce; with which last the power of taxation will, for the most part, be connected. The powers reserved to the several states will extend to all the objects, which, in the ordinary course of affairs, concern the lives, liberties, and properties of the people; and the internal order, improvement, and prosperity of the state. (*Federalist* no. 45)

As we have seen, the doctrine of enumerated powers has been ignored by all branches of the federal government, and parts of the Bill of Rights, especially the Second, Fifth, and Tenth Amendments, have been violated repeatedly.

When the scope and power of the federal government is limited, this also reduces the ability of local and state governments to exploit their citizens. Persons who are unhappy with government can vote with their feet (the exit option) by moving to another town, county, or state. The exit option has diminished in value as power has shifted from local and state governments to Washington.

In addition to explicit prohibitions (which have been largely ignored), the Constitution employs several strategies that make rent-seeking more difficult. The bicameral legislature makes it more costly and uncertain. "... a senate, as a second branch of the legislative assembly, distinct from, and dividing the power with, a first, must be in all cases a salutary check on the government. It doubles the security of the people, by requiring the concurrence of two distinct bodies in schemes of usurpation or perfidy, where the ambition or corruption of one would otherwise be sufficient." (*Federalist* no. 62) It is difficult to fashion legislation that will win approval in both the House and Senate because members of Congress serve different constituencies. Representatives from urban areas dominate in the House, and legislators from less-populated states hold the balance of power in the Senate.

Unfortunately, Congress has responded to constitutional obstacles by adopting rules and procedures that facilitate rent-seeking. Jonathan Macey provides a succinct summary of the problem:

> The Constitution determined the basic structure of government, but the Framers permitted Congress to design its own internal rules of governance.... The basic problem is that Congress has transformed itself, since the founding of the Republic, from a loose collection of unaffiliated individuals from all parts of the country, into a highly efficient, well-organized organization dedicated to effectuating wealth transfers to favored groups in order to insure the reelection of its incumbent members.[32]

The modern committee system allows special-interest groups to focus on the committees that deal with the matters that concern them. Members of Congress, in turn, typically seek committee assignments that permit them to benefit the groups they favor. When these organizational features are combined with the practice of logrolling, Congress bears only a faint resemblance to the institution envisioned by the founders. Members of Congress trade votes to gain support for legislation that might otherwise be defeated. The committee system helps to ensure that logrolling agreements will be kept. Once a law, policy, or agency is in place, the majority might prefer to rescind it. However, such proposals can often be bottled up in the committees that supported the legislation in the first place.

The executive veto is another constitutional impediment to rent-seeking. The president, who has a different constituency than members of Congress, can veto legislation that serves special interests. Congress often uses omnibus bills to reduce this threat to its power. Unrelated matters are packaged in a single bill. Thus, the president can veto special-interest legislation only by sacrificing legislation that he, presumably, supports. Omnibus bills also facilitate logrolling, since legislators cannot disapprove of some projects unless they vote against their own.

Judicial review is the final constitutional impediment to rent-seeking. This protection, however, has been mostly ineffective since the 1930s, when the Supreme Court began to refuse to protect property rights. Cases involving economic liberties receive the lowest scrutiny, which in practice often amounts to no scrutiny at all.

The Constitution was carefully designed to protect property rights and to make rent-seeking difficult:

> ... the most common and durable source of factions, has been the various and unequal distribution of property. Those who hold, and those who are without property, have ever formed distinct interests in society. Those who are creditors, and those who are debtors, fall under a like discrimination. A landed interest, a manufacturing interest, a mercantile interest, a moneyed interest, with many lesser interests, grow up of necessity in civilized nations, and divide them into different classes, actuated by different sentiments and views. The regulation of these various and interfering interests forms the principle task of modern legislation. ... (*Federalist* no. 10)

To protect property rights, the Constitution requires that rent-seeking legislation clear four hurdles: It must be approved by both houses of Congress; it must survive a possible executive veto; and the courts must not rule that it is unconstitutional. These constitutional protections were, for the most part, effective for 140 years, but their efficacy did not survive the change in intellectual climate that occurred in the 1930s.

The problem of rent-seeking requires a dual strategy: (1) structural reforms and (2) changing people's beliefs about the proper role of government. Structural reforms should raise the cost of obtaining wealth transfers so that more persons choose to forgo rent-seeking in favor of participating in wealth creation. Term limits and the line-item veto would be helpful. Special-interest groups seek long-term relationships with members of Congress (especially committee chairpersons), so that once gains are made they can be reasonably confident that the arrangements will be continued. When serving in Congress is a career, long-term support from special-interest groups is important to members of Congress as well. Turnover in Congress increases the uncertainty that special-interest legislation will be enacted or that it will not be rescinded once it is in place. In general, term limits would upset the comfortable, and mutually beneficial, relationships that many members of Congress have with special-interest groups.

The line-item veto would make the president more directly responsible for the passage of special-interest legislation. He could no longer claim that he had to sign a bill that includes legislation he opposes in order to obtain the legislation that he favors. The line-item veto also raises the cost of rent-seeking by creating uncertainty. Placing special-interest legislation in omnibus bills would not make a veto less likely. The line-item veto would help promote the general goal of making wealth creation through market exchanges a more attractive option than rent-seeking.

Ultimately, libertarians must believe that ideas do have consequences, and they must convince more people that wealth transfers are a negative-sum game. When members of Congress tout the pork-barrel projects they have secured for their constituents, voters should recognize that they do not benefit from this brand of politics. As I have noted (Section 13), transfers are not frictionless: It costs money to take money from Peter to give it to Paula. If it costs $1.50 to give Paula $1.00 (a conservative estimate), then most of us must be losers in the transfer game.

Second, lobbying costs are a deadweight loss to the economy. Lobbying diverts talented people from occupations where they would be creating wealth. When lobbying for wealth transfers is unsuccessful, both the rent-seekers and the persons who hired lobbyists to oppose the transfers have wasted their money. When lobbyists succeed in gaining wealth transfers that are beneficial to their clients, the rest of us lose.

Pointing out that rent-seeking is a negative-sum game engages the self-interest of voters. Libertarians must also make their case against state capitalism on moral grounds by attacking the liberal view that wealth transfers are morally acceptable. Most Americans are concerned about the moral decline that underlies many of our social ills. What libertarians must do is to make the connection between moral decay and big government. What kind of moral character does the government promote when politicians encourage persons to look to government to solve their problems instead of taking responsibility for their own lives? What kind of moral character does the government promote when it subsidizes irresponsible behavior such as unmarried teenagers having babies? What kind of moral character does government promote when health care "reform" means community rating that does not allow private insurers to discriminate between those who maintain healthy lifestyles and those who do not? Big government is incompatible with self-reliance and personal responsibility. Instead, big government reduces the penalties for irresponsible behavior, and it rewards people who seek to benefit from the wealth created by others. In other words, big government encourages dependence, irresponsible behavior, and greed. These are not the "moral virtues" we want government to promote, and in the communities where these vices are common, social pathologies abound.

I mentioned earlier that it was my belief in moral equality that first attracted me to libertarianism. Libertarianism, as I conceive it, embraces moral equality in its most fundamental sense—that persons have the *equal* right to be self-directing. On this account of moral equality, persons who oppose libertarianism are elitists who want to impose their conception of the good life on others. I think that persons who accept the moral view that I have called dualism have the only plausible reply to the charge of elitism. (Some opponents may simply be willing to admit that they are elitists. In this case, we will at least know where they stand.) Dualists maintain that there are two fundamental rights: the equal right to be free and the equal right to basic goods. Furthermore, dualists can argue that freedom has value only for persons who have access to basic goods. I have noted, however, that one can be a dualist in theory and a libertarian in practice. If basic needs were met by voluntary means, no one's rights would be violated, and thus the libertarian society is also the ideal dualist society. In other words, dualists can support tax-funded welfare programs only if basic needs cannot be met by voluntary programs. Thus, dualists should be libertarians (in practice) unless they hold the pessimistic view that ordinary persons cannot be trusted to make the right choices about whether to help others or how to take care of themselves. This pessimistic view certainly has the appearance of elitism. Finally, coercion requires justification, and thus the burden of proof lies with those who claim that voluntary programs to help the needy would be inadequate. No opponent of libertarianism has, to my knowledge, made a serious attempt to meet this burden of proof.

Notes

Introduction

1. John Rawls makes a similar assumption in *A Theory of Justice* (Cambridge: Harvard University Press, 1971): "Yet a society satisfying the principles of justice as fairness comes as close as a society can to being a voluntary scheme, for it meets the principles which free and equal persons would assent to under circumstances that are fair" (p. 13). I shall argue that Rawls falls far short of his goal of making society, as far as possible, a voluntary scheme.

2. From *Kant's Political Writings*, edited by Hans Reiss and translated by H. B. Nisbet (Cambridge: Cambridge University Press, 1970), p. 74.

3. John Stuart Mill, *On Liberty* (Indianapolis: Hackett, 1978), p. 12.

4. My thinking on these matters has been influenced by Christine M. Korsgaard, "The Reasons We Can Share," *Social Philosophy and Policy* 10 (1993), pp. 24–51.

5. For my contribution to the literature on this topic, see Lansing Pollock, "On Treating Others as Ends," *Ethics* 84 (1974), pp. 260–261.

Moral Foundations

1. Saul K. Padover, *The Forging of American Federalism* (New York: Harper and Row, 1953), p. 49.

2. See Friedrich A. Hayek, *The Constitution of Liberty* (Chicago: University of Chicago Press, 1960), pp. 64–65 and 159–161.

3. Good reasons for accepting a belief should include an understanding of the criticisms and objections that have been (or could be) raised against the belief. When the criticisms and objections can be answered, further grounds for holding the belief are provided.

4. Henry Sidgwick, *The Methods of Ethics* (London: Macmillan, 1970), p. 209.

5. R. M. Hare calls such holdouts fanatics. See *Freedom and Reason* (New York: Oxford University Press, 1965), pp. 157–185.

6. See Kurt Baier, *The Moral Point of View* (New York: Random House, 1965), pp. 108 and 135.

7. In the first edition of *The Moral Rules*, Bernard Gert claimed that the moral rules are the ones that rational persons would publicly advocate. Gert later concluded that this view erroneously combines two ideas: rationality and impartiality. See Bernard Gert, *The Moral Rules* (New York: Harper Torchbook, 1973), pp. xvii–xxi. See also Bernard Gert, *Morality* (New York: Oxford University Press, 1988), p. 78.

156   Notes

8. John Rawls, *A Theory of Justice* (Cambridge: Harvard University Press, 1971), pp. 150–175. Rawls claims that the choice of his two principles of justice does not depend on "a special attitude toward risk" (p. 172). Choosing the most conservative principles (the maximin strategy) reflects, I think, a special attitude toward risk. Just how conservative this strategy is is discussed in Section 4.

9. Jan Narveson, *The Libertarian Idea* (Philadelphia: Temple University Press, 1988).

10. T. M. Scanlon, "Contractualism and Utilitarianism," in Amartya Sen and Bernard Williams, eds., *Utilitarianism and Beyond* (Cambridge: Cambridge University Press, 1982), p. 110.

11. See Judith Jarvis Thomson, *The Realm of Rights* (Cambridge: Harvard University Press, 1990), pp. 188–189.

12. Another reason is to remove lawbreakers from society.

13. John Stuart Mill, *On Liberty* (Indianapolis: Hackett, 1978), p. 9.

14. Suppose that Jones will be unconscious for one hour. Is killing him morally permissible? We could argue that it is not because, as an autonomous agent, Jones has long-range plans. But suppose we know that Jones has no long-range plans. Since graduating from high school, he has had no idea what to do with his life. If asked, he will say that his life lacks meaning and that this is a source of real despair. Since killing him would not interfere with his long-range plans (because he has none), would it be permissible?

It is interesting to compare the libertarian view with that of Don Marquis. Marquis claims that killing is wrong because it deprives the victim of the value of his future. Libertarians emphasize that killing deprives the victim of an autonomous future. Whether the person will have a valuable future depends largely on what the person chooses to do. See Don Marquis, "Why Abortion Is Immoral," *Journal of Philosophy* 85 (1989), pp. 183–202.

15. This is the approach I took in *The Freedom Principle* (Buffalo: Prometheus Books, 1981), pp. 27–30.

16. Rawls, op. cit., p. 302. Page references in this section are to *A Theory of Justice*.

17. Rawls gives a similar argument for including the equal liberty of conscience in his list of basic liberties. *A Theory of Justice*, pp. 206–207. In Rawls's theory, the original position is the circumstances in which persons choose the principles of justice to regulate their society.

18. John Rawls, *Political Liberalism* (New York: Columbia University Press, 1993), p. 291.

19. *Ibid.*, p. 181.

20. *Ibid.*, p. 291.

21. For example, see pp. 298, 363, and 364 in Rawls, *Political Liberalism*.

22. *Ibid.*, p. 294.

23. For additional criticism of the principle of equal liberty, see H.L.A. Hart, "Rawls on Liberty and Its Priority," in Norman Daniels, ed., *Reading Rawls* (New York: Basic Books, 1974), pp. 230–252.

24. Are consequentialism and Kantianism the only reasonable alternatives? The answer depends on how broadly these two terms are interpreted. I have been deliberately vague about these matters because I am unsure what to say about egoism and religious justifications of morality.

25. John C. Harsanyi, "Some Epistemological Advantages of a Rule Utilitarian Position in Ethics," *Midwest Studies in Philosophy* 8 (1982), pp. 389–390.

26. *Ibid.*, p. 390.

27. This example is well worn, but it still provides a crucial test for moral theories. For a vigorous defense of utilitarianism, see R. M. Hare, "What Is Wrong with Slavery," *Philosophy and Public Affairs* 8 (1979), pp. 103–121.

28. Bernard Williams, *Ethics and the Limits of Philosophy* (Cambridge: Harvard University Press, 1985), p. 86.

29. John C. Harsanyi, "Morality and the Theory of Rational Behavior," *Social Research* 44 (1977), p. 647.

30. David O. Brink, *Moral Realism and the Foundations of Ethics* (Cambridge: Cambridge University Press, 1989). Page references in this section are to this book.

31. Bernard Williams, "A Critique of Utilitarianism," in J.J.C. Smart and Bernard Williams, *Utilitarianism: For and Against* (Cambridge: Cambridge University Press, 1973), pp. 116–117.

32. Alan Donagan, *The Theory of Morality* (Chicago: University of Chicago Press, 1977), p. 203.

33. Harsanyi, "Some Epistemological Advantages," note 34, p. 389.

34. Gert, *Morality*, p. ix.

35. Alan Gewirth, *Reason and Morality* (Chicago: University of Chicago Press, 1978), p. 260.

36. An analysis of Gewirth's moral theory can be found in Lansing Pollock, "Evaluating Moral Theories," *American Philosophical Quarterly* 25 (1988), pp. 234–237.

37. The reader should note that ranking the basic rules ahead of the other rules (in all cases) is not a realistic option. Given the rule utilitarian view that a rule may be broken only when it conflicts with another rule and given that the basic rules do not conflict with each other, this option would entail the implausible conclusion that the basic rules should never be broken.

38. Peter Singer, *Practical Ethics* (New York: Cambridge University Press, 1989), p. 168.

39. Gewirth, *op. cit.*, p. 332.

40. Brink, *op. cit.*, p. 250.

41. The "web of belief" metaphor is borrowed from Quine. See W. V. Quine and J. S. Ullian, *The Web of Belief* (New York: Random House, 1970).

42. See Jeremy Bentham, *An Introduction to the Principles of Morals and Legislation* (New York: Hafner, 1948, Ch. 1, Sec. 1.

43. A good critique of hedonism can be found in Brink, *op. cit.*, pp. 217–236.

44. Michael Harrington, *Socialism* (New York: Bantam Books, 1972), p. 421. Harrington's book *The Other America* was influential in engendering support for the war on poverty in the 1960s.

45. *Ibid.*, p. 454.

46. Since Harrington's tax proposals have the additional objective of equalizing wealth, it is not clear how the "free" goods and services would be paid for after the rich have been soaked.

47. Harrington, *op. cit.*, p. 454.

48. From *Kant's Political Writings*, edited by Hans Reiss and translated by H. B. Nisbet (Cambridge: Cambridge University Press, 1970), p. 74.

49. Milton Friedman, *Capitalism and Freedom* (Chicago: University of Chicago Press, 1962), pp. 191–192.

50. Robert Heilbroner, "Reflections After Communism," *New Yorker*, September 10, 1990, pp. 91–100.

51. Robert Nozick, *Anarchy, State, and Utopia* (New York: Basic Books, 1974), p. 217.
52. *Ibid.*, p. 206.
53. Rawls's discussion of eugenics is brief and what he says is (to me, at least) surprisingly favorable: "In the original position, then, the parties want to insure their descendants the best genetic endowment (assuming their own to be fixed). The pursuit of reasonable policies in this regard is something that earlier generations owe to later ones, this being a question that arises between generations. Thus over time a society is to take steps at least to preserve the general level of natural abilities and to prevent the diffusion of serious defects" (*A Theory of Justice*, p. 108).
54. Nozick, *Anarchy, State, and Utopia*, p. 214.
55. Christine Korsgaard, "The Reasons We Can Share," *Social Philosophy and Policy* 10 (1993), p. 24.
56. *Ibid.*, pp. 24–25.
57. *Ibid.*, p. 25.
58. James O. Grunebaum, *Private Ownership* (London: Routledge and Kegan Paul, 1987), p. 113.
59. For a similar line of criticism see Loren E. Lomasky, *Persons, Rights, and the Moral Community* (New York: Oxford University Press, 1987), pp. 139–140.
60. Korsgaard, *op. cit.*, p. 50.
61. In Norman Daniels, *Reading Rawls* (New York: Basic Books, 1974), p. 197.
62. Thomas Nagel, *Equality and Partiality* (New York: Oxford University Press, 1991), p. 36.
63. *Ibid.*, pp. 69, 107, and 121.
64. *Ibid.*, p. 100.
65. *Ibid.*, pp. 33–34.
66. *Ibid.*, p. 37.
67. *Ibid.*, p. 159.
68. Charles Murray, *In Pursuit of Happiness and Good Government* (New York: Simon and Schuster, 1988), pp. 80–82.
69. Nozick, *op. cit.*, Ch. 10. In *Principles of Political Economy* (Middlesex, England: Penguin Books, 1970), Mill recommends socialist experiments on a "moderate scale": "With regard to this, as to all other varieties of Socialism, the thing to be desired, and to which they have a just claim, is opportunity of trial. They are all capable of being tried on a moderate scale, and at no risk, either personal or pecuniary, to any except those who try them" (p. 366).
70. Rawls doesn't claim that his contract argument "justifies" his principles of justice. Instead, the contract is supposed to help us understand his conception of moral equality.
71. A contract argument for libertarianism can be found in Jan Narveson, *The Libertarian Idea* (Philadelphia: Temple University Press, 1988), Ch. 12–14.
72. This is too strong, but it is not as obviously counterfactual as some may think. First, I am concerned with what persons can believe when they think about the morality of their actions. Many persons who act immorally avoid thinking about morality. Second, excuses are not justifications. Persons who act immorally often look for excuses for their conduct, but when they do, they are admitting wrongdoing. If what you do is justified, you don't need an excuse.
73. Thomas Nagel, "Libertarianism Without Foundations" reprinted in Jeffrey Paul, ed., *Reading Nozick* (Totowa, N.J.: Rowman and Littlefield, 1981), p. 200.
74. Douglas J. Den Uyl, "The Right to Welfare and the Virtue of Charity," *Social Philosophy and Policy* 10 (1993), p. 205.

75. Thomas Nagel, *Equality and Partiality* (New York: Oxford University Press, 1991), p. 4.
76. Grunebaum has pointed out to me that this characterization probably does not apply to Kant's view of friendship.
77. David Schmidtz, "Reasons for Altruism," *Social Philosophy and Policy* 10 (1993), p. 53.
78. *Ibid.*, p. 66.
79. Peter Singer, "Famine, Affluence and Morality," *Philosophy and Public Affairs* 1 (1972), pp. 229–243.
80. Christine Swanton has produced the most thorough analysis of the various conceptions of freedom that I am aware of. See *Freedom* (Indianapolis: Hackett, 1992).
81. Rawls, *A Theory of Justice*, p. 51.
82. Sidgwick, *op. cit.*, p. 274.
83. *Ibid.*, p. 275.
84. *Ibid.*
85. *Ibid.*, p. 276.

Liberty and Government

1. Saul K. Padover, *The Forging of American Federalism* (New York: Harper and Row, 1953), p. 197.
2. The delivery of water and sewer services is often cited as an example of a "natural monopoly," since it is inefficient to have competing firms lay pipes to deliver these services. I discuss natural monopolies in Section 10. In the case of water and sewer services, strictly speaking, I do have other choices. For example, I could buy bottled water, and I could install a septic tank and hire someone to pump it out when needed. It is of course more convenient and less costly to have the city deliver water to my home. If I really wanted to avoid paying for water and sewer services, I could move to a rural area and dig my own well.
3. David Friedman, *The Machinery of Freedom* (New York: Harper and Row, 1973), p. xv.
4. Personal income exceeded $6 trillion for the first time in June 1995 (*Wall Street Journal*, August 1, 1995, p. 1).
5. An exception is a gasoline tax that raises revenue for the construction and maintenance of public streets and roads. I discuss this tax in Section 10.
6. John Stuart Mill, *Principles of Political Economy* (Middlesex, England: Penguin Books, 1970), p. 368.
7. *Ibid.*, p. 369.
8. *Ibid.*, p. 380.
9. David Schmidtz, "The Institution of Property," *Social Philosophy and Policy* 11 (1994), p. 45. See also David Schmidtz, *The Limits of Government* (Boulder: Westview Press, 1991), Ch. 2.
10. Joel Feinberg, *Rights, Justice, and the Bounds of Liberty* (Princeton: Princeton University Press, 1980), p. 265.
11. I do not mean to imply that I accept the details of Mill's solution. Mill was trying to give a utilitarian account of justice and I am not. See John Stuart Mill, *Utilitarianism* (Indianapolis: Hackett, 1979), Ch 5.
12. Karl Menninger, "Therapy, Not Punishment," in Jeffrie G. Murphy, ed., *Punishment and Rehabilitation* (Belmont, Calif: Wadsworth, 1973), p. 136.
13. *Ibid.*, p. 139.
14. Randy E. Barnett, "Restitution: A New Paradigm of Criminal Justice," *Ethics* 87 (1977), p. 287.

15. *Ibid.*, p. 288.
16. *Ibid.*, p. 289.
17. *Ibid.*
18. John Stuart Mill, *On Liberty* (Indianapolis: Hackett, 1978), p. 10.
19. Mill, *Utilitarianism*, p. 10.
20. David O. Brink, "Mill's Deliberative Utilitarianism," *Philosophy and Public Affairs* 21 (1992), p. 79.
21. Mill, *On Liberty*, p. 108.
22. *Ibid.*, p. 108.
23. *Ibid.*, p. 54.
24. Mill, *Principles of Political Economy*, p. 308.
25. *Ibid.*, pp. 311–312.
26. *Ibid.*, p. 314.
27. Mill also discusses (among other things) child labor laws and practical monopolies. I agree with most of what Mill says on these two topics.
28. Mill, *On Liberty*, p. 104.
29. *Ibid.*, pp. 105–106.
30. Mill, *Principles of Political Economy*, p. 320.
31. *Ibid.*, p. 320.
32. *Ibid.*
33. Mill, *On Liberty*, p. 106.
34. Mill, *Principles of Political Economy*, p. 334.
35. *Ibid.*, p. 333.
36. 468 US 8997.
37. Yale Kamisar, "The Sword of Damocles," *Law Quadrangle Notes* 29 (1984), pp. 1–3.
38. Padover, *op. cit.*, p. 269.
39. Richard A. Epstein, "A Common Lawyer Looks at Constitutional Interpretation," in Susan J. Brison and Walter Sinnott-Armstrong, ed., *Contemporary Perspectives on Constitutional Interpretation* (Boulder: Westview Press, 1993), p. 70.
40. *Williamson v. Lee Optical,* 348 US 343 (1955).
41. Stephen Macedo, *Liberal Virtues* (New York: Oxford University Press, 1990), p. 186.
42. Writing about the power of taxation in *Federalist* no. 56, Madison states: "Taxation will consist, in great measure, of duties which will be involved in the regulation of commerce." I should acknowledge that there is some dispute about whether this essay was written by Madison, Hamilton, or both.
43. Padover, *op. cit.*, p. 341. See also *Federalist* no. 41.
44. Padover, *op. cit.*, p. 46.
45. James D. Gwartney and Richard E. Wagner, *Public Choice and Constitutional Economics* (Greenwich, Conn.: JAI Press, 1988), p. 22.
46. Padover, *op. cit.*, p. 41. The quotation is from a letter to Jefferson, October 24, 1787.
47. This is discussed by Gwartney and Wagner, *op. cit.*, pp. 44–55.
48. Madison's answer to the legislative problem was to establish two branches, the Senate and the House of Representatives, with differing criteria of representation. (See *Federalist* no. 51.) However, the popular election of senators has eroded some of the differences. One way to make the two branches different is to require a supermajority, say two-thirds, for passage of legislation in the Senate. To some degree, the filibuster already provides this result.

49. Padover, *op. cit.*, p. 198.

50. David N. Mayer, *The Constitutional Thought of Thomas Jefferson* (Charlottesville: University Press of Virginia, 1994), p. 219.

51. See Mill, *Principles of Political Economy,* p. 239.

52. Milton Friedman, *Capitalism and Freedom* (Chicago: University of Chicago Press, 1962), p. 28.

53. *U.S. News and World Report,* June 21, 1993, pp. 56–63.

54. Friedman, *op. cit.,* pp. 101–107.

55. Loren E. Lomasky, *Persons, Rights and the Moral Community* (New York: Oxford University Press, 1987), pp. 177–178.

56. *Ibid.,* p. 175.

57. See S.J.D. Green, "Competitive Equality of Opportunity: A Defense," *Ethics* 100 (1989), pp. 5–32. Green calls for radical changes in early education in order to produce "competitive equality of opportunity." It is of course debatable how effective such programs would be in compensating for impoverished or abusive home environments. Green claims that competitive equality of opportunity is an ideal we should aim for even though it cannot be fully realized.

58. Lomasky, *op. cit.,* pp. 180–181.

59. Most analyses of equal opportunity assume that persons want to be successful and that success is measured in materialistic (economic) terms. Equality of opportunity looks very different if we assume that what is really important is strength of character as exhibited in such virtues as courage, determination, and fortitude. On this view, one can even argue that the child born into poverty has greater opportunities than the child with wealthy parents.

60. Joel Feinberg, *Harm to Self* (Oxford: Oxford University Press, 1986), p. 18.

61. Feinberg, *Rights, Justice and the Bounds of Liberty,* pp. 143–155.

62. See also Marvin Olasky, *The Tragedy of American Compassion* (Washington, D.C.: Regnery Gateway, 1992).

63. For example, see Tibor Machan, *Individuals and Their Rights* (La Salle, Ill.: Open Court, 1989), pp. 100–111. In this section, Machan refutes Sterba's claim that libertarian rights entail welfare rights. See James Sterba, "A Libertarian Justification for a Welfare State," *Social Theory and Practice* 10 (1985), pp. 285–306.

Liberty and Economics

1. Saul K. Padover, *The Forging of American Federalism* (New York: Harper and Row, 1953), p. 269.

2. Henry Hazlitt, *The Conquest of Poverty* (New Rochelle, N.Y.: Arlington House, 1976), p. 43.

3. *T. Rowe Price Report* no. 42 (1994), p. 6; *Insight,* October 4, 1993, p. 9.

4. Robert J. Samuelson, "How Our American Dream Unraveled," *Newsweek,* March 2, 1992, p. 35.

5. *Economist,* March 19, 1994, p. 3.

6. *T. Rowe Price Report* no. 42 (1994), p. 6.

7. *Insight,* October 4, 1993, p. 9.

8. Robert L. Bartley, *The Seven Fat Years* (New York: Free Press, 1992), p. 4.

9. *National Review,* November 7, 1994, p. 10.

10. *Economist,* January 6, 1995, p. 52.

11. *Reason,* July 1993, p. 27.

12. *Ibid.,* pp. 27–28.

13. *Ibid.*, p. 28.
14. *Ibid.*
15. George Gilder, *Recapturing the Spirit of Enterprise* (San Francisco: ICS Press, 1992), p. 7.
16. *Ibid.*, p. 39.
17. Lawrence Kudlow, "When Numbers Get Serious," *National Review*, March 6, 1995, p. 30.
18. Lawrence Kudlow, "It's Capital Formation, Stupid," *Wall Street Journal*, December 17, 1992, p. 14.
19. Gilder, *op. cit.*, p. 125.
20. Milton Friedman, *Money Mischief* (New York: Harcourt Brace Jovanovich, 1992), p. 215.
21. Milton Friedman, *Capitalism and Freedom* (Chicago: University of Chicago Press, 1962), p. 50.
22. *Wall Street Journal*, February, 23, 1994, p. 20. From 1991 to 1995, M1 (the narrow measure of money) grew at a much faster rate than M2 (the broader measure). This difference has intensified the debate over what is the best definition of money. For details on the numbers, see "Financial Indicators" in any issue of the Economist.
23. *Fortune*, October 4, 1993, p. 102.
24. The federal deficit for 1994 was $202 billion. See *Economist*, October 29, 1994, p. 31.
25. James D. Gwartney and Richard L. Stroup, *Economics and Prosperity* (Tallahassee, Fla.: James Madison Institute, 1993), p. 85.
26. Peter G. Peterson, "Facing Up," *Atlantic Monthly*, October 1993, p. 80.
27. For a general analysis of the cost of regulations, see *Economist*, October 10, 1992, pp. 21–24. Thomas Hopkins, professor of economics at the Rochester Institute of Technology, estimates that the total cost of regulations exceeds $600 billion a year (Economist, March 11, 1995, p. 25).
28. *Ibid.*, p. 21.
29. Robert J. Samuelson, "There's Still No Free Lunch," *Newsweek*, April 12, 1993, p. 49.
30. *Forbes*, June 6, 1994, p. 30.
31. *Insight*, May 10, 1993, p. 24.
32. *Economist*, October 10, 1992, p. 22.
33. Bartley, *op. cit.*, Ch. 2.
34. Gilder, *op. cit.*, pp. 55–56. Particularly influential was *The Limits to Growth*, issued by the Club of Rome in 1972.
35. Bartley, *op. cit.*, p. 39.
36. *Ibid.*, pp. 145 and 189.
37. *Ibid.*, p. 229.
38. *Ibid.*, pp. 230–234.
39. James A. Leach, "Clinton Capsized by the Arrogance of Power," *Insight*, April 11, 1994, p. 28. Congressman Leach is a representative from Iowa.
40. *Economist*, January 29, 1994, p. 84.
41. Paul A. Samuelson and William D. Nordhaus, *Economics* (New York: McGraw-Hill, 1995), pp. 652, 671..
42. *Economist*, January 15, 1994, p. 15.
43. *Economist*, September 11, 1993, p. 21; *Economist*, September 18, 1993, p. 57.
44. *Economist*, July 8, 1995, p. 99.

45. "Survey: Airlines," *Economist*, June 12, 1993, p. 10.
46. *Economist*, February 5, 1994, p. 69.
47. *U.S. News and World Report*, September 6, 1993, p. 59.
48. *Economist*, August 21, 1993, p. 51.
49. *U.S. News and World Report*, March 28, 1994, p. 60.
50. *Economist*, February 12, 1994, p. 74.
51. *Ibid.*, p. 75.
52. *Insight*, January 10, 1994, p. 9.
53. Kudlow, "It's Capital Formation, Stupid," p. 14.
54. *Economist*, March 12, 1994, pp. 14 and 19.
55. *Ibid.*, p. 20.
56. Gilder, *op. cit.*, pp. 156–164 and 215–244.
57. Bartley, *op. cit.*, p. 283.
58. *Economist*, February 26, 1994, p. 69.
59. *Wall Street Journal*, September 1, 1995, p. 4.
60. Cynthia Beltz, "The Big Picture," *Reason*, August 1993, pp. 58–59. See also *Economist*, February 26, 1994, p. 65.
61. Gilder, *op. cit.*, p. 149.
62. *Economist*, March 13, 1993, p. 31.
63. Milton Friedman and Rose Friedman, *Free to Choose* (New York: Harcourt Brace Jovanovich, 1979), pp. 121–122.
64. *Ibid.*, p. 119.
65. Perhaps the most prominent advocate of this "solution" has been Mickey Kaus, senior editor of the *New Republic*.
66. *U.S. News and World Report*, July 19, 1993, p. 41.
67. *Economist*, December 3, 1994, p. 33.
68. Lawrence Kudlow estimates that 4.4 million welfare recipients would have to participate in work programs if workfare were in place by 1996. See *National Review*, March 16, 1994, p. 26.
69. *Reason*, April 1994, p. 27.
70. *Insight*, April 12, 1993, p. 17.
71. Charles Murray, *Losing Ground* (New York: Basic Books, 1984), p. 15.
72. Charles Murray, "The Coming White Underclass," *Wall Street Journal*, October 29, 1993, p. 15; *U.S. News and World Report*, June 19, 1995, p. 17. The latest percentage is from the National Center for Health Statistics.
73. *Ibid.*, p. 15.
74. *Insight*, March 8, 1993, p. 19.
75. Murray, "The Coming White Underclass," p. 15.
76. *Ibid.*, p. 15.
77. Barbara Dafoe Whitehead, "Dan Quayle Was Right," *Atlantic Monthly*, April 1993, p. 66.
78. *Ibid.*, p. 77; *U.S. News and World Report*, November 8, 1993, p. 34.
79. Whitehead, *op. cit.*, p. 77.
80. Murray, "The Coming White Underclass," p. 15.
81. *Ibid.*, p. 15.
82. *Insight*, October 25, 1993, p. 32.

83. *Reason,* February 1993, p. 37.
84. A recent Census Bureau study found that in an average month of 1990, 35.2 percent of people in female-headed households were poor compared to 7 percent of those in households headed by married couples. Of the chronic poor (poor for every month of 1990 and 1991), only 1.4 percent lived in families of married couples. (*Wall Street Journal,* March 30, 1995, p. 16.)
85. *U.S. News and World Report,* March 8, 1993, pp. 59–61.
86. *Insight,* July 25, 1994, p. 37.
87. James L. Payne, *Costly Returns* (San Francisco: Institute for Contemporary Studies, 1993), p. 9.
88. James L. Payne, "Where Have All the Dollars Gone?" *Reason,* February 1994, p. 17.
89. Payne, *Costly Returns,* p. 21.
90. *Ibid.,* p. 24.
91. *Ibid.,* p. 25.
92. *Ibid.,* p. 26.
93. *Ibid.,* p. 29.
94. *Ibid.*
95. *Ibid.,* pp. 93–95.
96. *Ibid.,* p. 150.
97. See *Fortune,* September 6, 1993, p. 40.
98. Payne, *Costly Returns,* p. 11.
99. *Ibid.,* p. 36.
100. See Thomas Sowell, *Knowledge and Decisions* (New York: Basic Books, 1980), Ch. 3.
101. John C. Goodman and Gerald L. Musgrave, *Patient Power* (Washington, D.C.: Cato Institute, 1992), pp. 492–494. Britain has fewer than 350 cancer specialists (oncologists). The United States has 10 times as many per capita. See *Economist,* May 21, 1994, p. 67.
102. Goodman and Musgrave, *op. cit.,* pp. 522–523.
103. Elizabeth McCaughey, "Health Insurance for All," *Wall Street Journal,* April 28, 1994, p. 14.
104. Goodman and Musgrave, *op. cit.,* p. 360.
105. McCaughey, *op. cit.,* p. 14.
106. Richard A. Epstein, *Forbidden Grounds* (Cambridge: Harvard University Press, 1992), pp. 334–336.
107. *Buffalo News,* June 7, 1993, Sec. C, p. 3.
108. Goodman and Musgrave, *op. cit.,* p. 288.
109. *Ibid.,* p. 232.
110. Getting regulatory approval accounts for about two-thirds of the cost of developing a new drug (*Economist,* August 6, 1994, p. 65).
111. David S. Broder, "Kerrey Takes President to the Woodshed," *Buffalo News,* September 20, 1993, Sec. C, p. 3.
112. For Milton Friedman's analysis see *Wall Street Journal,* November 12, 1991, p. 20.
113. Goodman and Musgrave, *op. cit.,* p. 479.
114. George F. Will, "The Clintons' Lethal Paternalism," *Newsweek,* February 7, 1994, p. 64.
115. *Ibid.,* p. 64.

116. David S. Broder, "Listen to the Experts in Health Care Reform," *Buffalo News*, April 30, 1993, Sec. C, p. 3.

117. My evidence for this is anecdotal. It comes from talking to friends who are physicians.

118. *Wall Street Journal*, January 14, 1994, p. 10.

119. *Economist*, August 28, 1993, p. 23.

120. *Ibid.*, p. 24.

121. Thomas Sowell, "Patterns of Black Excellence," reprinted in Education: *Assumptions Versus History* (Stanford: Hoover Institution Press, 1986), pp. 7–38.

122. *Ibid.*, pp. 32–35.

123. *Ibid.*, pp. 32–33.

124. Allyson Tucker and Will Lauer, "Let States Lead Reform in Education," *Buffalo News*, May 2, 1994, Sec. C, p. 3.

125. *Economist*, April 2, 1994, p. 24; George F. Will, "Upgrading Education Begins at Home, Not D.C.," *Buffalo News*, February 18, 1994, Sec. C, p. 3.

126. *National Review*, September 26, 1994, p. 17.

127. Thomas Sowell, *Inside American Education* (New York: Free Press, 1993), pp. 8–9.

128. Richard J. Herrnstein and Charles Murray, *The Bell Curve* (New York: Free Press, 1994), pp. 428–429.

129. John E. Chubb and Terry M. Moe, *Politics, Markets, and America's Schools* (Washington, D.C.: Brookings Institution, 1990), p. 193.

130. *Ibid.*, Ch. 5. See also *National Review*, September 26, 1994. p. 17.

131. *Ibid.*, pp. 46–47.

132. *Ibid.*, p. 189.

133. *Ibid.*, pp. 186–187.

134. *Ibid.*, p. 227.

135. *Ibid.*, p. 29.

136. *Ibid.*, p. 36.

137. Friedman, *Capitalism and Freedom*, p. 89.

138. Chubb and Moe, *op. cit.*, pp. 221–222.

139. *Ibid.*, p. 225.

140. *Forbes*, June 7, 1993, p. 74.

141. *Ibid.*, p. 81.

142. *Insight*, November 16, 1992, p. 31.

143. *Ibid.*, p. 31. See also *Forbes*, June 7, 1993, p. 79.

144. *Insight*, January 10, 1994, p. 9.

145. Sowell, *Inside American Education*, p. 27.

146. *Forbes*, June 7, 1993, p. 7. Twenty-two percent is twice the national average. My own children went to public schools in Buffalo. We were able to get our children admitted to magnet schools, which provided a good education.

147. Mike Royko, "Where Good Sense Is in the Minority," *Chicago Tribune*, September 21, 1990, Sec. C, p. 3. Royko's column was picked up by *60 Minutes*.

148. Mike Royko, "Another Small Business Almost Failed," *Buffalo News*, October 1, 1993, Sec. C, p. 12.

149. Epstein, *op. cit.*, pp. 36–39.

150. Sowell, *Knowledge and Decisions*, p. 258.

151. *Ibid.*, p. 259.

152. *Ibid.* For a more recent analysis, see Epstein, *op. cit.,* pp. 254–259.
153. My wife, for example, belongs to a large church in the heart of Buffalo that has only a handful of black members.
154. Epstein, *op. cit.,* pp. 246–247.
155. Thomas Sowell, *Is Reality Optional?* (Stanford: Hoover Institution Press, 1993), p. 164.
156. Epstein, *op. cit.,* p. 352.
157. *Ibid.,* p. 319.
158. *U.S. News and World Report,* August 2, 1993, p. 52.

Liberty and Reality

1. Marvin Meyers, *The Mind of the Founder* (Hanover, N.H.: University Press of New England, 1973), p. 403.
2. Milton Friedman and Rose Friedman, *Free To Choose* (New York: Harcourt Brace Jovanovich, 1979), p. 37.
3. I discuss Social Security and the war on drugs in Section 18.
4. Nicholas Rescher, "The Environmental Crisis and the Quality of Life," in William T. Blackstone, ed., *Philosophy and Environmental Crisis* (Athens: University of Georgia Press, 1974), p. 101.
5. My thinking on this topic has been strongly influenced by Jan Narveson's essay "Resources and Environmental Policy," which will be published by *Proceedings of the Philosophic Exchange* at Brockport State College.
6. See *The World Almanac* (Mahwah, N.J.: Funk & Wagnalls, 1994). Holland's population density is 958 per square mile (p. 793).
7. See *The World Almanac* (1994). Japan's yearly birthrate is 10 per 1,000; the birthrates of Italy and Germany are 11 per 1,000. By contrast, Mexico's birthrate is 29 per 1,000, India's is 30 per 1,000, and Nigeria's is 46 per 1,000. The birthrate in the United States is close to replacement level at 14 per 1,000. See also *Insight,* August 22, 1994, p. 10.
8. *Buffalo News,* April 3, 1993, Sec. F, p. 12.
9. *Ibid.*
10. *Insight,* May 17, 1993, p. 26.
11. Robert L. Bartley, *The Seven Fat Years* (New York: Free Press, 1992), p. 40.
12. *Reason,* January 1993, p. 23.
13. *National Review,* November 7, 1994, p. 39.
14. *Ibid.,* p. 40.
15. For example, see the discussion with William Niskanen in *Reason,* June 1993, p. 45.
16. *Economist,* October 29, 1994, p. 31.
17. *National Review,* November 7, 1994, p. 41.
18. *Ibid.*
19. Warren Rudman, "Social Security's Fund Cannot Be Trusted," *Insight,* May 2, 1994, p. 21.
20. Peter G. Peterson, "Facing Up," *Atlantic Monthly,* October 1993, p. 81.
21. Gary S. Becker and Isaac Ehrlich, "Social Security: Foreign Lessons," *Wall Street Journal,* March 30, 1994, p. 18.
22. Friedman and Friedman, *op. cit.,* p. 124.

23. Milton Friedman, *Money Mischief* (New York: Harcourt Brace Jovanovich, 1992), p. 213.

24. *Ibid.*, p. 206.

25. *Ibid.*, p. 213.

26. The Harrison Act of 1914 prohibited the sale of opiates unless prescribed by a physician. The nonmedical possession and sale of marijuana were prohibited by Congress in 1937. *U.S. News and World Report* predicted that U.S. prison populations would top 1 million by the end of 1994 (June 13, 1994, p. 20). In that same year, the drug trade accounted for nearly 60 percent of inmates in federal prisons (*Economist*, April 23, 1994, p. 26). The United States has the highest incarceration rate in the world (*Economist*, July 23, 1994, p. 30).

27. Thomas Sowell, *Is Reality Optional?* (Stanford: Hoover Institution Press, 1993), p. 96.

28. Milton Friedman and Thomas Szasz, *On Liberty and Drugs* (Washington, D.C.: Drug Policy Foundation Press, 1992), p. 53.

29. *Washington Times* (National Weekly Edition), July 25–31, 1994, p. 32.

30. *Newsweek,* February 7, 1994, p. 64; *Wall Street Journal,* July 21, 1994, p. 14.

31. *Reason,* May 1994, p. 22.

32. Jonathan R. Macey, "Property Rights, Innovation, and Constitutional Structure," *Social Philosophy and Policy* 11 (1994), p. 205.

About the Book and Author

In the tradition of Milton Friedman's 1962 classic, *Capitalism and Freedom*, Lansing Pollock draws on moral, political, and economic theory to defend a libertarian vision of the good society. Pollock argues that mutual consent, derived from a fundamental Kantian moral equality, is the ideal standard for judging relations between persons. He contends that if the equal right of all persons to be free is taken seriously, most of the coercion by government that many take for granted is immoral.

Pollock situates libertarian moral theory in an American historical context, one compatible with the views of James Madison and Thomas Jefferson. Pollock argues that when the Constitution is interpreted according to the political philosophy of the framers, the modern welfare state is unconstitutional. Pollock goes on to demonstrate how free market economies promote human well-being, whereas government regulation is often counterproductive. In advocating a reduction in the size and scope of government, Pollock includes applied policy analyses of poverty and health care, among other topical issues. He also offers an innovative solution to the problem of funding a limited government without violating individual rights.

The strength of *The Free Society* lies in its synthetic achievement. In a book that is accessibly written and sure to appeal to scholar and lay reader alike, Pollock provides a compelling conception of the good society—one in which the libertarian vision includes moral, social, political, and economic perspectives.

Lansing Pollock is professor of philosophy at the State University College at Buffalo. He is the author of *The Freedom Principle*.

Index

Abortion, 2, 6, 119
Adoptions, 106
AFDC. *See* Aid to Families with Dependent Children
AFT. *See* American Federation of Teachers
Aid to Families with Dependent Children (AFDC), 105, 106, 142
Airlines, 100
American Federation of Teachers (AFT), 127
Americans with Disabilities Act, 97
Amish people, 43
Anarchy, 2
Anarchy, State, and Utopia (Nozick), 2
Aristocratic views, 10
Arthur Anderson, Inc., 111
Arthur B. Hill firm, 111
Assumptions, 30, 32, 33, 39, 45–46, 53
Attacking others, 7
Autonomous agents, 13–14, 52, 156(n14)

Baby boomers, 142
Ballard, Charles L., 111
Barnett, Randy E., 65
Bastiat, Frederic, 38
Beason, Richard, 101
Becker, Gary, 144
Beliefs, 6, 46, 47, 48, 53, 155(n3)
Benificence, 48. *See also* Helping others
Bentham, Jeremy, 1, 31
Bill of Rights, 79, 149
Birthrates, 140, 166(n7)
Blacks, 106, 123, 129, 130–131, 132
Brink, David O., 22–24, 30, 69
Brookings Institution, 100, 115, 124
Buckley, William F., 146
Bureaucracies, 124–125
Bush, George, 97

Canada, 99
Capital, locked–in, 94
Capital formation, 96
Capitalism, 31, 34, 35, 93, 101–102, 107, 108
    free market, 136–137, 138
    laissez–faire, 136
    state, 136, 137, 138
Capital punishment, 6, 67
Carter administration, 98
Categorical imperative, 42. *See also* Kant, Immanuel
Certification, 85
CETA. *See* Comprehensive Employment and Training Act
Character, 41, 69, 161(n59)
Charity, 50–51. *See also* Helping others
Cheating, 19–20, 23. *See also* Deception
Checks and balances, 78
Chicago, 130
Children, 13, 14, 41–42, 42–43, 53, 54, 70, 87, 105, 106, 107, 128, 139, 146. *See also* Education
China, 141
Choices, 8, 13, 47, 77, 87, 106, 107, 118, 119, 120, 125, 142, 147
Chubb, John E., 124–126
Civil disobedience, 64
Civil Rights Act of 1964, 131
Civil Rights Act of 1991, 97, 129
Classism, 87
Clean Air Act, 97
Cleveland's Free Clinic, 120
Clinton, Bill, 99, 128
    administration, 100
    economists' letter to, 121–122
Club of Rome, 139
Coercion, 1–2, 10, 11, 12, 17, 42, 43, 48, 52, 63, 153

171

Index

Coherence, 19, 27–30, 53
"Coming White Underclass, The" (Murray), 105–106
Communism, 83
Compassion, 32, 53
Competition, 70, 87, 93, 107, 118, 121, 125, 137, 161(n57)
Comprehensive Employment and Training Act (CETA), 104
Concern, 50
Conflicts. *See under* Values
Congress, 57, 78–79, 112, 142, 149–150, 160(n48)
   Senate, 75, 78, 149–150
Consent, 8–9, 13, 60
   hypothetical, 8, 44
   mutual, 1, 2, 10, 11, 17, 40, 52, 54, 138
Consequentialism, 1, 19, 38, 39, 40. *See also* Utilitarianism
Conservatives, 73, 147
Consistency, 6, 7
   Principle of Generic Consistency (PGC), 26, 29
Constitution, 57, 73–82, 149, 150–151
   amendments. *See* Constitutional amendments
   commerce clause, 76
   "general welfare" in, 76, 112
   original intent, 77
Constitutional amendments
   Second, 79–80, 149
   Fourth, 73, 80
   Fifth, 75, 149
   Ninth, 77, 79
   Tenth, 79, 149
   Sixteenth, 76
Contracts, 8, 34, 39, 44, 54, 131, 132
   contractualism, 40–41
Cooperation, 9, 42, 46, 52, 64
Copyrights, 84
Costly Returns (Payne), 110, 111
Creativity, 102, 121, 125, 141
Crime, 40, 63, 147
   and single–parent families, 106
   victimless, 67–68, 84
   See also Drugs, illegal; Lawbreakers; Law enforcement
Cypress Semiconductor, 93

Daniel Lamp Company, 130
Debt. *See* National debt
Deception, 1–2, 17, 20, 52, 84, 138. *See also* Cheating; Lying
Declaration of Independence, 73
Deficits, 96–97, 99–100, 107, 143
Definitions, 53
Democracy, 75, 81
   democratic vs. market controls, 124–126
Den Uyl, Douglas, 49
Dependency, 51, 103, 139, 147, 152
Depository Institutions Deregulation and Monetary Control Act (1980), 98
Deregulation, 100, 127. *See also* Regulations
Deterrence, 12, 66
Difference principle. *See under* Rawls, John
Disability Insurance Trust Fund, 143
Discrimination, 21. *See also under* Employment
Distribution, 1, 39, 43, 68, 74
Donagan, Alan, 25
Drugs, illegal, 167(n26)
   war on drugs, 136, 146, 147
Drugs, medical, 118, 164(n110)
Drunk drivers, 67
Dualism, 28–29, 34, 86, 152
Duties, 28, 29, 48, 50

EAW. *See* Employment, employment at will
Economic issues, 3, 77, 92–93, 114
   central planning, 35, 102
   economic equality, 42–43
   economic growth, 35, 93, 99, 107, 108, 131, 136, 138, 139, 144, 145,146
   free market economies, 30, 34, 35, 68, 75, 95, 136–137, 138
   government involvement, 41
   illegal activities, 67–68
   See also Inflation; Monetary system; Savings; Taxes
Economist, 99, 123
Education, 101, 106, 123–128
   dropout rate, 123
   private, 124–125, 128, 142
   public, 70–71, 86–87, 124–128, 136, 137, 142, 147

testing, 123, 124, 127
voucher system, 126, 142
EEOC. *See* Equal Employment Opportunity Commission
Egalitarianism, 10, 121, 127–128, 137
Ehrlich, Paul, 139, 141
Elites/elitism, 86, 87, 137, 138, 146, 152, 153
Empirical content, 19, 30–33
Employment, 92–93, 100, 107, 129–133
   benefits, 132–133
   discrimination in, 129–133
   employment at will (EAW), 130, 147
   government, 127
   make–work jobs, 105
   unemployment, 100
   work incentives, 103, 104
   working conditions, 137–138
   See also Workfare
Energy crisis of 1970s, 97
Energy Research and Development Adminstration, 98
England, 99, 115, 164(n101)
Entrepreneurs, 102
Environment, 141
Epstein, Richard, 75, 131, 132
Equal Employment Opportunity Commission (EEOC), 130, 132
Equality. *See* Egalitarianism; Inequalities, nondeserved;
   Morality, moral equality; Rights, equal right to be free; *under* Opportunity
Equal Pay Act (1963), 132
Eugenics, 37, 158(n53)
Europe, 100
Exclusionary rule, 73–74
Excuses, 63, 158(n72)
Expediency, 21
Experimentation, 139. *See also* Creativity
Experts, 119
Explanatory power, 19–25

Factions, 74, 75, 149
Fairness, 137, 155(n1)
Families, single–parent, 106, 164(n84)
Family Medical Leave Act (FMLA), 133
Federal deposit insurance, 99

Federalist, The, 74, 75, 78–79, 80, 149
Federal Reserve Board, 146
Feinberg, Joel, 62, 88
Feminism, 107, 129
First appropriators, 60–61
FMLA. *See* Family Medical Leave Act
Food and Drug Administration, 118
Food production, 100, 141
Fossil fuels, 141
France, 99
Freedom, 30, 38, 53
   of association, 97
   of contract, 131, 132
   See also Freedom principle; Rights, equal right to be free
Freedom principle, 10–15, 17–19, 20, 26, 27, 41–42, 53, 55, 60, 73
   and punishment, 62–63, 67
   vs. utility principle, 12, 15, 25
   See also Rawls, John, equal liberty principle; Rights, equal right to be free
Free rider problem, 49
Friedman, David, 59
Friedman, Milton, 84, 85, 95–96, 103–104, 126, 144, 145, 146, 147
Friedmanism, 34–35
Friendship, 50

Gates, Bill, 102
Gauguin, Paul, 47
GDP. *See* Gross domestic product
Generalization requirement, 7
General welfare. *See under* Constitution
Germany, 99, 166(n7)
Gert, Bernard, 26, 155(n7)
Gewirth, Alan, 26, 29
Gilder, George, 94, 101, 102
Global warming, 141
Golden Rule, 7
Goods, 39. *See also* Public goods; Rights, for basic goods
Good Samaritans. *See* Helping others
Gore, Al, 128
Governments, 3, 32–33, 41, 43, 135, 152
   role of, 58, 68, 69, 70–71, 73, 93, 115, 129–133, 148, 151. *See also* Government spending; Regulations; States (U.S.); Taxes

Government spending, 82, 93, 99, 136
Grains, 141
Great Depression, 95
Green, S.J.D., 161(n57)
Gross domestic product (GDP), 92, 99
Grunebaum, James O., 39
Gun control, 80
Gwartney, James, 96

Hamilton, Alexander, 78–79
Happiness, 1, 30
  deliberative, 69
  pursuit of happiness, 73, 77
  See also under Morality
Harrington, Michael, 31–32, 157(nn 44, 46)
Harrison Act of 1914, 167(n26)
Harsanyi, John, 20–21, 25
Hayek, Friedrich A., 35
Health care, 114–122. *See also* Health insurance; Medicare/Medicaid; Socialism, socialized medicine
Health insurance, 115–118, 133, 145, 148. *See also* Medicare/Medicaid
Hedonism, 30, 69. *See also* Pleasure/pain
Heilbroner, Robert, 35
Helping others, 28, 29, 48–49, 50–51, 107
  supply–sided vs. demand–sided accounts of, 49
Hispanics, 130
Hopkins, Thomas, 162(n27)
Hospital Insurance Trust Fund, 142
Housing, 108–109, 140
Human nature, 32, 33, 78, 136

Illegitimacy rate, 105–107
Impairment, temporary, 14
Impartiality (in moral theories), 50
Incentives, 117, 118. *See also* Employment, work incentives;
Taxes, disincentive costs
Income, 34–35, 39, 40, 68, 101, 118,139
  black, 131
  guaranteed, 104. *See also* Taxes, negative income
  per capita, 92, 107
  See also Poverty, poverty line

India, 141, 166(n7)
Individuals, 69, 80. *See also* Rights, individual
Inequalities, nondeserved, 37–38, 40
Inflation, 95–96, 98, 99, 100, 107, 145, 146
Institutions, 15, 26, 41, 58
Interests, 74. *See also* Special interests
Internal Revenue Service, 112–113. *See also* Taxes
Investments, 101, 111, 112, 144, 145
Italy, 166(n7)

Japan, 99, 100, 166(n7)
  Ministry of International Trade and Industry, 101
Jefferson, Thomas, 73
Judicial review, 76, 150
Justice, 36, 38, 40, 53–54, 62–72, 76, 136, 142, 143, 147, 155(n1), 156(nn 8, 17)
  economic/political, 68
  moral requirements concerning, 62

Kansas City, 123
Kant, Immanuel, 1, 19, 20, 42
Kaus, Mickey, 105
Keating Five, 99
Kennedy, John F., 105, 127
Kerrey, Bob, 118–119
Korsgaard, Christine, 38–39, 39–40
Kudlow, Lawrence, 163(n68)

Labor market, 101. *See also* Employment
Land use, 61
Lawbreakers, 12, 62, 63–67. *See also* Crime
Law enforcement, 58, 59, 83, 84, 145
Lawyers, 97
Leasing, 59, 83, 112, 145
Lee Optical (legal case), 77
Legislation, 81–82
  legislative excesses, 78–79
Legitimacy, 42, 44, 58–61
Liberalism, 34–44, 73, 74, 87, 132, 137, 138, 139, 143, 147, 152
Libertarianism, 1, 2, 3, 29, 32, 58, 60, 61, 63, 67, 83, 106, 137, 142, 143, 145, 146, 147, 151, 152, 156(n14)
  ideal libertarian society, 148

and liberalism, 139
objections to, 136
and poverty, 107–109
See also Freedom principle
Licensing, 68, 71, 85, 118, 126, 129
Life expectancy, 92
Limits of Growth, The (Club of Rome), 139
Lincoln Savings and Loan, 99
Line–item veto, 151
Living standards, 92, 99, 112, 136, 137
Lobbying, 97, 149, 152
Locke, John, 17, 38, 60
Lomasky, Loren, 86–87
Los Angeles Department of Water and Power v. Manhart, 133
Lying, 7, 8, 12–13. *See also* Cheating; Deception

McCaughey, Elizabeth, 117
McDermott, Jim, 118
Macey, Jonathan, 150
Machan, Tibor, 161(n63)
Madison, James, 5, 57, 73, 74–75, 79–80, 81, 82, 91, 135, 149, 160(nn 42, 48)
Majorities, 81–82, 135
Market control, 124–126, 148. *See also* Economic issues, free market economies
Marquis, Don, 156(n14)
Marriage, 107
Means/ends, 20, 39, 42
Medicare/Medicaid, 108, 116, 118, 119, 121, 142
Menninger, Karl, 63, 64–65
Methods of Ethics, The (Sidgwick), 53
Mexico, 166(n7)
Middle–class, 143
Militias, 80. *See also* Standing army
Mill, John Stuart, 1, 13, 60, 62, 139, 146, 158(n69)
on economic justice and government's role, 68–72
Minimum wages, 31, 68, 97, 100, 108
Minorities, 130–131. *See also* Blacks
Mises, Ludwig von, 35
Moe, Terry M., 124–126
Monetary system, 95–96, 146

Morality, 1, 62, 133, 143
being moral, 45–51, 158(n72)
and big government, 152
and happiness, 45, 46–47, 48, 51
moral equality, 10, 23, 25, 40
moral skepticism, 6–9, 19
moral theories, 19–33, 48, 49–50, 86, 136
See also Moral rules
Moral Realism and the Foundation of Ethics (Brink), 22
Moral rules, 155(n7)
basic, 7–8, 11, 20, 157(n37)
conflicting, 21, 22–23, 27
exceptions, 11, 12, 17, 52
See also Categorical imperative; Noninterference rule
Moynihan, Daniel Patrick, 106
Multiculturalism, 87
Murray, Charles, 42, 105–106

Nagel, Thomas, 34, 40–41, 42, 43, 48–49
Narveson, Jan, 8
National debt, 96–97, 145–146
National defense, 58, 59, 83–84, 145
National Education Association (NEA), 127, 128
Native Americans, 61
Natural gas, 98, 141
Natural monopolies, 84, 159(n2)
Natural resources, 2, 58–59, 60, 61, 68, 76, 83, 112, 139, 140, 145, 148
NEA. *See* National Education Association
New Deal, 75
Nigeria, 166(n7)
Nixon, Richard, 98
Noninterference rule, 10, 12, 17–18, 25, 41, 52, 67
Nonrejectability, 40–41, 42
Normal adults, 13, 53, 54
Norway, 99
Nozick, Robert, 2, 36, 38, 43

Occupational Safety and Health Administration (OSHA), 137
Offers, 10, 11
Oklahoma, 77

Old Age and Sickness Insurance Trust Fund, 143
Oncologists, 164(n101)
On Liberty (Mill), 13, 69
Opportunity, 130, 136
  equality of, 87, 137, 161(nn 57, 59)
Optimism, 32, 136, 141. *See also* Pessimism
Organ transplants, 23, 29
Orphanages, 106
OSHA. *See* Occupational Safety and Health Administration
OU. *See* Utilitarianism, objective

Parks, 85
Paternalism, 12–13, 14–15, 18, 32–33, 52, 54, 70, 88, 139, 143, 146
Payne, James, 110, 111
Pensions, 133
Perot, Ross, 110
Personal projects/relationships, 23, 24–25, 49, 50
Pessimism, 138, 139–140, 147, 152–153. *See also* Optimism
PGC. *See* Consistency, Principle of Generic Consistency
Phone service, 100
Pleasure/pain, 1, 30, 69
Plessy v. Ferguson, 132
Police misconduct, 74
Political Liberalism (Rawls), 16
Politics, Markets, and Public Schools (Chubb and Moe), 124–126
Poor Laws, 71–72
Population Bomb, The (Ehrlich), 139
Population growth, 140
Pork–barrel politics, 112, 151
Poverty, 3, 40, 50, 86, 103–109, 112, 120, 121, 139, 164(n84)
  antipoverty programs, 41
  libertarian solution to, 107–109
  poverty line, 104, 107
Presidency, 78, 150, 151
Prewar America, 92
Prices, 98, 114, 116, 117, 119, 129, 141
  market clearing price, 107–108

price controls, 98, 121–122, 129
  See also Inflation
Principles of Political Economy (Mill), 60, 69, 71
Prisoner's Dilemma, 110
Prisons, 167(n26)
Privacy, 113, 120, 145
Productivity, 100, 101, 108, 147
  agricultural, 141
Progress, 69, 140
Promises, 20, 22, 28, 48, 62
Property. *See* Rights, property rights
Prostitution, 67, 84
Psychological egoism, 48
Public goods, 58, 61, 76, 83, 112
Publicity requirement, 7, 8
Public schools. *See* Education, public
Public works, 82
Punishment, 12, 38, 67, 84, 136, 147
  vs. treatment/restitution, 63–66
  See also under Freedom principle

Quality of life, 140
Quotas, 131

Racism, 21, 87
Rangel, Charles, 113
Rationality, 1, 6, 7
  rational agents, 8, 26, 34, 69
Rationing, 114, 115, 119
Rauch, Jonathan, 149
Rawls, John, 1, 8, 39, 43, 53, 139, 147, 155(n1), 156(nn 8, 17),158(nn 53, 70)
  difference principle, 34, 35–36, 40
  equal liberty principle, 15–17, 37
  redress principle, 37–38
Real estate, 95
Recessions, 95
Reforms, 148, 151
Regulations, 41, 77, 80, 84, 97–101, 107, 108, 116, 117, 118, 119, 121,133, 138, 162(n27), 164(n110)
  regulatory failures, 97–98, 129–133
  See also Deregulation

Reich, Robert, 100–101
Relationships. *See* Personal projects/relationships
Rent-seeking, 81, 148, 149, 150–151
Rescher, Nicholas, 139
Respect, 50
Responsibility, 38, 40, 41, 51, 147, 152
Restitution, 65–66
Reversibility requirement, 7
Rights, 1, 2, 11, 26, 39, 62, 76
    for basic goods, 28–29, 86, 152
    bequeathable, 61
    equal right to be free, 1, 9, 28–29, 39, 50, 52, 54, 133, 136, 152. *See also* Freedom principle
    health care, 114
    individual, 73, 74, 81
    liberal rights theory, 87
    negative, 50, 73
    of procreation, 36–37
    property rights, 55, 58, 59–61, 68, 74, 75, 76, 150–151
    protection of, 58, 77
    to punish, 63, 84
    welfare rights, 3, 49, 88–89
Risks, 35, 115, 116, 120, 138, 156(n8)
Roads. *See* Streets/roads
Rodgers, T. J., 93
Royko, Mike, 130
Rules. *See* Moral rules

Sacrifice, 23, 29, 50
Samuelson, Robert, 92
S&L industry. *See* Savings and loan debacle
SAT. *See* Scholastic Aptitude Test
Savings, 93, 94–95, 96, 101, 112, 144, 145
Savings and loan (S&L) debacle, 95, 97, 98–99
Scanlon, T. M., 8, 34, 40, 42, 43
Schmidtz, David, 50, 60–61
Scholastic Aptitude Test (SAT), 124, 127
Segregation, 131. *See also* Discrimination
Self-defense, 11, 62
Self-interest, 45, 47, 48, 110
Self-reliance, 32, 53, 152

Sexism, 87
Sexual harassment, 132
Shipping, 83–84
Shoven, John B., 111
Sidgwick, Henry, 53–54
Silicon Graphics, 94
Simon, Julian, 141
Simplicity, 19, 25–27
Singer, Peter, 28, 50
Skepticism. *See* Moral skepticism
Slavery, 21
Slemrod, Joel, 111
Smith, Adam, 38
Socialism, 31, 35, 101–102, 139, 141, 147, 158(n69)
    socialized medicine, 114–115, 120, 121
Social Security, 88, 104, 108, 118, 136, 142–145
Sorum, Nikki, 111
South Carolina, 131
Soviet Union, 35, 58, 64
Sowell, Thomas, 123, 131, 146
Special interests, 149, 150, 151. *See also* Factions
Standard of living. *See* Living standards
Standing army, 79–80
Stare decisis priciple, 76
States (U.S.), 79, 80, 126, 149
    state mandates, 116, 117
Stealing, 7, 11
Streets/roads, 84–85, 148
Stroup, Richard, 96
Student loans, 85
Subsidies, 100, 110, 118, 119
Supply and demand, 114, 119
Supreme Court, 73–74, 77, 78–79, 150

Taxes, 29, 31, 39, 41, 43, 48, 49, 58–59, 72, 74–75, 76, 79, 86, 93–95, 100, 105, 107, 110–113, 138, 139, 143, 145
    capital gains, 94, 100, 101, 145
    compliance costs, 110–111
    disincentive costs, 111
    exemptions, 148
    gasoline, 85

and health insurance overconsumption, 117–118
negative income, 34, 103–104
payroll, 108, 142, 144, 145
property, 59, 112
resource, 59, 60, 83, 112, 145, 148
sales, 144, 145, 146
Social Security, 104, 108
See also Internal Revenue Service; User fees
Teachers, 126–127
Technology, 102, 141
Television, high–definition, 101
Term limits, 151
Theory of Justice (Rawls), 15, 35, 38, 155(n1), 156(nn 8, 17)
Threats, 10, 12, 52
Trade, 100
Training, 100, 101, 104
Trucking industry, 127

Unanimity, 42
Underclass, 105–106, 107
Unions, 100, 127
United States v. Leon, 173–174
User fees, 58, 59, 83, 85, 112, 148
Utilitarianism, 1, 17, 23, 31, 38, 67, 68
act, 20, 21, 25, 27, 28
objective (OU), 22, 23–24
rule, 20–21, 21–22, 27, 157(n37)
See also Freedom principle, vs. utility principle; Mill, John Stuart
Values, 14, 26, 46, 52
conflicts between, 47, 67
intrinsic/extrinsic, 22
theory of value, 22, 23, 31
Vetos, 150, 151
Virtue, 5, 41, 49, 152
Voluntary programs, 120–121, 153

Wages, 107, 108, 131, 133. *See also* Minimum wages
War on drugs. *See under* Drugs, illegal
Water/sewer services, 84, 140, 148, 159(n2)
Weinstein, David, 101
Welfare state, 76, 87
Welfare system, 71–72, 103–105, 109, 136, 147, 152. *See also* Rights, welfare rights; Workfare
Well–being, 26, 29
Whalley, John, 111
Whitehead, Barbara, 106
Will, George, 119
Williams, Bernard, 21, 24–25
Women, 132–133, 164(n84). *See also* Feminism
Workfare, 104–105, 163(n68)
Wright, Jim, 99